CHINA'S ONE-CHILD FAMILY POLICY

Also by Elisabeth Croll

FEMINISM AND SOCIALISM IN CHINA

THE POLITICS OF MARRIAGE IN CONTEMPORARY
CHINA

THE FAMILY RICE BOWL:
Food and the Domestic Economy in China

CHINESE WOMEN SINCE MAO

Also by Delia Davin

WOMAN-WORK:
Women and the Party in Revolutionary China

Also by Penny Kane

THE WHICH? GUIDE TO BIRTH CONTROL

CHOICE NOT CHANCE:
A Handbook of Fertility Control
(*with Beulah Bewley and Judith Cook*)

CHINA'S ONE-CHILD FAMILY POLICY

Edited by
Elisabeth Croll
Delia Davin
and Penny Kane

St. Martin's Press   New York

© Elisabeth Croll, Delia Davin and Penny Kane 1985

All rights reserved. For information, write:
St. Martin's Press, Inc., 175 Fifth Avenue, New York, NY 10010
Printed in Hong Kong
Published in the United Kingdom by The Macmillan Press Ltd.
First published in the United States of America in 1985

ISBN 0–312–13356–1

Library of Congress Cataloging in Publication Data
Main entry under title:
China's one-child family policy.
Includes index.
1. Birth control—China—Addresses, essays, lectures.
2. Population policy—China—Addresses, essays, lectures.
3. China—Social conditions—1976-   —Addresses,
essays, lectures.   4. Family policy—China—Addresses,
essays, lectures.   I. Croll, Elisabeth J.   II. Davin,
Delia.   III. Kane, Penny.
HQ766.5.C6C452   1985   363.9'6'0951   84–26756
ISBN 0–312–13356–1

Contents

Tables

Figures

Weights, Measures and Exchange Rate (1984)

one *jin* = 0.5kg or 1.1lbs.
one tonne = 1000kg
one *mu* = 1/15 hectare or 1/6 acre

There are approximately three *yuan* to one pound sterling and two *yuan* to one US dollar.

One billion = one thousand million

Abbreviations used in Notes

BR   *Beijing Review*
JPRS   *Joint Publications Research Service*
NCNA   *New China News Agency*
RMRB   *Renmin Ribao* (People's Daily)
SWB   *Survey of World Broadcasts*

Preface

The single-child family policy is one of the most momentous of the new policies which have transformed the face of China since the death of Mao in 1976. Its implications for the future social fabric and development of China are fundamental. The policy has its origins in the government's concern that unless population growth is slowed and ultimately reversed, China will not achieve the economic growth for which she is striving. Since 1979 all young couples have therefore been urged to limit their families to one child. To realise this ideal, heavy political and social pressure is employed and an elaborate set of incentives and disincentives has been evolved to reward those who comply with the programme and to penalise those who do not. However, as the policy conflicts sharply with traditional family values and with the belief that large numbers of children ensure the family's prosperity, it is difficult to implement. Its success or failure will have far-reaching implications for the economic, social and political development of China.

The issues raised by the study of the single-child family in China will be relevant to demographers, national and international family planners and development agencies. Values relating to family size, state manipulation of fertility norms, economic and political determinants of fertility and the ways in which couples make or vary fertility decisions are matters of considerable concern to theorists and policymakers.

In 1983, when the policy was already four years old, a review of its origins, problems and prospects seemed timely. A small group of specialists who had worked on this subject met in March of that year to discuss the policy and its implementation. Most of the chapters which make up this book were first presented as papers in this International Workshop. While the chapters each focus on a particular aspect of China's population planning, taken together they cover the single-child family in full. At this early stage, findings can only be tentative and there are still some differences in interpretation among our contributors. The introductory chapter provides the background to a more detailed discussion of the single-child family by summarising previous models of family size and their relationship to fertility. It presents the arguments employed by the government to justify such a radical programme and outlines the features which distinguish this latest phase of population policy from its predecessors.

So far in the first five years, it seems that the single most important determinant of response to the new policy is the location of the couple, whether they are resident in the rural villages or in the cities and larger towns. For this reason, the next two chapters examine in greater detail the factors specific to rural and urban China which make for this differing response. In the fourth chapter, H. Yuan Tien approaches the demographic data from a different perspective. He analyses provincial trends and patterns in fertility and explains some of the factors responsible for variations in population developments among the twenty-nine provinces, municipalities and autonomous regions of China. Pi-chao Chen describes in detail the birth control methods and organisation which have made possible the remarkable demographic transition of the 1970s. He argues that without the prior establishment of the health care infrastructure, this lower rate of fertility could not have been achieved, far less could the single-child family have been contemplated.

One of the factors identified in the first four chapters as a key determinant of the response to the single-child family policy is the problem of old-age security in a society where the elderly still depend so much on their children. Deborah Davis-Friedmann examines the level of provision for the elderly in the cities and villages and its likely implications for the single-child family policy. Perhaps the most distinctive feature of this new policy in China is the degree of State intervention in fertility decisions which it represents. What is not yet clear, however, is the extent to which this State intervention in the form of regulation, incentives and disincentives, as distinct from other socio-economic and political factors, will influence fertility decisions. It will only be possible to examine such questions in the detail required when more interviews and studies can be undertaken within China. In the meantime, the example of Singapore in South-east Asia, a city with strong cultural links with China, where the state has also intervened to reduce fertility is relevant. Janet Salaff in her chapter based on her detailed interviewing in Singapore, identifies some of the factors determining the response of couples there to stringent family planning policies and suggests their relevance to China. Finally, the book concludes with a first-hand report on the implementation of the single-child family policy in several locations within the Beijing Municipality.

The International Workshop was attended by a number of people whose work on China and in the general fields of demography, family and development enabled them to make valuable contributions to the discussion. We would like to express our appreciation to our fellow convenor, David Coleman, and to Hugh Baker, Penny Brook, Nigel Crook, Tim Dyson, Nuray Fincancioglu, Halvor Gille, Ed Goldwyn, Lado Ruzicka, Ashwani Saith, Ruby Watson, James Watson and Elizabeth Wright. Workshop participants were funded by the Queen Elizabeth House Contemporary China Centre, the International Planned Parenthood Federation, the Great Britain–China Federation and the Leverhulme Trust to all of which we would like to express our grateful thanks. We would also like to thank the Warden of Queen Elizabeth House, Dr Arthur Hazlewood, and the Director of the Contemporary China Centre, Neville Maxwell, for their generous hospitality.

ELISABETH CROLL
DELIA DAVIN
PENNY KANE

Notes on the Contributors

Professor Pi-chao Chen is a member of the Department of Political Science, Wayne State University. He is the author of *Population Growth and Policy in the People's Republic of China* and of numerous articles on China's demography.

Dr Elisabeth Croll, a Fellow at Wolfson College and a member of the Faculty of Social Studies at Oxford University, has spent over a decade engaged in research on China, where she conducted investigations in 1973, 1977, 1980 and 1983. She is the author of several books on China, including *Feminism and Socialism in China; The Politics of Marriage in Contemporary China; The Family Rice Bowl: Food and the Domestic Economy in China* and *Chinese Women since Mao*.

Dr Delia Davin is a lecturer in social and economic history at the University of York. She taught in Beijing from 1963 to 1965 and worked as a translator there from 1975 to 1976. She has written extensively on women in China and her publications include *Woman-work: Women and the Party in Revolutionary China*.

Dr Deborah Davis-Friedmann, Associate Professor of Sociology at Yale University, has done fieldwork in Hong Kong, Taiwan and the People's Republic on Chinese family structure and social welfare reforms. She is the author of *Long Lives: Chinese Elderly and the Communist Revolution*.

Penny Kane, who previously worked for the International Planned Parenthood Federation, is now a consultant on population and is a Visiting Fellow at the Australian National University at Canberra. She is the author of a number of books and papers on family planning, population and development and on China, including *The Which? Guide to Birth Control* and *Choice not Chance*.

Dr Janet W. Salaff, Professor of Sociology at the University of Toronto, has published widely in the area of family structure and population dynamics of the Chinese. She is the author of *Working Daughters of Hong Kong: Filial Piety or Power in the Family?* and her articles have appeared in *Population Studies, The China Quarterly* and *Journal of Social History.*

Professor H. Yuan Tien is a member of the Department of Sociology, Ohio State University. He is the author of *China's Population Struggle: Demographic Decisions of the People's Republic, 1949–69* and editor (with Frank Bean) of *Comparative Family and Fertility Research.*

1 Introduction: Fertility Norms and Family Size in China

ELISABETH CROLL*

In China today, the urgent attempt to reduce population growth rates is characterised by a dual approach. First the present government expects, as do most other developing countries, that as China develops and modernises there will be a consequent decline in fertility. It is thus determined that economic development and modernisation will rapidly proceed. Second, the present government also perceives that the process of development and modernisation in China is itself dependent on the degree to which China can reduce her population growth rates. To break this circle of interdependence the government has directly intervened and introduced a radical population plan the chief element of which is the single-child family policy. As its name suggests, this policy demands that except in extraordinary circumstances couples should have no more than one child.

Of all the policies introduced into China by the post-Mao government of the past five years, the single-child family policy is probably the most momentous and far-reaching in its implications for China's population and economic development. It is also of much wider interest to demographers, family planning agencies and governments elsewhere as there is some evidence that the widespread provision of family planning services and techniques facilitates the control of fertility and reduces unwanted fertility to meet the demand for 'small families', but of itself may have little effect in creating that demand. Hence those interested in the formulation and implementation of

*The research and writing of this paper was made possible by a generous grant from The Leverhulme Trust.

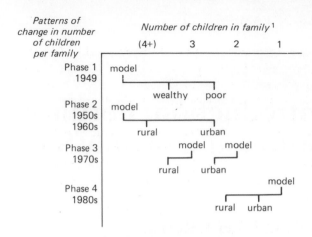

1   Representational only, figures not statistically plotted.

FIGURE 1.1   *Models of family size*

population policies have increasingly directed their attention towards values attached to family size and the manipulation of fertility norms in relation to images, norms and values about family size.

The analysis of models of family size and their relationship to fertility norms and rates is not a new area of interest among social scientists of China. Indeed twenty-five years ago, the late Professor Maurice Freedman, an eminent anthropologist of kinship, family and marriage in China, was moved to remark that the points of difference between models or ideal family size and real family size had been well enough made for the subject to be passed quickly over in the future.[1] What Professor Freedman could not have foreseen is that a quarter of a century later, the literature on models of family size and their relation to fertility norms and rates would acquire a new relevance with the recent introduction of a new nation-wide model of family size – that of the single-child family. This introductory chapter briefly summarises previous models of family size and their relationship to fertility as the background to a more detailed discussion on the generation of the 'small-family' model and especially of the 'one-child family' model in contemporary China. Other chapters in the volume will examine current and future relationships between the new model of family size and fertility.

MODELS OF FAMILY SIZE

Prior to the recent introduction of the single-child family model, it is helpful to distinguish three phases in the relationship between models of family size and fertility in China: the phase that ends with the establishment of a new government in 1949; a second phase covering the first two decades of Communist rule (1950–1970); and a third decade prior to 1979 when there was a sustained national attempt to establish a new model of family size based on the two- to three-child family. The introduction of the single-child family policy in 1979 marks the beginning of a fourth phase. (See Figure 1.1.)

Phase 1: The Joint Family Model

In China before the mid-twentieth century, ideals of family size, structure and function can confidently be represented by one dominant model which was well-nigh universal throughout China. It was based on Confucian prescriptions for a large, complex and extended or joint family. (In this chapter the term family (*jia*) refers to the kin-related unit bounded by a common budget and cooking stove. It is used interchangeably with the term household (*hu*), although a household may also include persons not related by kinship.) It was patrilocal, patrilineal and formed by the co-residence of as many generations and married brothers as possible, and each male was encouraged to have many sons to fulfil his obligation to his father and his father's lineage, or as folk usage has it 'to continue the incense smoke at the ancestral shrine'. Indeed of the traditional charges against an unfilial son, the failure to provide descendants was the 'gravest of unfilial acts'. For women too, the status attached to motherhood and especially to the birth of sons was an incentive to bear many children. All grown sons, their wives and children were encouraged to reside under the same roof to manage the household's corporate political, economic and social resources jointly and to worship their common ancestors. This combination of the various generations and large numbers of siblings and their wives and children all residing in one large household or family compound made up of rambling courtyards and gardens was for a long time the prevailing image of the Chinese family among nineteenth century observers of China. Even the first avowedly sociological descriptions of the Chinese family fastened upon the large or joint household as the common form of domestic organisation throughout China. It was not until the surveys and community studies of the 1920s and 1930s revealed that the joint family form was not so common that the dominant image of the large and complex family compound began to fade.[2]

The belief that the Chinese family tended to be large in size and complex in organisation with several generations living under the same roof was first substantially challenged by surveys of farm families undertaken by Professor J. L. Buck and his associates in the 1920s. According to a survey conducted among 12 456 farm families from twenty-two localities in eleven provinces, the mean size of the farm family was 5.25 persons and of the household, 5.42 persons (see Table 1.1). Indeed the majority of farm families numbered between three and six persons (see Table 1.2). The results of a larger survey covering 38 256 farm families in twenty-two provinces conducted in the same year were recently re-analysed by Irene Taueber to show that the average family size again was 5.2 persons. She calculated that domestic units of up to six persons constituted 76 per cent of the families; those of seven to nine persons constituted 17.6 per cent of all families and only 6.5 per cent of families were composed of ten or more persons.[3]

Later surveys and community studies continued to place the average size of the family household at between four and six persons which suggested at the most a composition of two or at most three generations and of one to three children.[4] Most of the more detailed village studies confirmed that only a very small proportion of families were complex in form with more than one married son in residence. More revealing though than the average size of family household was the range in family size over a period of time and the fluctuations in membership occasioned by the births, marriages and deaths and divisions of its members.

Social scientists came to distinguish between two quite distinct developmental cycles through which households moved in Republican China before 1949. In one cycle the marriage of each son added to the membership of the family group all of whom drew benefit from the corporate political and economic resources to which they had access by virtue of their family membership. The partition of the estate might be delayed until the death of the surviving parent led to division and the establishment of new households which were themselves relatively complex in form. The repetition of this pattern of one partition per generation 'meant that few nuclear or conjugal families emerged as separate households'. Here in skeleton form was the mechanism by which 'joint' families persisted. The alternative cycle differed from the

TABLE 1.1   *Mean and median size of farm family and household[1]*

	Family		Family	
	Mean	Median	Mean	Median
China	5.25	4.48	5.43	4.49
North China	5.55	4.49	5.78	4.56
South China	5.03	4.20	5.18	4.39

[1]   Based on survey of 12 456 farm families in twenty-two localities, eleven provinces, China 1929–31.

SOURCE   Chiao, C. M., 1934, *Rural Population and Vital Statistics for Selected Areas in China 1929–1931* (Shanghai, 1934, 13.)

TABLE 1.2   *Percentage distribution of farm families by size[1]*

Number of persons in family	China	North China	South China
1	3.1	3.8	2.6
2	8.3	8.8	7.8
3	14.6	13.4	15.5
4	18.7	16.3	20.4
5	17.5	15.5	19.0
6	13.8	13.7	13.9
7	8.6	8.9	8.4
8	5.2	6.1	4.6
9	3.4	3.6	3.3
10 +	6.8	9.9	4.5
	100.0	100.0	100.0

[1]   Based on survey of 12 456 farm families, twenty-two localities, eleven provinces in China 1929–31.

SOURCE   Chiao, C. M., *Rural Population and Vital Statistics for Selected Areas in China 1929–31* (Shanghai 1934) 13.

first in that the cycle of development was short and nuclear families emerged rapidly from more complex units. Only one son might survive or continue to stay and reside with his father so that when the head of the household died there was little reduction in the complexity of household structure. All the available evidence from surveys and community studies suggested that despite the coincidence of the tratitional model of family size with the first cycle, the number of families which adhered to the first of these two quite distinct cycles was small compared with the numbers of families which followed the shorter and simpler cycle of development.

Once social scientists had established the statistical frequency of the 'smaller' as distinct from the 'larger' cycle of development, they turned their attention to the relationship between the dominant model of family size encouraging the co-residence of many generations and the birth of many children and the prevalence of the 'smaller' family. Why should there be such a discrepancy between models of family size and fertility? Analyses showed a direct correlation between family size as determined by both co-residence and fertility and economic resources and socio-political status. That is to say, they directly correlated wealth and high socio-political status with 'large' family size and complexity of structure, and poor and low status families with small family size and a short cycle of development. Their studies identified the *jia* estate, which included land (usually the most significant feature of family's property for all but the poorest families) and other items such as residences and enterprises, household effects, farm structures and tools and livestock, as the crucial components determining family size. Not only was the *jia* estate the main form of economic support for family members – and its size thus determined the number of dependents – but in addition the absence of a *jia* estate large enough to support more than one son forced other sons to disperse and migrate. Access to common economic resources and corporate social and political interests proved an effective counter to tensions between father and son and between brothers and their wives, which in less favourable circumstances made for division into smaller units. The correlation between *jia* estate and family size was not just based on a crude association of the comparatively greater riches of the gentry and merchants and their larger family size and complexity, for even within the peasantry, field research showed a definite correlation between size of landholdings and family size. Both Notestein and Buck related size and structure of household to access to land, and without exception found that the larger the landholdings, the larger the family size.[5] Table 1.3 compiled by Gamble from his village studies in north China showed that the size of household was directly related to family income and holdings.[6]

Olga Lang correlated class and family structure in both the cities and villages and her findings show that the number of joint families increased with social class (see Table 1.4).[7]

A major factor reducing the complexity of family structure among the poorer socio-economic groups was the mortality rate which per-

TABLE 1.3 *Size of farm and persons per family*

Number of mu	Size of family[1]	Number of mu	Size of family[2]	Number of mu	Size of family[3]
1–9	4.7	1–10	3.8	0	4.1
10–29	6.4	11–20	4.8	under 25	4.7
30–49	7.8	21–30	6.2	25–49	6.7
50–99	10.6	31–40	6.7	50–74	10.6
100 +	12.9	41–50	8.4	75–99	14.1
		51–100	9.4	100 +	13.2
		100 +	13.5		
Average	6.9	Average	6.3	Average	5.2

[1] Based on survey of 515 families
[2] Based on survey of 400 families
[3] Based on survey of 1220 families

SOURCE Gamble, S. D., *Ting Hsien, A North China Rural Community* (Stanford University Press, 1954) 55.

TABLE 1.4 *Family type and social class*

	Number of families	Family type (as %)		
		Conjugal	Stem	Joint
Villages in North China[1]				
Farm labourers	61	54	35	11
Poor peasants	163	41	44	15
Middle peasants	125	27	44	29
Rich peasants	58	17	42	41
Landlords	51	12	35	53
Non-industrial cities in North China[2]				
Wage-earners	426	58	34	8
Lower middle-class	251	51	36	13
Middle class	496	50	34	16
Upper class	192	52	28	20

[1] Based on survey of 458 families
[2] Based on survey of 1365 families (mainly Beijing)

SOURCE O. Lang, Chinese Family and Society (Yale University Press, 1946) 136.

TABLE 1.5   *Number of generations per household*

Number of generations	Percentage of families		
	Rural	*Urban*	*All*
1	7.8	20.2	13.4
2	51.6	58.3	54.8
3	37.7	20.7	29.9
4	2.9	0.7	1.8
5	0.04	0.1	0.05

SOURCE   Smythe, Lewis C. 'The Composition of the Chinese Family', Nanking Journal, 5, 1935, 380.

mitted few members of the older generation to survive long enough to preside over households containing sons and grandsons. Thus the overwhelming majority of peasant families were made up of only two generations. Taueber's analysis suggested that three-fifths of farm families had only two generations[8] and Smythe's study of 2422 rural and 2027 urban Chinese families shows that the majority (or more than two-thirds) of the rural and urban households were made up of one or two generations. (See Table 1.5).

Economic factors and especially access to land and other material resources were found not only to affect the co-residence of generations and of siblings, but also the birth and survival rates of children within each generation which limited the potential expansion of family size and complexity. Although the old adage that 'to have many sons was the greatest of blessings' persisted, most surveys and studies show that the number of births per couple declined with their resources and social status and that the survival of just one son to maturity was not uncommon. The scant data on differential fertility in China before 1949 illustrated that the number of surviving children was directly related to access to economic resources. In 624 complete conjugal families of Lang's urban informants in North China, the wage-earners and lower middle-class families had 1.9 children, middle-class families 2.4 children and upper class families 3 children. The average number of children in the 140 rural conjugal families surveyed who were mainly poor and middle-class peasants in North China, was 2.4.[9] Dr Smythe's sample of 670 poor urban conjugal families revealed an average of 2.1 children per family – a figure close to Lang's.[10] The average number of children in 620 rural families (mostly poorer groups) was 2.5.[11] There were several factors keeping poorer families

TABLE 1.6 *Family fertility and size of farm*

Size of farm	Number of children born
Small	503
Medium	506
Medium large	528
Large	535
Very large	551

SOURCE Buck, J. L., *Land Utilization in China* (Nanking, 1937) 385.

TABLE 1.7 *Fertility and size of farm* *

Size of farm (mu)	Children aged 1 – 10 years
1 – 10	0.6
11 – 20	0.8
21 – 30	0.9
31 – 40	1.3
41 – 50	1.4
51 – 100	1.9
100 +	3.2
Average	1.1
Owners	1.3
Part-owners	0.9
Tenants	0.6

* Based on survey of 400 farm families.

SOURCE Gamble, S. D. *Ting Hsien, A North China Rural Community* (Stanford University Press, 1954) 84.

from unlimited expansion. The first of these was that there seems to have been a smaller number of children born or at least who survived in the poorer families.

In his study of 10 700 women aged 45 years or more, J. L. Buck established a slight correlation between size of farm and number of children born (see Table 1.6).[12] Gamble also found that the amount of land farmed by the family appeared to have a definite correlation to the number of children born (see Table 1.7).[13]

Again in the cities, surveys such as those summarised in Table 1.8 show a direct correlation between number of children born and social class (see Table 1.8).[14] When Lang correlated the educational levels of husbands and wives with number of children born, she found that

TABLE 1.8   *Fertility and social class*[1]

Class	Total	Living	Dead	Number of mothers
Upper Class	6250	4570	1680	438
Lower Class	4700	2300	2400	1000

[1]   Based on survey of 1438 married urban women of 40 years and older, 1929–31.

SOURCE   Herbert D. Lamson, 'Differential reproduction in China', *The Quarterly Review of Biology*, 10,3, September 1935, 308–21.

husbands and wives who were both illiterate had an average of 5.15 births; where literate husbands had illiterate wives, the average number of births was 5.67, and where both husband and wife were literate the average birth rate per couple was 6.29.[15]

Of the children born, many died, the poor of course losing most. There are no exact figures for child and infant mortality in China before 1949, but most estimates place the rate of infant mortality somewhere between 30 and 50 per cent. Treudley's study in Sichuan in the mid-1940s showed that the average number of children 'ever born' was 4.99, but that the average number of children who survived was 2.35, a proportion which placed the infant mortality rate of the market town at 47.3 per cent.[16] In a Guangdong village, C. K. Yang found a mortality rate of about 300 per 1000 live births. The incidence of death bore more heavily upon the infants of the poor than upon the well-to-do because of poor nutrition and lack of medical care. In this village, poor couples considered themselves fortunate if they were able to raise two children to maturity out of six, seven or even more live births.[17] Martin Yang in the northern province of Shandong also found that the death rate was two or three out of every six or seven children born. In the village about which he wrote the survival of all children in a family was thought to be unusual, and most couples thus expected to lose a child or children. Indeed only if a family lost more than half of its children – for example three out of five – did they think that there must be something larger than fate at work.[18] The death rate was highest among children under the age of three and it gradually tapered off between the ages of 5 and 10, so that in most regions the ages of 3 and 10 or in some cases, 12, were considered to be critical milestones in survival. Indeed the fear of tempting fate by registering the child before these ages was one of the factors which produced under-reporting in local censuses, registers and other like data. The high infant and child mortality rate meant that a couple would need three sons to ensure the survival of one to adulthood, and to have three boys, a family would need to have an average of six children.

Folklore suggests that the poor were well aware of their limited ability to support many children. As one old folk saying suggested: 'To feed a family of five a peasant must work like an animal. But even with whipping, an animal couldn't support a family of six'. Couples and especially poor couples thus took steps to limit the number of children as a precaution against poverty. As in most other societies, there was a well-developed repertoire of folk remedies believed to prevent conception or encourage abortion which passed from generation to generation. In China these ranged from the almost unbelievable method of swallowing quantities of live tadpoles to various herbal mixtures which – tried for centuries – are now being tested for their efficacy by more scientific methods. There were customs of temporary sexual avoidance after the birth of a child and of permanent avoidance after the marriage of the eldest child to maintain an orderly kinship hierarchy. A common method of limiting the number of children in addition to withdrawal, abstinence and abortion was female infanticide.

Throughout China there was a universal preference for sons. They continued the family line; on marriage they remained within the parental household and supported the older generation and finally they tended the ancestral shrines. Parents were thus dependent on sons and in the competition for scarce resources it was daughters who were sacrificed. Female infanticide was practised throughout China both directly by intervention at birth and indirectly as a result of the malnutrition and sickness from which girls suffered disproportionately because of the unequal distribution of family food and medical attention. One local study of a village where there was pressure of population on land revealed that in the first five years of life the number of boys outweighed the girls in proportion of 100 to 35.[19] Doubtless this was an exceptional situation. However without accurate data on the sex ratio at birth, it is impossible to gauge the scale of female infanticide. Data from Beijing in 1917 shows that the female mortality rate in the first year of life was nearly 30 per cent higher than that of males. The death rate of females from 1 to 5 years of age was 152 per 1000 and for males 122 per 1000 so that in this case the supposition of neglect is strong.[20] The very poor lost their daughters not only at birth or shortly after, but many were also later sold into slavery, prostitution and as child-brides. The higher the income of the family, the more likely the girls were to remain in the household as valued members until marriage. Just as the employment of means to reduce the number of child dependants was intensified with poverty, so the number of children supported became a measure of and symbol of wealth and status. As an eminent Chinese social scientist of the time noted: 'Nothing so much indicates the social status of a household in the Chinese countryside as its size, which is a matter of pride, and especially when it contains a large number of sons'.[21]

In sum all the available evidence suggests that a number of economic and demographic factors inter-related to affect family size, the number of surviving generations within one household and the number of children born and surviving within each generation. A minority of 'households' with many sons formed a contrast with the majority where only one son survived to maturity in each generation. Marion Levy who studied family size and structure in the 1940s argued that although the literature on family and kinship has been preoccupied with the ideal structures which call for maximum proliferation along the vertical and horizontal axis, the dominant model was largely irrelevant to the developmental cycle of the majority of the population.[22] However the behaviour of the socially mobile suggests that the joint family model was only irrelevant so long as economic and demographic circumstances prohibited its appropriation. It remained an aspiration and was taken up as soon as the expansion of the *jia* estate permitted. Additions to the *jia* estate and changes in social status permitted expansion in family size and complexity, and in turn the attainment of the ideal family model was itself a mark of approbation and status. Indeed Francis Hsu concluded from his studies that movement towards the large Chinese family was a tendency inherent within Chinese social organisation, which expressed itself as soon as the economic foundation of the family made such an expression practical.[23]

C. K. Yang also thought that although the joint family was only associated with classes having social, economic and political dominance, it served as an exemplary model of traditional family organisation for the rest of the population to be sought whenever economic conditions permitted. As soon as there was enough land or other forms conditions permitted. As soon as there was enough land or other means of production to employ married sons, they would remain in the the process of expansion of the small household unit into the 'large' family unit was set in motion. In this sense, C. K. Yang likened the Chinese family to a balloon, ever ready to expand whenever there was wealth enough to inflate it.[24] Those remarks written in 1950 or so were prophetic, for from that time forward economic and demographic conditions were such that in the countryside peasant families began to follow the larger cycle of development in that they became larger and more elaborate at least for a significant phase of their developmental cycle.

Phase 2: The Complex Peasant Family Model

In the first twenty years after the establishment of the People's Republic of China, no new dominant model of family size was clearly articulated or incorporated into the ruling ideology by the communist government although it did have a great deal to say about the introduction of new ideals underlying intra-familial relations and the reduction of gender and age hierarchies. Any definition of the 'ideal' family emphasised the relations within it to the exclusion of its economic and political functions and structure. In the 1950s and 1960s, the domestic group was defined as 'mainly a unit of life in which the husband and wife share their married life together, rear and educate their children and care for their elder near relatives together'.[25] The implications of this definition for the size and structure of the domestic group are far from clear, and the new ideology left vague the number of persons or the projected form which the residential group or family formation and division should take.

Virilocal marriage, or the recruitment of wives to the domestic group in which the husband resided prior to marriage, was widely practised in traditional China and nowhere were new rules of post-marital residence stated. Rather, the domestic group or household was said 'to stem from the marital bond in that either it functions to establish a new household completely or it perpetuates an old household for a further generation'.[26] In the urban areas, education for later marriage and the allocation of housing to young couples on marriage encouraged the formation of neolocal households, but in the rural areas the absence of any such intervention or alternative prescriptions did nothing to discourage the continuation of the old virilocal post-marital residential patterns.

In the second decade there had been some discussion of a smaller family of two to three children, but this had not resulted in any very specific or clear directions being given as to the number and spacing of births within marriage. There were a number of birth control campaigns from the mid-1950s which were only interrupted by the events of the Great Leap Forward (1958–9) and the Cultural Revolution

(1966–9), but these campaigns had primarily advocated family planning with the emphasis on planning of fertility rather than population reduction. Just as individuals and couples were encouraged to plan their work, study and leisure, so they were encouraged to plan their child-bearing. Even the campaigns to raise the age of marriage were presented and rationalised in terms of the benefits to women and children, rather than fertility reduction and the consequent elimination of one or two generations every century. Thus the campaigns concentrated on delivering contraceptives and other family planning services to encourage spacing and fertility limitation for couples who had already completed their desired family size. Contraception, abortion and sterilisation became widely available to those who voluntarily chose to avail themselves of these services. Family planning workers might visit families to advise them, but the decision to limit and space the births was very much left to the couples themselves.

The account of family planning in one locality in the early 1960s illustrates both the more advisory and more voluntary nature of family planning in the first twenty years. There the women in charge of family planning in the village interpreted their brief as entirely a matter of educating the villagers about the types of contraceptives available and they only directly intervened in households where women with several children who wished to prevent further births were opposed by their husbands. They usually succeeded in persuading the husband to agree to use contraceptives in the interests of merely postponing or spacing births rather than the more radical step of permanently limiting further births. As one family planning cadre in the village noted, they were powerless to interfere in the birth plans of families where both parents wished to have many children 'We can't do anything there. The whole thing is voluntary. The chief thing is to have a healthy family, and that the mother feels all right'.[27] What was recognised throughout these two decades was that family planning in the interests of spacing and limiting unwanted births was a private family matter in which the individual couples themselves took decisions according to their own personal circumstances and wishes. There was no national population plan or new dominant model of family size and structure to substitute for the larger joint family ideal, and in the absence of a new model, the older joint family remained the ideal structure. Moreover as a result of new demographic and economic factors, a higher proportion of peasant families came closer to realising that ideal for at least a phase of their developmental cycle than they had at any time during the recent past.

A number of public health campaigns, measures to improve sanitation and hygiene, the increased stability of food supplies for the major portion of the population, and expanded medical services all contributed to a decrease in malnutrition and epidemic diseases which had taken such a toll before 1949. Improvements in diet, health, preventive medicine and general welfare had the combined effect of lengthening the life-span and reducing infant-mortality rates. Life expectancy which was well below 40 years of age before 1949 had increased to somewhere between 55 and 60 years by the early 1970s and a cut-off in migration after the first few years meant that fewer family members dispersed in the search for employment. The infant mortality rate dropped drastically in the first two decades.[28] A current slogan reflected the attention directed towards infant and child health: 'One pregnancy, one live birth; one live birth, one healthy child'. By 1957 the proportion of child births attended by trained health workers was estimated to have reached 60 per cent or so in rural areas and 95 per cent in the large cities.[29] The sex ratios too became much more normal which suggests that infanticide was no longer widely practised. China had entered a well-recognised phase of the demographic transition in which a decline in the mortality rate had not yet been matched by a decline in fertility rates.

In the new stability and security of times in the 1950s, children not only constituted a source of personal pleasure, but were also a symbol of the new-found wealth and status. All these demographic factors which contributed to the expansion of family size by both encouraging the number of births within each generation and expanding the number of generations which could potentially reside under one roof were reinforced by the new economic policies of the mid-1950s which directly encouraged an expansion in peasant family size.

The removal of the land base of the *jia* estate and the collectivisation of land and the establishment of the commune, production brigade and production team as effective units of production, distribution and accounting contributed to some decline in the socio-economic and political functions of the individual peasant household. Indeed as earlier references revealed, the very definition of the family or household itself omitted any reference to its property base or the socio-economic functions to do with production and consumption. In the 1950s social scientists abroad forecast that the diminution of the *jia* estate or economic basis of the joint family, the payment of individual wages, the collective ownership of land and the collective organisation of production would all weaken the economic base of both the

TABLE 1.9   *Demands on labour resources of peasant household (before 1978)*

Collective sector		Domestic sector
Production	Sidelines[1]	Servicing
		Food processing and cooking
Cropping	Private plot	Child care
Livestock	Livestock	Water carrying
Industries	Handicrafts	Sewing
Transport	Transport	Laundry and cleaning
		Fuel collection

[1]   Mainly for subsistence, surplus for local exchange and for sale to the State.

traditional complex and 'smaller' peasant family.[30] Yet a closer examination of the peasant household revealed that the economic organisation of rural China continued to demand that peasant households mobilise their individual resources in order to find solutions to two organisational problems, namely production in and for the collective or for subsistence and for local exchange and the transformation of materials for consumption and the provision of basic needs (see Table 1.9).

The peasant household was indeed still a unit of production although somewhat reduced by collectivisation and the primary unit of consumption. Furthermore the economy of the domestic group no longer relied on the exploitation of the *jia* lands and estate, although private plots were distributed for family use, so much as on the waged and domestic labour of each member of the household. Those who worked for the collective contributed their incomes to the household budget. Other family members, in addition to undertaking domestic labour and child care, contributed to the household economy by tending the private plot, raising domestic livestock or undertaking handicraft occupations all of which provided an important source of food and cash income for the household. The sum of all the demands on the peasant household and the consequent economic interdependence of young and older members encouraged the expansion of the peasant household. Marriage and the birth of children added to the membership of the peasant household, and a joint phase in the developmental cycle served as a unique opportunity for the household to maximise its labour resources and specialise or diversify its economy in order to accumulate wealth in this period prior to any subsequent household or family division.[31]

In any community where labour forms the major part of the total means of production and where control over labour is the major source of social differentiation, the recruitment and reproduction of labour itself is in constant demand. Where the individual and private hiring of labour is prohibited by law as it was within the People's Republic of China, then the highest value is placed on the reproduction of family labour. In the 1950s and 1960s peasant families saw little need to revise the adage which equated more children with more blessings. At the level of the household and where family planning services were available, fertility decisions are sometimes categorised as rational decisions in which political, cultural and socio-economic determinants are integrated into a single framework centring on the supply and demand for children. The costs of child-rearing in the countryside were relatively small. Children were normally allocated a grain ration equivalent to that of an adult and child care was usually undertaken by family members. Older children soon contributed to the household economy and finally, as wage-earners, they fully contributed to the family budget eventually supporting their parents in their old age. Thus it was frequently said that it is 'better to produce a little flesh dumpling (a baby) than produce work points yourself'.[32]

The traditional preference for sons remained and peasants desired at least one or preferably two sons. This continuing preference for sons was not just a survival of the feudal ideology as Chinese leaders sometimes thought, for there were very good economic reasons for such a marked preference. Patrilocal post-marital residence or the recruitment of the bride into the groom's household on marriage meant that it was only sons who could be relied upon to continue the family line and provide for their parents in their old age. Moreover the removal of the narrow property base of the peasant's household which had encouraged out-migration in the past, the expansion in local employment opportunities provided by the collective and the official limits placed on out-migration have all meant that sons were more likely to remain in the same village as their parents.

The scarce data on preferred family size implies that peasant women may have desired between four and six children, and data on average family size for these two decades suggest that the average number of children ever born per peasant woman was around 4, 5 or 6 although not all of these might survive (see Figure 1.1). It is known that the birth-rate had fluctuated between 33 and 38 per 1000 for these two decades and that in 1963 almost 40 per cent of the population was less than 15 years of age.[33] Villagers had always seen and could still see for themselves that even in the new economic conditions of the coun-

TABLE 1.10   *Some socio-economic determinants of decreased demand for children*

Income rise and redistribution
Demand for female labour
Reduced demand for child labour
Compulsory education
Increased educational opportunities
Increased opportunities for social mobility
Alternative sources of investment
Alternative sources of status
Increased urbanisation
Decreased infant mortality
Industrialisation (separation of production from household)
Increased social security and pensions
Increased direct and indirect costs of children

tryside, the richer households were commonly the larger households. This apparent correlation between family size, income and welfare was an incentive to follow suit and at least to maintain, if not increase, the number of children raised and to delay household division until the marriage of a younger son or the birth of a number of children to the oldest son. In increasing their family size, peasants did not just aspire to following the old model of the joint family. A number of economic incentives had encouraged the peasant household to expand and a number of new demographic factors permitted it to do so.

In urban areas there was not the same premium on the labour resources of the individual household and many of the socio-economic factors associated with a declining fertility elsewhere were operating within Chinese cities in the first two decades. (See Table 1.10.)

With the establishment of the State, co-operative and neighbourhood factories and enterprises and the ensuing separation of production from the urban household the demand for family labour decreased. Simultaneously the demand for female labour outside the home increased and widespread schooling occupied the children. Infant mortality dropped significantly, the costs of raising children increased and the competition for scarce educational and health and material resources encouraged parents to invest in fewer rather than more children. Most importantly, secure incomes and the introduction of a pension system plus the establishment of community services meant that adults were less reliant on the younger generation in the provision of basic needs. In the cities, post-marital residential patterns

were generally neolocal with the allocation of housing and the formation of separate households on marriage. In many of the cities there
was an acute housing shortage which sometimes led young couples to
reside with the parents of one of the partners, but this was presumed to
be only a temporary expedient. Moreover, both housing – which is not
usually privately-owned in the cities – and jobs are allocated, and their
location may not therefore be in such close proximity to the parents as
in the bounded village community.

In comparison with the rural areas, the economic interdependence
of the generations and the private and domestic demands on labour
were much reduced in urban areas and these factors had repercussions
for fertility decisions. The birth rate is frequently reported to be lower
in the cities than in the rural areas. By 1971 the birth rate in Shanghai
municipality had dropped from 23 per 1000 in 1963 to around 7 per
1000 in the city proper and from 41 to 18 per 1000 in the rural
suburbs.[34] A survey of urban women in Hubei province in 1959 also
revealed that urban women past child-bearing age had averaged one to
two children fewer than their rural counterparts.[35]

In sum, it was the contrasting socio-economic functions of the
household in rural and urban areas that can be said to have given rise to
a new dual familial form in contemporary China. By the end of the first
two decades , in 1970, the main differences in family size and structure
were no longer between social classes as formerly, but between urban
and rural China. Family size and the structure of the household in each
can be correlated directly to their respective socio-economic functions.
In urban areas where there was a minimal private sector of the
economy and where there were institutionalised state and community
provisions for retirement and for servicing and sharing in the mainte-
nance of the household, the functionality of the household as a
socio-economic unit had diminished. It was less a unit of production
and consumption than its rural counterpart and the residential patterns
tended towards those of the nuclear or conjugal type at the time of
marriage. In rural areas, where the individual household is still called
on to maximise its resources in order to perform a number of socio-
economic functions, marriage is still virilocal and household division
may be delayed.

In peasant and urban households developmental cycles differed. In
urban areas there tended to be no joint phase although conjugal
households might become stem at a later stage when, after the marriage of sons or daughters, a widowed parent might move into the
household of either a married son or daughter. In contrast, in rural

areas, the developmental cycle tended to pass through a joint phase although household division might eventually create a combination of conjugal and stem households. Although residential arrangements in urban and rural areas might eventually take the same form, it seems as if the developmental cycle of the domestic group may pass through different sequences in rural and urban areas. Each form had repercussions for fertility decisions. On the basis of available data it is a fair estimate that couples in urban areas tended to avail themselves of family planning services after the birth of one, two or three children; in suburbs after two, three or four children, and in the rural areas, after the birth of three, four or five children. During its first two decades the government of the People's Republic had made an impressive start in making services available to couples wishing to reduce unwanted fertility or the supply of children. What it had not yet aimed for was a reduction in the demand for children which is by far the most difficult step. By the beginning of the 1970s, however, it was clear to the government that if it planned to reduce the birth rate substantially in China it would have to redefine the fertility norms and models of family size themselves in favour of fewer children and the 'small' family.

Phase 3: The 'Small' Family Model

The early 1970s marked the beginning of a sustained attempt to implement family planning in China as part of a national population policy to reduce the birth rate to 2 per cent. To translate the objectives of the national population policy into meaningful and manageable goals, a new nation-wide model of family size was introduced which was encapsulated by the slogan 'late, spaced and few'.[36] The new model was based on late marriage, at about 27 and 25 years of age respectively for men and women in the cities and 25 and 23 years in the countryside. Such a rise in the age of marriage would of itself make for later child-bearing and over time the elimination of one generation per century. The second characteristic incorporated into the new 'small' family model was the spacing of at least four years between births which again would reduce the number of births in child-bearing years. Finally the slogan ended with a direct reference to the goal of fewer births per couple. The decade of the 1970s marks a departure from the past in that the recommended number of births for all couples is now quantitatively defined with the introduction of the slogan: 'one's not too few, two will do and three are too many for you'.[37] In fact the two-child family emerged as the official model in the cities although three were allowable, and in the countryside the family size model tended to hover around three children although again more were allowable especially if the previous births had all been girls.

To redefine family size in favour of the two- to three-child family and introduce new fertility norms, the government embarked on a series of national campaigns to educate and persuade the population to adopt the new models. These campaigns coincided with the establishment of nation-wide organisational network to make available and deliver family planning services. Thus committees for planned birth work were set up at every administrative level from the national to the regional, and within urban and local communities, cadres were made responsible for the family planning education. The delivery of contraceptives was closely tied in with the provision of basic health care by local clinics and particularly by the barefoot doctors. Thus records of women's fertility histories, cycles, contraception and future birth plans were all kept on wall-charts in the local clinics and simultaneous developments in family planning technology enabled barefoot doctors to deliver low-dosage pills daily in the fields during agricultural labour. Other widely available means of birth control were the IUD, barrier methods and both abortion and sterilisation. These were all provided for individual couples without charge.

Throughout the 1970s family planning education was aimed at those who were at the height of their fertility and especially those who could be expected to space their children adequately and those who already had completed a two- or three-child family. The means employed by the government to institutionalise the new norms – and perhaps one that is distinctive to China – was the small group combining the personal approach and peer group pressure. In factories, in enterprises, in urban streets or in rural villages, women were divided into small groups each of which was placed under the charge of a family planning worker (usually a mature woman who had completed her family) who organised the meetings and met with each woman member individually in her home. Whereas in the first two decades family planning had been voluntary and the final decision to adopt birth control methods left to the couples themselves, now there was some attempt to implement a national population plan according to a quota system.

In this system national, regional and local birth planning committees calculated desirable target quotas for the areas under their control.

Birth quotas or the number of births to be allowed in the next few years were passed downwards through the family-planning administrative hierarchy until finally each small group based on residence or enterprise received its allocated number of births. Local groups held periodic meetings to distribute the permitted number of births to members on the basis of 'late, spaced and few'. It is not clear how widespread the operation of the collective birth plan was, but there were certainly accounts of the groups' existence in the cities and suburban communes. Even if its operation was then limited, the collective plan marks an important precedent in that the decision to limit family size became a joint decision subjected to intervention by the state in the form of controlled peer or group pressure.

By the late 1970s, the redefinitions of old ideals and propagation of new models of family size, advances in contraceptive techniques and their delivery, and the operation of the collective birth plan had all begun to reduce the birth rate, especially in the cities. By 1973, the birth rate in the majority of the cities had fallen to below 20 per 1000.[38] Not unexpectedly many of the factors which had begun to affect the birth rate in the cities in the previous two decades continued to reduce the demand for children in the 1970s.[39] The birth rates for the cities visited by Pi-chao Chen in the mid 1970s ranged from 6.3 in Shanghai to 22 in Anyang city and the proportion of couples practising contraception ranged from 90 per cent in Shanghai to 40 per cent in Anyang. [40] In a random survey of children per couple, H. Yuan Tien found that the average was 3.24 and for those couples aged more than 40 who could be expected to have completed their fertile period, the average was 4.25.[41] Among the younger generations though, the two-to three-child family seemed to have emerged as the norm in the cities.

In the rural areas also the birth rate had declined although not as sharply as in the cities. Most estimates of the rural birth rate places it somewhere between 15 and 20 per 1000 in the suburban communes and figures in excess of these, or 20 to 30 per 1000 in the rural villages. Again the estimates of the proportions of couples practising contraception are wide – ranging from 20 per cent or so in the villages of Guangdong province to some 60–90 per cent in the suburban communes.[42] There had been little change in the economic organisation of rural China which continued to favour those peasant households with considerable family labour resources. It is true that this demand for family labour may have been affected by the new limits placed on domestic sideline production and the reduction of the child's grain ration, but apart from these small modifications, economic policies remained much the same and peasant households continued to prefer several rather than fewer children and to prefer sons rather than daughters.

The decade had been marked by the introduction of the new 'small' family model but rural economic policies had continued to encourage the demand for children. Although overall there had been a substantial decline in the national birth rate from 30 to 20 per 1000,[43] as the decade drew to a close the new post-Mao government viewed China's projected population growth-rate with increasing concern, and population and family planning once again became the focus of major new policies and campaigns. The major reason for the introduction of new population goals and a new model of family size based on one child only was the new government's ambitious plans for development and modernisation in the face of current and anticipated population growth-rates.

Phase 4: The Single-child Family Model

In the late 1970s the post-Mao government had embarked on a new and much-heralded phase of socialist modernisation the general aim of which was to turn China into a powerful and modern socialist society by developing four sectors of the economy: agriculture, industry, science and technology and defence. Although statements on the goals of socialist modernisation referred to a new 'Long March' in the development of China, in 1978 the pace of economic development was designed to be rapid. To this end individual policies emphasised the importance of production, professionalism, skills, scientific and technological research, profitability and the operation of economic incentives in the planning, management and expansion of production. Of course, plans and indeed ambitious plans to promote development and increase production were not new in China, but what was novel was the degree to which plans to develop and modernise China were thought to be contingent on China also taking drastic steps to reduce her population.

The basic problem according to the present government was that unless the population to be fed, housed and clothed was reduced, the goals of any development strategy in China were bound to fail. This official concern with population and its relation to development in the late 1970s reflected the increasing alarm of the present government over the total sum of the population of China – nearing one billion persons – and present and projected rates of population growth.

The other factor which made the introduction of radical family planning policies imperative was the age structure of China's population with some 50 per cent and 65 per cent of the population under the ages of 20 and 30 years respectively. Growth rates were expected to be unprecedently high in the near future. As a result of birth peaks in the mid-1950s and subsequently in the mid-1960s, it was expected that some 20m persons would enter marriageable and child-bearing age annually between 1979 and 1982, and again from 1987 to 1996, which was double the rate of recent years. On the basis of the present average birth rate of 2.3 children per couple, Chinese demographers calculated that the total population would reach some 1.3bn after twenty years and 1.5bn after forty years (see Table 1.11).[44]

The government also calculated the costs of educating, training and employing the younger generation and the costs of providing basic needs for an ever-expanding population. It estimated that the total cost of nurturing and educating a child to 16 years of age (not including college) and according to the general standard of living in China to be 1600 *yuan* in the countryside (87 per cent of the population), 4800 *yuan* in the small towns (4.2 per cent) and 6900 *yuan* in the cities (8.6 per cent). On the basis of these rough estimates, the government reckons that it has cost more than 1000bn *yuan* to bring up the 600m children born since 1949.[45] Given that 30 per cent of the national income has been spent on reproducing the labour force, just to employ the 6–10m young people entering employment each year will require a large capital investment in the means of production amounting to billions of *yuan* annually.[46] If present birth rates continue, these costs will act as a formidable barrier to accumulating the necessary capital for economic development and modernisation.

Demographic projections and their correlation with material and social resources show that land ratios and per capita grain rations will decline. For instance, the past thirty years have already seen a decline in cultivatable land from 2.6 to 1.5*mu* per capita,[47] and it can be expected to decline further in the future (see Table 1.12). Again, although grain production has more than doubled in the same period from approximately 110m tonnes in 1949 to nearly 318m tonnes in 1980, so has the population doubled – from 500m to 1000m.[48] There has consequently been little change in the average grain output per capita between 1956, when it was about 307kg, and 1980, when it was still around 307kg.[49] Government reports estimate that in the future, for grain production to keep pace with present population growth, the

TABLE 1.11   *Projected population growth*

Average birth rate of every married couple[2]	Population figure, year 2000[1] (in millions)	Number of increase over 1979 (in millions)
3.0	1414	444
2.3	1282	312
2.0	1217	247
1.5	1125	155
1.0[3]	1050	80

[1] Population figures do not include Taiwan and overseas Chinese
[2] Presumed from 1979 that the birth rate is maintained without variation
[3] Presumed from 1979 that the birth rate will decline and from 1985 be maintained at average of one child per couple

SOURCE   Zhongshan Daxue Xuebao Zhexue Shehui Kexue Ban (Zhongshan University Journal, Philosophy and Social Science Edition) no. 4, 1980, Trans. JPRS 1981.

TABLE 1.12   *Family size and basic needs in year 2000*

Average births per couple[1]	Average arable land[2] (mu per person)	Average jin of foodgrain per person per year[3]	Average number of children entering primary school annually 1996–2000 (in millions)	Total nurturing expenses incurred[4] (100 million yuan)
3	1.05	618	1.8	9768
2.3	1.16	682	1.4	6864
2	1.22	718	1.3	5434
1.5	1.32	777	0.9	3410
1	1.42	833	0.7	1760

[1] See Table 1.11
[2] Calculated on the assumption that by the year 2000 the country's arable land can be maintained at 1.49bn *mu*
[3] Calculated on the basis of a progressive yearly production increase of 10bn *jin*
[4] Calculated on the basis of an average of 2200 *yuan* in nurturing expenses for each person born between 1979 and 2000AD

SOURCE   'One married couple, one child seen as necessity', Zhongshan Daxue Xuebao-Zhexue Shehui Kexue Ban (Zhongshan University Journal) no. 4, 1980.

total grain output would need to be 480m tonnes by the end of the century, or 50 per cent more than the total output for 1980.[50] Similar calculations have been made for the provision of housing.

As a result of these projections, the government not only emphasised production but also redefined it to include both the production of material goods and the reproduction of human beings themselves. The government constantly quoted Engels in support of its twofold definition of production:

> Social production itself is of a twofold character: on the one hand, the production of the means of subsistence of food, of clothing and shelter and the necessary tools; and on the other the production of human beings themselves, the propagation of the species.[51]

Current slogans thus directed cadres and the population to 'grasp the two kinds of production' and be aware of the consequences of allowing the population to increase out of step with China's productive capacity.

> If we do not implement planned population control and let the population increase uncontrollably, rapid population growth is bound to put a heavy burden on the state and the people, cripple the national economy, adversely affect accumulation and State construction, the people's living standard and their health and slow down progress of the four modernisations.[52]

On this basis, 'planned and proportionate' development not only called for the planned development of the production of material goods but also for planned development of the production of human beings. The potential for simultaneously achieving these twin goals was conceived to be one of the unique strengths of the socialist mode of development and again one long ago identified by Engels.[53] He had forecast that because the public ownership of the means of production already subjected the production of goods to State planning, it was but a natural consequence to take planning one step further and if necessary include reproduction within national economic plans. This analysis, simple as it was, offered an immediate explanation for the apparent lack of development in China in the past decades when the 'unchecked growth of population' and the resulting imbalance between the 'two kinds of production' had been allowed to violate the socialist principles of a planned economy. It also offered a plan for the future achievement of planned and proportionate development. To fulfil the current national population targets of reducing rates of growth to 1 per cent by the end of 1979, 0.5 per cent in 1985 and zero population growth by the turn of the century, the present government felt it had no alternative but to adopt the rule – only one child.[54]

The government is aware of the sacrifice which this policy demands of the younger generation in China today. The policy is usually identified as an emergency measure or 'social payment' which will have to remain in force for the next twenty to thirty years to make up for the lack of population control in the previous twenty to thirty years.[55] Although both the present Constitution and the Marriage Law promote family planning and refer to the 'duty' of both husband and wife to practise family planning, there is as yet no national family planning law applicable throughout the entire country. A family planning law was drafted and was originally to be presented to the Fifth National People's Congress when it met in 1980. However, the law was never published apparently because there were still a number of unresolved problems and a lack of consensus surrounding its provisions.[56] Nevertheless, it is likely that general guidelines were communicated to the provinces and municipalities each of which has published its own set of rules and regulations enacting the single child family policy over the past few years. A study of these suggests that three features distinguish this new policy from its predecessors.

One Child

The first distinguishing feature is its novel, universal and singular recommendation – one child – which was deemed to be the 'fairest' means of reducing the birth rate. However any success in promoting the one-child family is determined by the accompanying policies and measures to reduce the number of second and additional parity births. The published sets of rules and regulations on family size uniformly advocate the birth of one child and categorically 'prohibit', 'eliminate' or 'ban' the birth of a third child. That is, there are no conditions under which the birth of a third child is officially permitted in either rural or urban areas. What is not yet so clear or so uniform throughout China are the policies towards the birth of a second child. Yet it is precisely the acceptability or otherwise of a second child which will be the key determinant of the success of the single-child family policy.

Official policies towards second parity births include programmes which aim to 'control' and 'regulate' the birth of second children in order to 'reduce' their number. The slogans range from 'no second child' to 'no more than two', and there is a range of circumstances, by no means uniform throughout China, under which a second child is allowed. The regulations usually read:

> Among government cadres, workers and urban residents each couple shall have only one child, with the exemption of those who for special reasons have obtained permission to have more than one child. In rural areas, couples should limit themselves to a single child, but some couples may be given permission to have a second child if their requirements can be justified on account of practical difficulties which can be examined and approved. No one is allowed to have a third child no matter what.[57]

There are a number of very particular conditions under which the birth of a second child is permitted and these usually include situations in which the first child either has a congenital defect or has been adopted because of presumed sterility or one partner of a re-married couple is childless.[58] These conditions apply equally to urban and rural couples, but in rural areas there are additional circumstances under which a second child might be born. These usually allow a second child 'if an individual commune member is having true or real difficulties'; a state which is to be defined and approved by county government officials and can therefore be variously interpreted throughout China. What is interesting about the more recent regulations is not only the breadth of conditions under which a second child is permitted, but the concessions to kinship and the continuation of the family line here, which are incorporated into the range of permitted circumstances.[59] It is a fair guess that much of the opposition within the government to a national law centres on the conditions under which a second child is permitted and the severity of the penalties to be attached to the birth of a second child.

Incentives and Disincentives

The second distinguishing feature of the single-child family policy is the number of economic incentives and disincentives which have been incorporated into this policy. The inclusion of quite punitive economic sanctions to be taken against those not adhering to any official regulations is a departure from past practice in China. Of course the circumstances under which couples can be induced to limit their families to one child is a matter of considerable interest, and one of the means by which the government has sought to encourage a preference for one child only is to reduce the cost of this first child and dramatically increase the cost of subsequent children. Official regulations introducing the single-child family policy in provinces and municipal authorities include lists of incentives and disincentives which reward those couples with one child who pledge to have no more, and penalise households not limiting family size to one child.[60]

Over the past three years or so, rewards have gradually become more standardised over much of China, so that in all provinces and cities, couples with one child who apply for a single-child family certificate can now expect to receive a cash health or welfare subsidy. This is paid to the parents by their units of employment either as a monthly or annual subsidy or is payable at each periodic distribution after the harvest in rural areas. There are a number of other privileges and subsidies to which the single-child family is entitled. The single child has priority of admission to nurseries, schools, hospitals, clinics and in job allocation and all educational and medical fees from birth onwards are to be waived or at least reduced. The single-child family is to receive a larger grain ration, a larger private plot and priority in allocation of housing or housing plots. Parents of a single child can expect to receive special financial aid on their retirement.

The rewards are to be paid directly by the husband's and wife's unit of employment and the exact proportion paid to each parent depends on the level of ownership of their units. For instance where both are employed at the same level, the payments are to be equally shared, but if one member is employed in a state-owned enterprise and the other by either a rural or urban co-operative, then the state factory is likely to pay the whole subsidy. Potentially the economic rewards can be quite considerable, and in one commune it has been calculated that a couple with one child could augment its total collective income by a quarter or even a third through the benefits and rewards available to the single-child family.[61]

A key question in the analysis of any incentive scheme is the degree to which it is practically operative and in particular the source and extent of its funding. With the exception of the monthly cash subsidy, other incentives are very much determined by the resources of the unit of employment and the funds it has at its disposal. The government has undertaken elaborate calculations to show how the cost of making economic rewards might be met, but these are usually based on the national savings resulting from each child not born because of the new policy. These savings are estimated to range from 2000 *yuan* per child in the cities, 1000 *yuan* per child in the towns and 400 *yuan* per child in the countryside.[62] However in real cash terms these savings are somewhat hypothetical.

The economic penalties for a subsequent or additional child are the reverse of the incentives. An 'excess child levy' is to be made on the income of couples as a form of economic compensation to the state and the collective for the extra burdens caused by the birth of those children. Thus the regulations permit employment units to deduct 5 to 10 per cent of the total income of a couple for somewhere between ten and sixteen years after birth, a proportion which rises to 15 per cent for a fourth and 20 per cent for a fifth child. In a few regions a single cash levy or fine is payable at the time of birth. In addition, the offending family must bear all the costs of the birth and subsequent medical and educational expenses incurred by the extra child, and it enjoys no priority in admission to any educational or medical institutions. The grain ration for the excess child is either reduced or available at a higher price and the family with more than one child is not eligible for any additional housing space or private plots. Finally parents who reject the single-child family policy are not eligible for promotion or a bonus for a number of years and cannot apply for subsidies in cases of hardship.

Potentially then the economic sanctions are quite considerable and what makes them even more exacting is the requirement that, in addition to these sanctions, the value of the rewards received for the single-child by certificate-holders are with few exceptions also to be paid back on the birth of a second child. Again what is not clear is the extent to which these penalties are exacted on the birth of a second child. There have been no such cases reported in the media and it seems that local regulations range from those where a second pregnancy is not permitted to proceed to term, to those where local authorities take a softer line, allow the birth of a second child and do not exact any penalties. In the media most of the reports on the operation of penalties refer to the births of a third, fourth and fifth child among cadres and Party members who are supposed to be setting an example. In such cases, the couples have been demoted, their salaries reduced and an abortion or sterilisation ordered. The operation of the penalties could amount to a financial loss of several hundreds or even thousands of *yuan*.[63] However it does seem that where second and third parity births are prohibited, government intervention may take place at an earlier stage and that the pressures brought to bear on offending couples are such that they are more likely to terminate the pregnancy than to proceed to term and be penalised.

State Intervention

The third distinguishing feature marking out this policy from its predecessors is the degree of State intervention in fertility decisions which it represents. In China it can be said to mark a fourth phase in the relations between state and the reproductive unit in which the present Chinese leadership regards fertility decisions as too important to be delegated to the reproductive unit, the family:

> The population plan of the whole country is based on the reproductive activities of individual families and the family birth plan must be co-ordinated with the national population plan.[64]

The incorporation of family plans into a national population plan means that the control of births and family size becomes the prerogative of the state. This attempt by the government to acquire an exclusive measure of control over fertility decisions, family planning and family size represents an almost unique attempt by any government anywhere to regulate fertility behaviour and reduce the demand for children by direct authoritative regulation and political control. Indeed, taking the spectrum of policy instruments available to any government to decrease fertility, China has broken new ground in employing direct regulation. One of the main ethical and political issues raised by policies to depress fertility centres on the very incompatibility of population control and reproductive freedom or the point at which policy options cross the line from voluntarism to coercion. What the present government in China hopes is that the introduction of the single-child family model will be freely accepted by the population of China as a new norm and of itself regulate fertility behaviour. For this reason the government has devoted enormous effort to present the case for the single-child family to the population at large.

In 1979 the government embarked on a massive educational campaign designed to publicise and popularise the idea of the one-child family, and all aspects of the media have been marshalled in its support.[65] The main aim of the educational campaign has been to convince the present population of China that it is the 'objective' conditions of China rather than the Communist Party or the present leadership that do not permit the birth of more children. To this end, the government has taken great pains to identify and explain the dimensions of the problem to the population at large.

What is interesting about the case which the Chinese government has presented in these campaigns is that all demographic calculations and their correlations with projected demands on resources are calculated in terms of family size rather than large and national population aggregates. Indeed the general aim of the educational materials is to link the responsibility of the individual couple directly with the welfare of the collective and the nation. According to the present government, one of the problems in the past was that all too often couples were only acquainted with family circumstances and made their individual decisions on family size without reference to national conditions and constraints.

To communicate and popularise the objects of the new policy, the National Family Planning Association has taken special responsibility for the nation-wide administration and implementation of the single-child family programme. It already had a national network providing comprehensive services throughout China which could be activated in support of the new policy. It is the task of this network to persuade families to accept new norms and take practical steps to implement the policy.[66] The degree of pressure applied to couples varies considerably. In some areas, individual women, their husbands and their mothers or mothers-in-law may be visited time and and again until all sources of resistance are worn down. In other areas, however, the new policies once expounded and explained are not followed up with quite the same vigour.

The degree to which the new policy is successful will depend very much on the success of the government in persuading those of child-bearing age to accept the necessity for the single-child family and thus establish new fertility norms. The emphasis on education and establishing a new norm of behaviour reflects the quite central belief in China that ideology and organisation can introduce and maintain momentum in social change. The government believes that if the population can be persuaded by education to accept the new norms in the long-term national interest then change will be possible even if it directly counters their family interest in the short-term. However, present attempts to persuade the peasant household by employing a new ideology may well prove to be more difficult to implement in the coming decade than in the past. This present leadership faces a central problem – that of the credibility of the state in effecting long-term social change. Employing any ideological campaign to persuade peasant households to disregard their short-term interests in favour of long-term goals has been made all the more difficult by repeated and substantive changes in official policies over the past twenty-five years. These have generated some malaise and cynicism especially among the younger generations or those entering child-bearing age, who now display a distrust of the government's power and will to hold any policy universally constant over place and time. In the case of the single-child family, not only does this uncertainty affect the way that the rules and regulations are regarded, but also the degree to which incentives and disincentives operate and are effective.

In the implementation of the single-child family the national government is reliant on the local or basic level family-planning cadres to operate the policy on its behalf. It has not been uncommon in the past for the government to hold basic-level cadres responsible for the tardy implementation of national policies within the local socio-political arena and indeed many a failure has been attributed to faulty leadership. At the present time, reports on family planning throughout the country all stress that one of the central factors determining the success or failure of the single-child family policy will be the quality of local leadership:

> Positive and negative experience indicates repeatedly that the success of planned parenthood still depends heavily on leadership.[67]

In the last analysis however it is the response of individual couples to the policy which will finally decide the establishment of new fertility norms and fertility behaviour. During the first five years this response has been highly variable. The single-child family has been deemed the most unpopular policy introduced into China over the past five years. There are those who view it as one more measure of state control over the individual, 'You are in charge of the earth and the sky and now you still want to take charge of child-bearing'.[68] There are others who although they do not like the policy defend it as a radical but necessary solution to China's problems of population growth, modernisation and development. Estimating the proportions of those who accept the policy and those who refuse it is very difficult, given the problems of definition and of compiling statistics in China. Overall, the government claimed that by the end of 1979 some 6m out of 14m couples with one child had taken out single-child family certificates; by the end of

1980 it was 11m out of 20m and by mid-1981 it was 12.5m out of the 22m eligible.[69] Of course those who already had more than one child in 1979 were not eligible, and some single-child families had already decided to have but one child long before the current policy. It is probably too soon to ascertain in any detail the response of different sections of the population to this policy, but the data already available does suggest certain trends. So far it seems that the largest single factor determining the response of an individual couple to the new policy is the location of their residence – whether they be urban- or rural-based.

NOTES AND REFERENCES

1. M. Freedman, *Lineage organisation in South-eastern China*, LSE Monographs in Social Anthropology (London: Athlone Press, 1958) 19.
2. See F. Hsu, 'The Myth of Chinese Family Size', *American Journal of Sociology*, vol. 48, May 1943; Fei Hsiao-tung, 'Peasantry and Gentry', ibid., vol. 52, July 1946.
3. I. B. Taeuber, 'The Families of Chinese Farmers' in M. Freedman, (ed.) *Family and Kinship in Chinese Society* (Stanford University Press, 1970).
4. C. K. Yang, *Chinese Communist Society: The Family and the Village* (Boston: Massachusetts Institute of Technology, 1959), 7; M. Freedman, 'Chinese Domestic Family Models' in *VIe Congrès internationale des sciences anthropologiques et ethnologiques*, Paris, 1963, vol. 2. Pt 1, 97–100.
5. F. W. Notestein, 'Population' in J. L. Buck, *Land Utilization in China* (Nanking: University of Nanking, 1937), 363–71.
6. S. D. Gamble, *Ting Hsien, A North China Rural Community* (Stanford University Press, 1954), 21–59.
7. O. Lang, *Chinese Family and Society* (Yale University Press, 1946) 134–54.
8. Taueber, 'The Families of Chinese Farmers', 83.
9. Lang, *Chinese Family and Society*, 149.
10. L. C. Smythe, 'The Composition of the Chinese Family', *Nanking Journal*, 5, 1935, 12 and 14.
11. Ibid.
12. Buck, *Land Utilization in China*, 385–6.
13. Gamble, *Ting Hsien.*, 84.
14. H. D. Lamson, 'Differential Reproduction in China', *The Quarterly Review of Biology*, 10, 3 September 1935, 308–21; also in J. Salaff, 'Institutionalised Motivation for Fertility Limitation', *Population Studies*, vol. XXVI, no. 2, July 1972.
15. Lang, *Chinese Family and Society*, 152.
16. M. B. Treudley, *Men and Women of Chung Ho Ch'ang* (Taipei, 1971), Table II.
17. C. K. Yang, *Chinese Communist Society*, 18.
18. M. Yang, *A Chinese Village* (Columbia University Press, 1945), 11.

19. Fei Hsiao-tung, *Peasant Life in China* (London, Routledge Kegan Paul 1939), 34.
20. S. D. Gamble, *Peking: A Social Survey*, (New York: George H. Doran, 1921), 45.
21. Chen Ta, *Emigrant Communities in South China* (New York, 1940), 125.
22. Marion J. Levy, *The Family Revolution in Modern China* (Harvard University Press, 1949) 45–60.
23. F. Hsu, 'The Myth of Chinese Family Size' 561.
24. C. K. Yang, Chinese Communist Society, 9.
25. Yang Liu, 'Reform of marriage and family system in China', *Peking Review*, 13 March 1964.
26. Lu Yang, *Ruhe zhengque duidai lianai, hunyin, jiating wenti* (The Correct Handling of Love, Marriage and Family Problems) (Jinan: Shandong People's Publishing House, 1964), 7.
27. Jan Myrdal, *Report from a Chinese Village*, (Harmondsworth: Penguin Books, 1967), 292–3.
28. Han Suyin, 'Population Growth and Birth Control in China', *Eastern Horizon*, vol. 12, no. 5; 1973, 8–16.
29. Lim Kahti, 'Obstetrics and Gynaecology in the Past Ten Years', *Chinese Medical Journal*, 79, 5. (November 1959) 375–83.
30. See Elisabeth Croll, *The Politics of Marriage in Contemporary China*, (Cambridge University Press, 1981), 144.
31. Ibid, 142–64.
32. Han Suyin, 'Population Growth and Birth Control' 9.
33. Liu Zheng, Song Jian et al. *China's Population and Prospects* (Beijing: New World Press, 1981), 5.
34. Pi-chao Chen, 'China's Population Programme at the Grass Roots Level,' *Studies of Family Planning*, vol. 4, no. 8, August 1973, 220.
35. Salaff, 'Institutionalised Motivation for Fertility Limitation' 96.
36. See H. Yuan Tien, 'Wan, Xi, Shao: How China Meets its Population Problem', *International Family Planning Perspectives*, vol. 6, no. 2, June 1980, 65–73.
37. Ibid, 68.
38. Pi-chao Chen, *Population Growth and Policy*, Occasional Monograph Series no. 9 (Washington: Interdisciplinary Communication Programme, Smithsonian Institute, 1976), 107–18.
39. Carl, Djerassi, 'Fertility Limitation through Contraceptive Steroids in the People's Republic of China, *Studies in Family Planning*, vol. 5, no. 1, January 1974, 28.
40. Pi-chao Chen, 1976, *Population Growth and Policy*, 111 and 113.
41. H. Yuan Tien, 'Planned Production, Family Formation and Fertility Decline', Paper read at Annual Meeting of the Population Association of America, New York, 19 April 1974; 8.
42. Djerassi, 'Fertility Limitation'.
43. Liu Zheng et al. *China's Population*, 5 and 68.
44. For a lengthy discussion in English on the characteristics of China's population, see Liu Zheng et al., *China's Population*.
45. Chen Muhua, 'Population Control', *RMRB* (People's Daily) 11 August 1979.

46. 'Population Situation: Theory studies from an Economic Angle', *Jingji Yanjiu* (Economic Research) 20 May 1979; 'Population Control Important to Economic Planning', RMRB, 2 June 1980.
47. Chen Muhua, 'Population Control'.
48. Li Shiyi, 'Development Trends in Chinese Population Growth' *Beijing Review*, (BR) 11 January 1981.
49. Ibid
50. Ibid.
51. Engels quoted in Liu Zheng, 'Problems of China's Population Growth' in *Jingji Yanjiu*, 20 May 1979.
52. Editorial, *RMRB*, 8 July 1978.
53. Chen Zhongli, 'An Analysis of the Large Population Policy', *Gongren Ribao* (Workers' Daily) 4 October 1979.
54. 'Population Control and Modernisation, *Jiefang Ribao* (Liberation Daily) 30 July 1979; Liu Zheng *et al., China's Population.*
55. Li Shiyi, 'Development Trends'.
56. New China News Agency (NCNA), 13 September 1980.
57. 'Central Committee and State Council Urge Better Family Planning', *NCNA*, 13 March 1982.
58. For example, 'Shanghai Planned Parenthood Regulations,' *Jiefang Ribao*, 10 August 1981, *Survey of World Broadcasts*, (*SWB*) 31 August 1981 (FE/6815/B11/1).
59. 'Shanxi Planned Parenthood Regulations,' *Shanxi Ribao* (Shanxi Daily), 17 November 1982 in SWB 16 December 1982 (FE/7210/B11/3).
60. For example see 'Sichuan Regulations in Family Planning', *SWB*, 16 March 1979 (FE/6068/B11/9).
61. Ashwani Saith, 'Economic Incentives for the One-child Family in Rural China', *China Quarterly*, September 1981.
62. Gui Shixin, 'Population Control and Economic Policy', Shanghai Teachers' Journal, *Zhexue Shehui Kexue Ban* (Philosophy and Social Science) 25 April 1980 (Trans. (JPRS) May 1980).
63. 'Problems in Family Planning Work in Zhejiang', *RMRB*, 11 April 1980.
64. Liu Zheng, 'There must be a Population Plan', *RMRB*, 2 June 1980.
65. For full discussion of arguments in support of the policy, see Gui Shixin, 'Population Control and Economic Policy'.
66. See 'Family Planning in Tianjin', *Tianjin Ribao* (Tianjin Daily) 22 July 1979; 'Family Planning in Shanghai', *Wenhui Bao* (Shanghai) 18 January 1980.
67. Editorial, *Shanxi Ribao*, 12 April 1982.
68. 'Take Urgent Action to Reduce the Birth Rate', *Tianjin Ribao* 4 August 1979.
69. Beijing Centre of Communications and Family Planning, *Renkou Lilun xuanzhang* (Topics in Population Theory) 40.

2 The Single-child Family Policy in the Countryside

DELIA DAVIN

As 80 per cent of China's population is rural and 87.2 per cent of births in China occur in the countryside it is ultimately there that the battle to control population growth will be won or lost.[1] Far greater efforts are needed in the villages than in the towns, not only because peasants vastly outnumber city-dwellers, but also because while some conditions historically associated with a rapid fall in fertility are present in the towns, this is not the case in the countryside. In the 1960s, China's planners, like planners in many other developing countries, saw efficient delivery of the contraceptives and contraceptive education as the main tasks in population control. By the 1970s they had recognised that motivation was the fundamental problem.

Early attempts to change the desired family size of the peasants relied heavily on reasoning, persuasion, group pressure and appeals to a sense of the public good. When in the late 1970s it was clear that these methods had proved insufficiently successful, interventions designed to change the economic costs and benefits of having children were made. The incentives and penalties introduced as part of the two-child campaign in the late 1970s and greatly expanded at the start of the single-child campaign in 1979 can be seen as an attempt to bring about rapidly, through state intervention, changes in fertility and population growth rates which in the west came about largely in conjunction with industrialisation and urbanisation.

The single-child family policy is far more ambitious than anything which went before it. While earlier campaigns aimed to push the peasants a bit further and faster along a path which they might anyway have been expected to take, the present campaign demands a radical break with tradition. When the policy was introduced in 1979, the particular difficulty of implementing it in the countryside was recognised in the comparitively modest goals set. Rural areas were to aim for a 50 per cent rate of one-child families (among those couples who had not already had more) whereas urban areas had to try for an 80 per cent rate.[2] These targets were soon raised however. In February 1980, Vice-Premier Chen Muhua, Director of the State Birth Planning Commission stated:

> We will try to attain the goal that 95 per cent of married couples in the cities and 90 per cent in the countryside will have only one child in due course, so that the total population of China will be controlled at about 1.2 billion by the end of the century.[3]

Enormous pressure is exerted on peasant couples to restrict their families to one. Only a tiny minority can, in very special circumstances, apply to have a second. This means that 50 per cent of couples are being asked to face old age without a male heir and to accept that their family line will end in their generation, while all families are required to curtail their future supply of labour. Obviously if this state-induced demographic transition is to succeed, policy-makers need a clear understanding of fertility motivation in Chinese society and an ability to calculate accurately the interventions necessary to alter the motivation. These are the issues with which this chapter is mainly concerned.

Despite the oft-cited Chinese desire to have sons and the fact that women married early in rural society, marital fertility among Chinese peasants was suprisingly low in the first half of the twentieth century, a fact which may reflect a spontaneous response to the deteriorating population: land ratio.[4] Death rates were very high and most demographers believe that population growth in the century prior to the establishment of the People's Republic in 1949 was very slow.

However, as a remarkably far-sighted American report of 1950 pointed out, China's high birth-rates and death-rates contained a huge potential for population growth if a strong central government capable of instituting public health measures were to be established.[5] The report also surmised that the lack of consciousness among educated Chinese of the population problem faced by their country, together with the simplistic marxist position that 'people are wealth', meant that no government was likely to come to grips with the problem in the immediate future

These predictions proved correct. After 1949 death rates fell especially among the young age-groups and population began an accelerating climb, while the government only began to pay serious attention to the problem of population after the loss of two decades which in retrospect can be seen to have cost it dear. Enormous population growth had taken place creating a situation by the middle 1970s where 65 per cent of the population was aged 30 or younger and 38.6 per cent was under 15 years old.[6] Given this population structure and lowered death-rates, only the most draconian measures could slow growth and there was no immediate prospect of halting it. Even population projections based on a universal single-child family show that China cannot reach zero population growth until the year 2000.[7] However it is worth remembering that this period of unrestrained population growth lasted only two decades, not long in terms of the time needed to generate a spontaneous demographic response. It does not prove Chinese peasants would not in time themselves have made some adjustment to the deterioration in the population: land ratio brought about by falling death-rates, especially infant mortality rates, still less that they could be expected to reject government attempts to persuade them to do so.

THE PEASANTS' DESIRE FOR CHILDREN

A knowledge of the costs and benefits of child-rearing in rural China and of the peasants' reasons for having children are necessary to an understanding of China's present population policy and its chances of success. Prior to the single-child family programme the cost of each additional child impinged on the rural family less than on its urban counterpart and there were certain economic advantages in a large family. Each peasant family received an allocation of grain distributed on a per capita basis. Although part of the value of the grain was deducted from the family's collective income for the year, it was possible to go into 'overdraft'; that is a household could draw its grain allowance even in a year in which it earned less than the full value of the allowance. The amount owed would be carried over to the follow-ing year. Couples with numerous young children could thus rely on what was in effect 'free credit' until their children began to enter the labour force and the family's finances improved. Allocation of land for private plots and for housing was also made on a per capita basis. Houses in most villages are privately owned so that peasants, unlike city-dwellers, can extend their houses or build new ones when they expand their families.

Although woman's role in Chinese agriculture is often considerable, the fear of curtailing the woman's earnings did not act as a very effective brake on fertility.[8] In most peasant families, young mothers could still find some way to engage in remunerative activity. They might take their babies to the fields, do handicraft work at home or tend the private plot. Grandparents or elder siblings could care for a baby or toddler if their earning potential was less than that of the mother's. Where women's labour was in demand, collective childcare was sometimes available, although in rural areas this was still the exception. Thus village mothers have several alternative ways of getting infants cared for and older children are allowed to roam more freely in the rural areas than they would be in the cities where traffic constitutes such a hazard.

Despite subsidies from collective welfare funds, school and medical fees could be a problem for the peasant family with several young children.[9] However in well-off communes or brigades they were sometimes waived for families in economic difficulty while in the poorest parts of the country enrolments were so low and health facilities so scanty, that the fear of such expenses would not have affected fertility.

The wholly dependent period of a child's life does not last long in a Chinese village. Children make themselves useful very early by caring for their younger siblings, feeding livestock, weeding private plots, fetching water and gathering fuel. Although obviously these are simple tasks and thus within a child's capabilities, they are all essential to the household economy. If there is a child to perform them, an adult is freed for some more remunerative task. Often also a child would start to earn work-points by hoeing and gleaning in the fields or taking livestock into the hills even before the official end of primary school. But children also represent a long-term investment for their families. Sons at least grow to join the family labour force, continue the family line and offer their parents security for their old age. When the fields were tilled collectively, fertiliser and machinery were purchased by the collective and household enterprise was discouraged; children were thus not just the best, but the *only* large-scale investment which peasants could make.[10]

Recently, for obvious reasons, Chinese social scientists have begun to show an interest in the peasants' reasons for wanting children. Three main ones are commonly cited (see Table 2.1). When young married couples look to the future they know that they need at least one son to survive to adulthood. Given high infant mortality rates, this meant for security two or preferably three male births. If more than one son

TABLE 2.1   *Survey of 808 persons in rural Hubei:* reasons for wanting many children*

Reasons	Percentage
To produce sons for support in old age	51
To produce successors for the ancestral line	25
To increase the household labour force	21
Liking children	3

* The methodology of such surveys tends not to be satisfactorily explained and their findings are frequently tantalising in that they raise as many questions as they answer, but this one does summarise the facts basic to an understanding of Chinese rural demography.

SOURCE   Cheng Du, 'Fertility Survey in the Rural Areas of Hubei Province', *Renkou Yanjiu*, no. 5, 1982.

reached adulthood, probably only one would reside with his parents but all would contribute to their upkeep, producing an improved standard of living for the old people. Improved survival chances for children have now reduced the upwards pressure on fertility by the 'insurance' factor. The *number* of sons a peasant couple wants is negotiable but the desire for a minimum of one boy to take care of his parents and to assure the continuance of the family line is unwavering.

As at least one son normally remains with his parents after marriage and the birth of his own children, stem families are common in the countryside. The parents of a new bridegroom are likely to be in their forties. They will be still more aware than the young couple of the need for a male infant whose labour can begin to replace that of his grandfather as the latter withdraws from the labour-force in his late fifties. Nor is the influence of the older generation confined to pressing for male offspring. Conscious of the passage of time, older people have tended to be a source of opposition to the government's advocacy of late marriage and wide spacing between children. Any measure which lengthens the age-gap between the generations increases the danger to the individual family that it will get caught in the situation where one working generation (the parents) must support two non-working ones (the grandparents and the children). It comes as no surprise that rural three-generational households have been found to have to produce more children than two-generational ones.[11]

Each peasant family needs a son rather than a daughter because a boy will stay in his father's household, supporting its older members, carrying on the family name and in his turn supplying a male heir in the next generation. A daughter by contrast marries out and often away from her village, becomes part of the labour force of another family, cares for her parents-in-law in their old age and bears grandchildren to them. Despite all the effort made to improve the position of women in China since 1949, the system of virilocal marriage remains intact and the peasant preference for sons over daughters is therefore inevitably unaltered.[12]

This is not to say that when peasant families could still, without problems, produce several children, a daughter was altogether unwelcome. After all, her labour before marriage did go to the family. Where there were a lot of children or household sidelines in which female labour was employed she might be very useful. In collective labour girls or boys of nine or ten could sometimes earn three, four or even five workpoints a day (to a man's ten) and unmarried teenage girls were often on higher workpoint rates than married women. Given her own contribution to the family budget, the collective's hidden subsidies to child-rearing and the bride-price to be expected, a daughter must normally have produced a net gain for her family by the time of her marriage.[13]

When a girl marries in the countryside, her parents usually receive a bride-price which far outweighs any expenditure they undertake for her wedding and which may indeed be used by them to meet the very high expenses they incur in arranging a marriage for her brother.[14] It is a paradoxical manifestation of the way women's worth has risen since the revolution in association with their greater economic role, that bride-price, despite vigorous official opposition to its very existence, appears to have increased considerably. A family with a daughter of marriageable age therefore finds it easier to finance the longed-for marriage of a son, a family without daughters will need to save for longer. This relationship and system of priorities in which a son is vital and a daughter useful was reflected in the findings of a survey in rural Hubei in 1981. Of 747 couples each with two daughters, who were questioned, 62 per cent still wanted a son whereas of 710 couples each with two sons, one third still wanted a daughter. Given the new one-child policy however, of 543 childless couples polled, only 2.2 per cent wanted a daughter.[15]

The general, but not total, preference for boys was reflected in another survey, carried out in northern Shanxi province in 1981. Nearly 1000 couples who had produced a second child outside the plan were questioned. Of these couples, 42.61 per cent had already had one boy, 57.39 per cent had had a girl. Asked why they had had a second

TABLE 2.2   *Urban and rural crude birth rates in China 1971–8 (per 1000 population)*

	1971	1972	1973	1974	1975	1976	1977	1978
Urban areas	21.9	20.1	18.1	15.1	15.3	13.6	13.9	14.0
Rural areas	31.9	31.2	29.4	26.2	24.8	20.8	18.7	18.8
National average	30.7	29.9	28.1	24.9	23.1	20.0	19.0	18.3

SOURCE   Pi-chao Chen and Adrienne Kols, 'Population and Birth Planning in the People's Republic of China', *Population Reports*, series J, no. 25, 1982, 599.

child, 50.5 per cent of respondents gave answers which implied they had wanted a boy (support in old age, ancestral line and labour power) but 11.4 per cent specifically stated that they had wanted a girl. (Their rationale was an interesting combination of the emotional, practical and economic. The investigators were told, 'Girls are close to their parents, they look after old people well and they can do embroidery'.[16]

Before the advent of the one-child policy, China achieved a fall in the official crude birth rate from 30 to 20 per thousand in the space of only five years between 1972 and 1976.[17] The family planning campaign of those years employed the slogan 'late, spaced and few' (wan, xi, shao) and relied mainly on persuasion, although some incentives were introduced. Urban and rural crude birthrates for the period show rural areas lagging about five years behind in birth reduction (see Table 2.2).

Although even this programme required a considerable modification of peasant reproductive behaviour, its flexibility made it far easier to promote than the present policy with its universal prescription of one child. Under the earlier policy those who already had two boys or a boy and a girl could often be persuaded to stop, those who had one girl could still try again and only those who had two or worse three girls presented an intractable problem. For them an old Chinese strategy for families lacking a male heir, that of uxorilocal marriage was mooted, it seems with little success. In the 1970s, judging from foreign visitors' reports and my own impressions, only surburban communes could produce instances of such marriages and even so they were rare.[18] Further away from the big cities it was possible to visit communes where there had been no recent cases. Not surprisingly peasants remained reluctant to rely on being able to find a 'live-in' son-in-law, and births 'outside the plan', that is of a third or higher parity child or of a second child born less than three years after the first, were probably concentrated in families to which only girls had been born. Those with the strongest motivation for refusing to comply with family-planning policy were still at this stage a clear minority.

The success of the 1970s is thus impressive but understandably so given that the objective of the family planning campaigns before 1978–9 was much less out of line with peasant wishes than is the present policy. Even without the family-planning campaign, desired family size might have fallen and could in some land-short regions have reached three, or even two, providing that there was a boy among the children. As early as the 1930s the anthropologist Fei Xiaotong found that villagers in his Yangzi valley village were not even willing to bring up a second *son* because of land shortage and avoided doing so by abortion or infanticide, producing the figure of only 1.3 children under 16 per household in the village.[19] This phenomenon although atypical for the time does indicate the potential responsiveness of Chinese peasant fertility to economic conditions.

By the 1970s, land shortage had become a pressing problem in many more areas. Officially it is estimated that per capita availability of arable land had fallen to only 1.5 *mu* compared with 2.71 *mu* in 1949.[20] Efforts to extend the area of cultivated land have proved extremely expensive and there is little or no unused land left which is suitable for this traditional Chinese style of intensive cultivation. Pressure in the most congested areas cannot be relieved by migration since movement into the already overcrowded cities is strictly controlled, and until very recently the prohibition on the hire of labour prevented peasants seeking a living elsewhere in the countryside. The great majority are still in effect tied to the commune in which they were born. Social changes such as the spread of literacy and greater political participation by women, which American demographers as early as 1950 had forecast would tend to reduce the birth rate have presumably begun to take effect.[21] All these factors predisposed the peasants to accept the call for smaller families. The government provision of a rural health network to supply the means of family planning therefore met with enough response to produce an impressive decline in the birthrate.[22]

THE ORGANISATION OF FAMILY PLANNING WORK IN THE RURAL AREAS

All cadres are supposed to be responsible for family planning prog-rammes, but the day-to-day work is carried out by cadres at the team and brigade level responsible for women's affairs and by health workers.[23] At the lowest level the women's team leader pays regular house-to-house visits to propagate family planning and to check on the situation in each household. She is expected to know which women are using contraceptives, what method they use, which women are eligible to give birth and which have become pregnant. She reports up to the brigade women's leader who records the information in registers which she takes to a monthly meeting of the commune birth-planning committee. One of the criticisms now made of earlier family planning campaigns was that they were often left entirely in the hands of women's affairs cadres who lacked both power and prestige. It is now emphasised that birth-control work should be the concern of all cadres and to underline this the commune birth-planning committee normally includes some important commune leaders. At the county, regional and even national levels, the same pattern can be seen. Meetings on family planning are attended by important government and Party figures in an attempt to convey the message that birth control is everybody's business.

The enormous intrusiveness of family planning work is well-documented. The careful records enable the village family planning worker to identify her 'targets' precisely. Unmarried young people are persuaded to postpone marriage, childless couples are visited and urged to 'await their turn' to try for a pregnancy, and those who already have a child are asked to practise contraception or accept sterilisation. Sterilisation is the solution urged on all couples with more than one child.

Officially, since voluntarism is the principle of the programme, family planning workers must limit themselves to persuasion but this can amount to extremely heavy pressure. A foreign journalist who visited Fengyan county in Anhui province in 1982 was told by county officials that women who get pregnant out of turn would be taken to commune headquarters and criticised until they agreed to an abortion.[24] An account of the campaign in a village in Guangdong province in 1979 describes how seventy-four 'target couples' who refused to practice contraception were told to attend discussion meetings at which thirty cadres attempted to wear down their resistance.[25] The meetings lasted seven hours a day for five months. The couples were paid regular workpoints for three days after which the husbands were excused from further meetings. The women had to continue to attend without further pay unless they capitulated. Absence was penalised by a fine of one yuan – slightly more than a day's pay. These seventy-four couples were the 'hard cases' who refused to comply and were drawn from a base of 1500 families so their experience cannot be cited as typical. It does however show how harsh pressure can be. Other reports indicate that peasant women who seek to carry an unapproved pregnancy to term so fear the pressure under which they will come that they seek to conceal themselves in cities. Elsewhere the line has certainly sometimes been crossed into straight compulsion, and there have been reports of forced abortions. The IUD used in China can only be removed by skilled medical personnel, and, once she has had it fitted, a woman is not supposed to have it removed except with official approval.[26]

Family-planning work is relentlessly maintained but it is given certain peaks which reflect the fertility patterns of the Chinese year. Propaganda is intensified just before festivals especially the Chinese New Year, a favourite time for conviviality, family reunions and for weddings. January of 1982 was named as 'family-planning month' and throughout the last weeks of 1981 and the first ones of 1982 every possible means was used to publicise it.

THE MEANS OF BIRTH PLANNING IN THE COUNTRYSIDE

Several forms of contraception are employed in the countryside and use-patterns differ from one province to another for reasons which are not always very clear. Recent figures show that of China's 170m married women capable of bearing children, 110m are currently practising contraception. Of these 50 per cent have IUDs while 33 per cent rely on sterilisation – both low-cost and reliable methods.[27] The pill is a less important method, especially in the rural areas. It is costlier and in remote regions supply can prove a problem. The highest rural user-rates are in communes close to the big cities. In the past the use of the pill was sometimes regarded as an appropriate way to postpone a second child in order to achieve spacing. Now that women are urged to produce only one child and can be expected in rural areas to do so within a year or two of marriage in their early twenties, a contraceptive is required which will give twenty or more years of safe protection. As Chinese medical opinion does not favour the protracted use of hormones, the IUD can be expected to maintain its predominance.

Sterilisation is the second most important method of contraception in the countryside, but may decline wherever a high single-child family rate is achieved. Prior to the single-child family campaign, sterilisation was primarily accepted by older couples who had completed their families with the birth of a third or a fourth child. The pressure on young couples to accept sterilisation after a second birth was also heavy at that time, and a sterilisation bonus was sometimes offered.[28]

It seems unlikely however that many parents of only children will accept sterilisation because they would then be unable to replace the child in the dreaded event of death or disablement. In many cases they may also be hoping for a relaxation of population policy which would allow them to produce a second child at some time in the future. In 1980, Xiangdong People's Commune in Fujian province offered parents who accepted sterilisation after a first birth, a sewing machine, 30 *yuan* in cash and 25 kg of rice – a considerable bait in a commune whose average per capita income had been 68.10 *yuan* in 1979, but there were few acceptances.[29] The problem has been recognised by medical experts who are searching for a method of cheap and easily reversible sterilisation, but until their efforts meet with success, few parents of only children will be prepared to accept the risk. Meanwhile sterilisation will certainly continue as couples who defy the family-planning campaign by having two children are now under greater pressure than ever to accept sterilisation and in Guangdong may even be *ordered* to do so.[30]

Complaints from men (and indeed their wives) that vasectomies caused them to 'lose their strength' seem to have been a greater problem than complaints about the side-effects of female sterilisation.[31] Female sterilisations performed have outnumbered male sterilisations by 3:2 but vasectomies have been performed on a wide scale in Sichuan, the province which has achieved the greatest success in reducing its birth rate. Vasectomy by injection, a quick and simple technique has been pioneered in China and is regarded as especially suitable for the rural areas.[32]

Induced abortion, although officially stated to be a back-up method in the event of contraception failure rather than an independent method, is of considerable importance. Abortion rates will presumably rise with the number of one-child certificate holders if, as predicted, few of them accept sterilisation. Another factor likely to keep the rate high is that those who wish for a second or higher-order child and embark on a pregnancy come under such irresistible pressure to terminate.

THE SINGLE-CHILD FAMILY: REGULATIONS IN THE RURAL AREAS

Despite the successes of the family-planning campaign of the 1970s, fear of the upwards pressure likely to be exerted on the birth rate as earlier 'bulge' generations came of age, in 1979 drove the government to announce the stringent new target of one child per family. There was no illusion that the implementation of this new policy would be easy, so incentives and penalties designed to facilitate its acceptance were a part of the new programme from its inception.

As the family which restricts itself to one child is, at least in the countryside, making a considerable economic sacrifice, the offer of material incentives is logical and can be seen not only as an inducement but also as a sort of compensation. Similarly the penalties to which couples who have more children than they are allowed are liable would, if enforced, serve to cancel out the economic advantage which might otherwise ultimately accrue to their households. For a state to offer incentives and penalties designed to promote family limitation implies that the perceived balance between the economic costs and benefits of raising children will not of itself produce the level of fertility favoured by the state. It therefore intervenes to alter that balance in favour of fewer children. It is significant that in the 1970s campaign, such intervention was made only in the rural areas and was quite sporadic. In the ambitious single-child campaign, intervention has been considered necessary in both urban and rural areas.

Any discussion of the incentives and disincentives used to promote the single-child family policy or of the conditions under which families may be exempted from the policy is complicated by the fact that there is no single national package. A national family-planning law setting out a programme of incentives and disincentives intended to promote the one-child family was proposed in 1979 but never passed.[33] Calls for national legislation incorporating greater uniformity of incentives and disincentives continue, but in the meantime the campaign relies for its legitimacy on strong backing from the Party and the State.[34] The provincial authorities have issued regulations on planned parenthood which include guidelines for incentives and disincentives while communes (and sometimes counties) draw up their own more detailed regulations just as enterprises do in cities.[35]

The various provincial regulations promise all couples who accept the one-child family certificate a package of benefits which looks something like this:

1. A nutrition or welfare allowance reckoned monthly in cash or in workpoints from the birth of the child or the time when the parents sign the one-child pledge.

   5 *yuan* is a figure commonly encountered for this at least on 'model communes' visited by foreigners

2. A single payment.

   In one commune I visited in Guangdong Province, this was as high as 300 *yuan*. The 20 *yuan* recorded in a Suzhou commune by Ashwani Saith would certainly be more typical.[36]

3. Paid maternity leave or extra paid maternity leave.

   The length of maternity leave has never been standardised in the countryside and the majority of communes do not offer it with pay. Those which do, seem often to double it for mothers taking out the single-child certificate, while others offer paid leave only for such families.

4. An allocation of private plot land and housing land for the single-child family equal to that normally given for two children, or where land is short, 1.5 children.

5. A full adult grain ration.

6. Free medical, educational and kindergarten facilities for the child.

In addition, many communes meet the medical expenses of birth for a single-child family. Where there is rural industry, priority for jobs in commune or brigade workshops and factories is promised for the only child or its parents. To counter the concern of those who look to the future, the few well-off communes which are able to introduce pensions now sometimes do so only for the parents of an only child or they offer higher rates to such people. A further refinement of this is to offer the highest rate to the parents of only daughters.

All regulations insist that if a second child is born to a peasant family which has received single-child benefits then all those benefits must be repaid. The benefits can therefore be seen not only as an inducement to couples to sign the pledge, but as a device to make backsliding prohibitively expensive for those who have signed. As long as the system is being properly administered those have received the benefits are in effect locked into it. The position of those who give birth to a second child without having signed the pledge is less clear. The official slogan is:

We must universally promote late marriage and one child for every couple, exercise strict controls about having a second child and resolutely do away with having more than two children.[37]

The meaning of 'strictly control' is of course vague. Regulations for Fujian province, dating from early 1979, urged that couples should 'ideally have only one child and two at the most'.[38] Only the birth of the third child was strictly forbidden and would provoke the imposition of economic sanctions. In spring 1980 in Xiangdong People's Commune in the south-west of Fujian province, while the single child was promoted as the ideal, no penalty was imposed for a second child provided that it was born at least five years after the first.[39] Again it was only on the birth of the third child that economic sanctions were imposed. That child could not be registered either for a grain ration or private plot land.

Provincial regulations now lay down penalties which are far more severe and appear to be intended to apply even to second births except in the rare cases where approval has been given. Examples of penalties include:[40]

1. A deduction of 20 per cent of the couple's income to apply from the date when a second pregnancy is discovered. The deduction money is repaid if abortion is accepted.
2. A deduction of a set percentage (5 per cent in Sichuan, 10 per cent in Shanxi) of the couple's wages until the child reaches a specified age (7 in Shanxi and Qinghai). This is less severe than the level of urban penalties, presumably because many peasants live so close to subsistence that higher rates were thought unnecessary and perhaps unenforceable. Deductions from income are set at even higher levels for the third, fourth and subsequent children.
3. No per capita allowance of grain, private plot, responsibility plot or housing land for children born outside the plan. (This penalty may be imposed in the case of the second birth even where income reductions are reserved only for third and higher parity births).

In addition to the provisions for incentives and penalties, most sets of regulations include a list of conditions under which a couple may be permitted to have a second child. Some of these, categorised as 'special circumstances', enable any couple whether urban or rural, to apply for permission to have a second child. These usually include the following circumstances:

1. where the first child suffers from a medically-certificated, non-hereditary disability and is not expected to grow up to be an able-bodied labourer;

2. where one spouse has a child by a previous marriage but the other does not;
3. where a couple believed to be infertile adopt a child after years of marriage and the woman subsequently becomes pregnant;
4. both spouses are of minority nationality;
5. both spouses are overseas Chinese who have returned from abroad.

Significantly regulations designed for the countryside include a further category of 'real difficulties' which permit couples to apply to have a second child. They are vaguely enough defined to allow cadres some discretion in their interpretation. The set issued for Shanxi province in 1983 provides an interesting range of exceptions.[41] Rural couples may apply to have a second child if:

1. the husband has settled in the home of his wife's parents and she is an only child;
2. they live in sparsely populated mountain villages disadvantaged both in terms of transport and natural conditions;
3. the husband is the only one among three brothers to be capable of fathering a child;
4. the husband is the only son of someone who died for the revolution;
5. one spouse has a major disability.
6. the family has had only one son in a generation for three consecutive generations;
7. both spouses are themselves only children.

The conditions are noteworthy both for the concessions they make to the interests of the traditional male kinship system and the belief in the family line which passes through the male, and for the challenge that they make to those beliefs by rewarding husbands who move in with their in-laws. The possibility of exceptions may give rise to great differences in the percentages of second births approved in different areas as the regulations will doubtless be interpreted with varying degrees of severity. It is certainly surprising that even within such an advanced region as Beijing municipality, exemptions are being allowed in some areas because they are poor and mountainous (see Croll's study of Beijing in Chapter 8).

Interesting as the exceptions and penaties are, the incentives will probably prove to be the most important part of the regulations. Exceptions by definition apply only to a minority; penalties seem, for the moment at least, not to be applied very consistently, whereas millions have already taken out the single-child certificate and begun to benefit from the incentives.

It is not just by chance that the monthly allowance to the certificated family is called a 'welfare' or 'nutrition' allowance or that medical and educational expenses are prominent among the other benefits. The authorities believe that part of their struggle must be to persuade the peasants to prefer quality to quantity. The first step of course is the achievement of infant mortality rates low enough for peasants not to want an extra child as an 'insurance' but beyond that, the authorities would like to show that the family which can concentrate its resources on a single child will bring up a healthier, better-qualified heir than one which has several.

The precise value of the certificated family of the single-child family benefits is certainly substantial although difficult to generalise about. One observer estimated that in Zhangqing People's Commune, Suzhou municipality, the family which took the single-child pledge could augment its total income by one quarter or even one third over the family which went on to have a second child.[42] My impression is that elsewhere, even where a full programme of incentives is being operated, the difference may be less. Moreover when incentives and penalties are pegged commune-wide at a uniform cash level, their impact on particular families must differ considerably. In Stonewell Commune, Guangdong province where uniform cash incentives were on offer in 1981, incomes in the richest brigade averaged 4.7 times those in the poorest brigade and the highest individual earner in the commune had made 1449 *yuan* in the previous year where the lowest had made 308 *yuan*.[43] These variations in total and per capita household income are based not only on production levels but also on the labour power and dependency ratio in each household and are typical of rural China. On a national scale, inequalities are even greater.[44] As enormous regional disparities also exist, a single national package of incentives and penalties would seem to be out of the question, despite the pleas for greater standardisation which have been made.[45] Even if a national Birth Planning Law is one day enacted it will have to allow considerable regional autonomy in the details of its implementation.

The planners are obviously aware that the level at which incentives are set will bear on their effectiveness but are constrained from raising them too high by the fear of excessive cost. Incentives are supposed to be paid out of commune and brigade welfare funds, augmented by fines imposed for unauthorised births. Thus ironically, the greater the success of the programme, the greater the expense to the unit implementing it as the amount paid out in benefits rises and receipts from penalties fall. To make things more difficult in some localities cadres have been instructed to hold the amount collected for welfare in check.[46] Some Chinese commentators have suggested that the state should set up a fund to back the single-child programme whose success they believe is endangered by the problem of finance. State backing, they argue, would eliminate arbitrary differences in benefit produced by differences in what the unit can afford.[47]

State backing for the programme would however be a major departure from Chinese practice which has been to encourage the organisation of rural welfare on a local, self-financing basis and to avoid central direction and standardisation. Instead concern at the expense of the programme is met with arguments that it will more than pay for itself:

> At first some cadres in the production teams had reservations. 'Where is the money and the grain to come from?' they asked, when material awards were considered for single-child families. Their worries were dispelled when they were shown the facts and figures. In terms of grain, for every two children the production team had to provide 10 920 *jin* of grain from the time of their birth until they were sixteen years of age. For one child, the team provided half that amount, and rewarding the parents of one child with 504 *jin* meant that the total was only 5964 *jin*. The production team saved 4956 *jin*. Another illustration was a financial comparison. According to local standards, 5200 *yuan* had to be spent on bringing up two children from time of birth until they reached sixteen years of age. If 30 per cent came from the state and the collective, that came to 1560 *yuan*. If one child was born, the state and the collective had only to spend 780 *yuan*, and if 5040 workpoints (10 workpoints make one workday), worth say 400 *yuan*, were given as a reward for having only one child the total only came to 1180 *yuan*, which would be a saving of 380 *yuan*. This showed that the state and the collective saved grain and money if material rewards were made to encourage each couple to have only one child.[48]

The problem of course with this 'projected savings' argument is that the sums saved are mere accountants' figures, while the cadres have still to produce the finance for the programme. For the moment, single-child benefits represent a transfer of income away from the majority of households to those which contain a couple who have taken the single-child pledge. If the policy is widely accepted as time goes by, the minority will grow, the burden on welfare funds will be very great and the temptation will be to rely more heavily on the penalty system because it is cheap. Some benefits which entail preferential treatment will lose their value automatically if take-up is too high. It will not be possible to give whole cohorts of children sought-after jobs in rural industry or the best educational chances. Other problems with incentives and penalties have emerged as a result of new rural policies: the responsibility systems and household sideline production.

RESPONSIBILITY SYSTEMS

Responsibility systems are an attempt to link remuneration more closely to the quantity and quality of the work done. It is argued that only by rewarding the effort and skill of good workers and by allowing them to earn significantly more than less capable peasants can agricultural production be raised as quickly as the needs of the economy demand. The system of remuneration based on work collectively performed and measured in terms of workpoints is critically referred to as having 'allowed everyone to eat from the same big pot'. It is said that it failed to reward hard work, skill and enterprise sufficiently; allowed malingerers to rely on the efforts of others and did not offer the incentives necessary to produce rapid growth in productivity.

The range of responsibility systems is very wide. Their bewildering variety makes them difficult to generalise about. All involve contracting some responsibilities which formerly lay with the production team or even the brigade, to some smaller unit such as the work-group, the individual or, most commonly, the household. Most also allow the contracting party to retain all or a proportion of any above-quota production and penalise the contracting party if production falls below the set quota.

The following six fairly distinct varieties of the system can be identified:[49]

1. *contracting output to the household (baochan dao hu)*
    Collective accounting is maintained at least in theory. The household contracts with the team to produce a set output at set costs for a specified number of workpoints. It undertakes to do this on a given area of land determined by the number of mouths in the household or the number of labour powers or some combination of the two;

2. *contracting land to the household* (*baogan dao hu*)

   Still more decentralised. The household agrees to contribute a given amount or a given proportion of what it produces to the team and may retain the rest;

3. *contracting output to the labourer* (*lianchan daolao*)

   Similar to the system of contracting output to the household except that the contracting party is an individual;

4. *contracting to output to workgroups* (*baochandaozu*)

   Another variant of number one in which the contracting party is a group of peasants.

5. *specialised contracting to the household, individual or workgroup with payment according to output* (*zhuanye chengbao lianchan-jichou*)

   Used for the production of specific commodities or performance of specific tasks (tea production or the use of tractors, associated with a developed diversified rural economy);

6. *short-term contracting* (*xiaoduan baogong*)

   The contracting of specific jobs with payment based on quotas, used in the slack season where other systems are in use or for minor jobs.

In September 1983 it was reported that responsibility schemes were in use in over 98.3 per cent of China's production teams.[50] Six months earlier it had been claimed that they were used by 92 per cent of production teams and that household responsibility systems had been established in 78 per cent of all production teams.[51] Given the difficulties of gathering figures, the problems of definition and the fact that many teams use two or more systems simultaneously, such estimates may be expected to differ. However, all reports seem to indicate that responsibility systems have been set up in the great majority of China's villages and that most of them are based on the household.

This dominance is interesting because responsibility schemes based on the household, especially the highly devolved system of contracting land to the household, were accepted only cautiously at first, tending to be identified as suitable for poor areas where the collective economy was not yet highly developed. Despite this they have clearly gained ground widely at the expense of other systems since 1980. Specialised contracting often, but not always, based on the household, is common in the richer more diversified economies of the model communes most often visited by foreigners. The minor forms of contracting, though less important, can still be found, often used in combination with household forms. There are significant differences between the various forms of responsibility systems, but one can usefully generalise about some of their implications while bearing in mind that not everything suggested will apply to each system.

All the responsibility systems involve devolution, usually to the household. The extent of the devolution will be more or less limited according to the system in use and indeed the local interpretation of that system.

At its most extreme, when *land* is contracted to the household, much planning and decision-making power goes with it. Even collective property in the form of machinery and draught animals may be shared out (it is true that there has been considerable criticism of such developments, but in the interests of stability, it may prove difficult to go back on them). In any event, the whole system of workpoints is abolished, and the team, instead of functioning as an accounting unit, merely collects a fixed amount of output for state procurement together with a levy for collective services – it acts in fact as a tax agency. In the less extreme form of household contracting, contracting production to the household, the team retains more power as leadership, planning and accounting remain in its hands. But this collective accounting may be a book transfer only – at the margin the distinction is arbitrary.

What both systems have in common is the renewed importance which they give to the household. Even when the contracting party is the individual or the workgroup, this still tends to be the case – the day-to-day deployment of labour, the division of labour between work in the fields and sideline production, the allocation of tasks between different family members, all decisions in which the team-leader once had the main say, now revert to the household head.

HOUSEHOLD SIDELINE PRODUCTION

Another area of change and expansion in the Chinese countryside is that of household sideline production and the marketing of its output.[52] Until the late 1970s this sector of the rural economy was severely discouraged or even in places wholly suppressed. Private peddling and marketing was frowned on but the prices given for the products of household sidelines by state purchasing agencies were often too low to provide a sufficient stimulus. Peasants who did succeed in making money from sideline production risked being criticised for showing a selfish spirit and neglecting the interests of the collective. As one recent Chinese source put it:

We were also afraid of the commodity economy and even the raising of a few chickens and the selling of a few eggs in the countryside were not allowed.[53]

Although the degree to which the free market was suppressed varied noticeably from one area to another it was everywhere under pressure. The furtive peasant squatting by the roadside in the mid-1970s, ready to snatch up his wares and flee at any sign of officialdom, is in sharp contrast to the raucous self-advertisers of free markets today.

Household sideline production having been held back in the past is capable of rapid expansion. It now meets with official favour because it satisfies pent-up demand at low cost to the state since investment is provided by the household. In addition to a wide variety of goods such as pigs, poultry, eggs, rabbits, fruit and so on produced on private plots, sideline products include handicraft products as diverse as baskets, embroideries, fans and raw silk. The gathering and sale of bird dung for fertiliser, grass for fodder and herbs for medicinal use also count as sideline production.

In the past, in those areas where profitable sideline production was possible because of special local features or resources or accessible markets it might supply as much as 15 per cent of household income.[54] Given official encouragement, the expansion of market and credit facilities and the possibility for those peasants who wish to drop out of collective labour altogether a far higher percentage is now possible. Figures from the State Statistical Bureau show that the proportion of peasant household income produced from domestic sidelines rose from 27 per cent in 1978 to 38 per cent in 1982 (see Table 2.3). This development is again one which boosts the importance of the household as a unit of production and as the primary economic unit to which each individual belongs and is tied by bonds of dependency and loyalty. It can indeed be argued that household sidelines, being still less under collective control than contracted agriculture, are even more conducive to household autonomy.

SOME IMPLICATIONS OF THE RURAL REFORMS

The strengthening of the household has inevitably meant a challenge to collective authority. In some areas difficulties have been experienced in maintaining the welfare and education systems because the peasants were not willing to pay for them.[55] The criticism of the old collective system which accompanied the introduction of responsibility

58

TABLE 2.3   *Average per capita net income of peasant households*

	1978	1979	1980	1981	1982
(1) Average per-capita net income (*yuan*)	133.57	160.17	191.33	223.44	270.11
From the collective	88.53	101.97	108.37	116.20	140.12
From domestic sideline production	35.79	44.00	62.55	84.52	102.80
From other non-borrowing incomes	9.25	14.20	20.41	22.72	27.19
(2) Percentages (Take the total net income as 100)					
From the collective	66.28	63.66	56.64	52.00	51.87
From the domestic sideline production	26.79	27.47	32.69	37.83	38.06
From other non-borrowing incomes	6.93	8.87	10.67	10.17	10.07

NOTE   'Income from the collective' refers to the total income the peasants get from the collective, including all incomes from the production teams, production brigades and the communes. Also included in this category is the income the peasants get through signing contracts for collective production with the collective. 'Other non-borrowing incomes' refers to cash and things sent back by household members who work in other places, state subsidies for households with difficulties, for labourers working on public projects and for disabled servicemen, etc.

SOURCE   Sample survey of peasant households selected by the State Statistical Bureau on a national basis. The sample size was 6095 in 1978 but was increased each year and stood at 22 775 in 1982. The survey was summarised in *Beijing Review*, 26 October 1983.

systems tended to discredit by association the authority of cadres who had worked in the old structure. In the early days of contracting, a lot of anti-cadre feeling seems to have emerged. Peasants were reported to be refusing to contribute towards their stipends saying, 'Who needs cadres now that we have responsibility land?'[56] In some places cadres no longer received a stipend but were allocated a share of responsibility land. Not unnaturally they tended to neglect official duties and concentrate on cultivation.

There were reports of various violations of collective authority in pursuit of short-term individual interests from all over China: peasants cut down trees planted in earlier afforestation campaigns, built houses illegally on land officially assigned to grain production, grazed hillsides too heavily and so on. It comes as no surprise to learn that family planning was another area in which individual or family interest began to assert itself. Peasants began to say that as long as they farmed their own contracted land, their children were their own business.[57]

The economic advantages of having more children, though diminished by the abandonment of pro-natalist practices such as the per capita allocation of grain, private plot and housing land, were in some ways boosted by the new rural policies. Households wanted to increase their labour force in order to increase the yield from their responsibility land and to make more from household sidelines. As long as the hire of labour remained prohibited this could only be done by increasing the numbers in the family. The prohibition was lifted and the press now contains references to conditions under which households may hire assistants or apprentices.[58] Never the less the normal way for a household to enlarge its labour-force is still by increasing the number of family members. Of course under the old collective system, a household's income was also related to the size of the labour-force which it could deploy. The connection has now been made even closer, as it must be by any policy which increases incentive by increasing the return to labour.

There has also been a significant change in the moral climate. The acquisition of wealth is socially approved: the model households are the prosperous ones. When '10,000 *yuan* households' are held up for emulation those doing less well are, by implication, failures. In such a climate a primary loyalty to the family is harder to challenge and the individual is reluctant to look further than the short-term interests of the household. Appeals to a sense of selflessness and the public good no longer seem appropriate.

The rural reforms have also had a direct effect on the operation of the single-child family programme in the villages. The packages of incentives and disincentives introduced to promote the single-child family were for a time disturbed or even became inoperable. This was most serious where land was contracted to the household because collective accounting ceased and it became harder to ensure the payment of incentives to certificate-holders and to impose penalties. Moreover where peasants had contract land, private plots lost some of their former importance and the grant of housebuilding land was less significant, according to the press, because unauthorised house-building flourished.[59] This meant that extra shares of private plot and house-building land for those who committed themselves to one child became less tempting. Where difficulties were experienced with financing nursery, educational and health facilities, the offer of privileges in these areas tended to lose credibility. Paid maternity leave was no longer workable once collective accounting had ceased. In areas where household sidelines offered exceptionally high returns even the lure of jobs in rural industry was reduced.

Another important effect of strengthening the household must be on power relations within the household. Unfortunately since Chinese researchers have shown extraordinarily little interest in the effects of the reforms on intra-household relationships this remains largely an area for speculation. In claiming that the autonomy of the household has increased under the present reforms, I do not wish to imply that its functions under the former collective system were negligible. On the contrary, it is clear that the government found the institution of the household extremely useful and did not hesitate to acknowledge it as the basic unit of society. Collective income for example was normally paid out on the basis of the household, the household was required to send representatives to meetings and most commune, brigade and team leaders would give population and income figures in terms of households with far greater fluency than in terms of individuals. The household remained the main unit of consumption, of reproduction and in a minor way was still a unit of production. Even the institution of the household head, usually defined as the oldest working male, continued to be used in rural government and thus to enjoy *de facto* official recognition. The question of how the household head should exercise his power sometimes came under discussion, especially during the cultural revolution, and it has been government policy to support the freedom of the individual against him in issues such as marriage. Such challenges however were short-lived or specific, and the house-hold head continued to represent the household in discussions with authority, received the collective income of all the household's working members, and was named as the head on the forms for household registration and the census.[60] None the less, under the former collective system, the authority of the household head was balanced or in certain contexts even eclipsed by the team head or other rural cadres. That balance of power has been altered in important ways.

Young adults who are now part of a family workforce first and of a production team second, are more completely under the authority of the household head and are less likely to appeal for outside support in disputes with him. The influence of the older generation over marriage and procreation, already considerable, has thus been reinforced. As the older generation generally favour early marriage for their children and the promotion of late marriage has been an important part of China's birth control programme, this is not an encouraging development. Given that many young couples live with the bridegroom's parents the older generation are also in a position to press for more grandchildren. (It is noteworthy indeed that much Chinese family planning propaganda is aimed at grandparents).[61] The distressing reports of the maltreatment of young women who have given birth to daughters, or who desire against the wishes of their in-laws to limit their families to one child, frequently implicate the grandparents.[62] In such disputes, the new rural policies which tend to strengthen the household head and to reduce the daily contact of peasants with others outside their family, leave young people more vulnerable to pressure from the older generation.

The introduction of the responsibility system must have increased the determination of ordinary peasants to avoid ever becoming dependent on collective welfare because the weakening of team and brigade power seemed for a time to threaten the survival of the system.[63] Under the collective system, those who had no close relatives on whom to rely and who were too old to work (or were incapacitated in some other way) could rely on the 'five guarantees' (food, clothing, shelter, the bringing up of children and burial) which formed the basis of the rural welfare system. However this was looked on as a last resort because:

1. only those unfortunates who had no close relatives to help were eligible;
2. support was at a minimum standard;
3. reluctant and therefore resentful relatives were sometimes made to contribute;
4. a feeling of loss of face was involved.

Son-preference

The five guarantees have therefore never provided a satisfactory alternative to relying on the support and care of a co-resident adult son and his family, a system sanctioned not only by tradition, but also by the law which imposes on children the obligation of supporting aged parents.[64] In practice of course the obligation falls most heavily upon the sons and hence son-preference in undiminished in rural areas despite all the attempts since 1949 to change it. With the introduction of the single-child family policy the consequences of this preference became tragic. Reports began to come in from many regions of the maltreatment of women who have given birth to girls, and even of female infanticide.[65] Although rusticated cadres in the 1970s occasionally encountered cases of female infanticide and there are other indications that it may have survived on a small scale after 1949, it seems probable that instances were only isolated.[66] Most families have been able to afford to bring up their girl-babies since 1949 and have been willing to do so.

The single-child family policy has brought back the threat to female infant life. Now if a peasant family brings up a daughter it must sacrifice its chances of a son, or suffer the penalties for giving birth to a second child outside the plan. In these circumstances some have preferred to rid themselves of a girl in order to try again for a boy.

It is difficult to assess the extent of this tragic problem. It has received an enormous amount of official attention in China and press attention abroad, but this is not necessarily an indication that female infanticide is widespread. In China a high level of media attention has clearly been directed towards producing a revulsion against the practice and an increased regard for women which is recognised as necessary for the success of the one-child policy. Some official reports on census data have stated that nationally the sex ratio is normal and unaffected by the family planning campaign.[67] Locally however there have been reports of highly distorted sex ratios.[68] Census data on the sex ratio at birth point to gloomy conclusions. Nationally a figure of 108.5 male births to 100 female ones was reported instead of the expected 105–107.[69] The sex ratio at birth varied by region. Shanghai, where for socio-economic reasons son-preference should be weak, reported a reassuring 105.4:100 and various border regions where population policy has been less strict produced figures well within the normal range like 106.1:100 for Xinjiang and 106.8:100 for Guizhou.

However, the figure for the southern province of Guangdong was a depressing 110.5:100, while the poor, non-urbanised province of Guangxi and Anhui reported 110.7:100 and 112.5:100 respectively. These figures indicate a pronounced discrimination against baby girls and show what a difficult and unpopular policy the one-child family is. To implement it, the Chinese have to overcome the problems which result from the new economic policies, the problems associated with son-preference and old-age-support, and the problem of leadership in the villages.

DEALING WITH THE PROBLEMS

Given the urgency and importance constantly attributed by the Chinese to their population problems it does appear extraordinary that a set of rural policies with implications for fertility could have been introduced without, it seems, any initial awareness of those implications. However it did not take long for this sort of awareness to develop and many articles have since appeared which discuss the negative effects of responsibility schemes on family planning while household sidelines have also received some attention.[70]

This recognition has been complicated by the controversy which surrounded the introduction of the responsibility systems. Those who favoured them have had to defend themselves against accusations that they want de-collectivisation and a return to family farming. They respond with firm denials and with claims that there need be no irreconcilable contradiction between responsibility systems and family planning if the correct solutions are adopted.[71]

The main solution still being pressed in such discussions is that of building family limitation into responsibility schemes, an idea which has been given authoritative support by the Central Committee:

> A contract should also contain items such as the amount of labour to be contributed for public construction purposes, *tasks concerning family planning* and unified and assigned planned purchase tasks.[72]

Other documents talk of assigning both reproductive and productive tasks or of contracting for land as well as for births. Translated into action this means that in many areas, birth-control undertakings are built into household production contracts. They commit couples with one or more children to using an effective contraceptive method. Childless couples are required to wait their turn before embarking on a pregnancy.

The incentives and penalties laid down in provincial regulations have been updated to take account of the responsibility systems. One-child families can now be rewarded with extra land and lower production quotas to meet. Those who have an unauthorised child are liable to be punished by having a part of their responsibility plots withdrawn and by being given higher quotas to meet.[73] Again there appears to be an uncertainty over how to treat second births. Under some regulations they are to be penalised fully with higher production quotas, less contract land and even the withdrawal of a share of private plot land.[74] Other regulations reserve such severity for third and higher parity births merely ruling that the second child will not be entitled to a share of responsibility land or private plot land.[75] The situation still appears to be under review and the introduction of other links between responsibility systems and birth planning is possible. It has been urged that where the double contract on production and reproduction is made with the workgroup, all members of the group should suffer a penalty if any member of the group breaks the contract by having an unauthorised child, and this is beginning to appear in some commune regulations as is shown in Croll's study of Evergreen commune, Beijing, in chapter 8 of this book.[76]

It is not true then that without a workpoint system no economic sanctions can be applied, however, it is by no means apparent that they are easy to apply. Even at the most basic level of incentive, cadres were still allocating responsibility land on a per capita basis as late as mid-1982, despite appeals they they should stop doing so.[77] Any reallocation of responsibility land would entail problems. To induce the peasants to farm their land properly, they need the confidence that they will hold it for long enough to make investment worthwhile.[78] If they believe that it may be taken away from them after a year or two, the temptation will be to exhaust it by working it too hard. Chinese discussions of contracted production show an acute awareness of this problem and emphasise the benefits of stability, indeed a Central Committee directive of January 1984 indicated that land contracts should last for as long as fifteen years in order to encourage peasants to invest in and care for their plots.[79] An effective reward and penalty system on the allocation of responsibility land would involve frequent redistribution of the land which, if it had to be done on a large scale, would undermine this stability.

LAND SHORTAGE

It may yet turn out that the system of contracting land ultimately contributes to the peasants' acceptance of the need for a family-planning programme. There is no doubt that with a national per capita average of only 1.5 *mu* of arable land the situation is serious.[80] Only Japan and Egypt have less arable land per head. Decreasing returns to labour and even to other outputs must be occurring widely in most of the congested regions where the Chinese population is concentrated. There was of course a consciousness of land shortage under the collective system, but this may well be a case where 'everybody eating from the same big pot', really did reduce a sense of individual concern. Each peasant family could hope that *other* families would not exacerbate the situation by having too many children. It was also possible to see the matter of future livelihood as 'a problem for the cadres'.

Where each household holds its own responsibility plot, especially if that plot is held unvaried over a number of years, and decline in the population: land ratio will be felt in a far more immediate way by the individual family than it was under collective cultivation. The emergence of a surplus of rural labour as a result of the responsibility system has already been commented on in the press.[81] Where there is still scope for a significant expansion of household sidelines or for more intensive use of labour on the land, the decline may not have this effect, but in other cases there will be a greater receptiveness to family planning. A study of Guangdong Province in the 1970s found that the family-planning campaign had been best accepted in the villages which were most short of land.[82] A comparison could also be made with Taiwan where, it has been argued, uniformly small holdings reduced both the need and the opportunity for the employment of children, thus contributing to the success of family planning.[83]

Land shortage receives much attention in propaganda designed to persuade the peasants that the one-child family is necessary. The press grinds out national, provincial and county statistics designed to show how much less arable land there is now than there was in 1949, and how much richer people would have been if there had been less population growth.[84] These unsophisticated calculations assume that the growth in grain production and other growth indicators would have been the same even with an entirely different rate of demographic increase, but doubtless they serve to put across the general point that population growth has hampered economic progress.

Local cadres are urged to do the same sort of calculation for their own villages so that peasants can see how much the per capita area of arable land they farm has fallen and what the situation will be like in twenty years or thirty years if present trends continue.[85] Put in terms of the area of responsibility land a household must be expected to subsist on in a generation's time, the dimensions of China's population problem can perhaps be grasped by the peasants. In this way the responsibility system itself is being put to use in the campaign to persuade China's peasants to modify their reproductive behaviour.

There is another way in which the restoration of the individual family's interest in the farming enterprise may ultimately serve to reduce the peasants' desired family size. Under the collective system fertilisers and machinery were purchased by various levels of the collective. The team, brigade or commune made the decisions about investment and found the funds to finance it. Some smaller scale investment at least is now made by the household which can also purchase equipment for use in domestic sidelines. Thus it is no longer the case that the only productive investment the household can make is in labour power; indeed children and investment goods could now be perceived as competing alternatives. Given the peasant family's slender resources, it may well forego children it would otherwise have wanted if the sacrifice allows it to buy fertiliser or machinery. The expansion of the production of appropriate industrial goods in support of agriculture will therefore contribute to China's population campaign.

However the acceptance of the need for family planning and a greater willingness to limit the numbers of children do not of course imply the acceptance of the single-child family. Even when peasants are no longer interested in a large labour supply, they still crave security in old age. We return to this as the fundamental obstacle to the implication of the one-child family programme.

THE PROBLEM OF SUPPORT IN OLD AGE

If the one-child family is to win wider acceptance in the villages, the state must develop acceptable methods of extending adequate economic support and care to the elderly which do not depend on kinship bonds. A few general observations are needed for my argument here, although the problem is dealt with at length by Davis Friedmann in Chapter 6.

Prior to the single-child family campaign only the most prosperous communes had introduced pensions for their members. Now that the authorities make explicit connections between pensions and the single-child family campaign there is more pressure on communes to institute them.[86] However communes with such provisions are a small minority. In villages where collective accounting and the workpoint system still exist, any additional burden on collective funds lowers the value of the workpoint and may thus reduce work incentives. When land is contracted to the household and collective accounting has ceased, cadres, as we have seen, may have problems extracting finance for existing collective services. Extra calls on the collective purse are therefore unwelcome both to cadres and peasants. The dilemma is expressed in the contradictory calls now appearing in the press to introduce pensions or improve the way old people are cared for under the five guarantees on the one hand, and to stabilise or reduce the amount spent on welfare on the other.

A new development is the payment of pensions only to those who restrict their families to one child.[87] This would initially involve low expenditure as for the moment there are few parents of only children who are of pensionable age and the scheme would never become as expensive as universal pensions. It could therefore be introduced in less prosperous communes.

For the time being it seems that the majority of communes will continue to rely on the five-guarantee system to relieve destitution among the elderly. As we have seen, this was never a very satisfactory system and the erosion of team and brigade power which occurred with the introduction of responsibility systems brought it fresh difficulties. Significantly the authorities have been quick to insist that the five guarantees must not be allowed to collapse, and have indeed specifically linked them with family-planning campaigns, recognising that the peasants will never accept the single-child family if society allows old people without children to live in destitution. For example the governor of Guizhou province is reported to have said in a speech at a family-planning conference:

> We must take good care of rural households enjoying the five guarantees and get rid of some people's fears of disturbances in the future in order to promote the smooth development of planned parenthood.[88]

There have been many articles on the importance of checking and strengthening five-guarantee work; it has even been stated that the income of childless old people should not be allowed to fall below average per capita income in any locality.[89] As usual unfortunately these idealistic prescriptions fail to offer any solution to the problem of finance.

Whatever the difficulties, the five-guarantee system is by far the most important system of social support to the elderly in the countryside although pensions systems are developing. Homes for the elderly, although much discussed in the press, remain insignificant statistically.[90] There are occasional experiments. In Stone Wall Commune in Guangdong province for example, families who take a non-related old person into their homes are paid a 'fostering allowance' from the welfare fund.[91] Other communes have apparently evolved a system in which welfare relief itself is assigned on the basis of a responsibility system.[92]

In the communes people speculate on the possibility that when the children of a single-child family grow up, each young couple may live with four older people and worry about the problems which will arise.[93] The most dramatic version of this nightmare appeared in a Shanghai paper:

> In the not-too distant future, when the rule of the one-child family has become a reality, a young couple will have to support twelve old people, four parents and eight grandparents. What is to be done?[94]

The demographic literature scoffs at such a scenario and attempts to meet the concern by population projections which show the dependency ratio will fall steeply until the year 2000 and will not reach its current level of over 0.90 until 2034.[95] According to such projections not until 2040 would one working person be supporting one non-working person and the proportion of elderly would not reach 50 per cent until 2080 when the proportion of working-age people would still be 43 per cent. This reasoning concludes with the reassurance that by then modernisation will have increased productivity to such a level that a higher dependency ratio is supportable.

A more specific projection designed to show how the age structure will change in Shifang county in Sichuan province (a model birth planning county) if the one-child family is generally adopted has been published in a similar attempt to reassure (see Table 2.4). These projections may help to reduce the anxiety of cadres and planners who are considering the future for whole communities, but it is hard to imagine that they will do as much for the couple with an infant

TABLE 2.4   *Projections of the population of Shifang County*

Year	% of pop. under 19	20–59	Over 60
2000	21%	63%	16%
2020	11%	58%	31%

SOURCE   Lin Fude and Zhou Qing, 'Family Planning in Shifang County', in Liu Zheng *et al. China's Population.*

daughter concerned about their own support when she grows up.

The other solution for peasant households still sometimes offered by the media, and also apparently by family-planning workers, is that of uxorilocal marriage which as we have seen was first promoted for the two-child family in the 1970s. Not surprisingly, now that a universal one-child family is in prospect the peasants ask cynically where the bridegrooms will come from. It is hard to imagine any peasant family allowing a son who was an only child to leave to join his wife's family. The strongest official promotion of uxorilocal marriage can be seen in some provincial regulations which give families in which the husband is a 'living-in son-in-law' the extraordinary privilege of being allowed to have a second child.[96]

Finally, there have been suggestions that the peasant family which has a daughter first time may be allowed to try again. Even some regulations appear to envisage the possibility; 'peasant parents with only one daughter who are in real difficulty', are among the categories of parents allowed to apply for permission to have a second child in some provinces. The implication is still that these would be exceptional cases, but the regulations seem to empower cadres to interpret 'real difficulty' at their own discretion.[97] The moderate view was mentioned in the People's Daily in February 1982,

> Many demographers advocate that more couples should be given special permission to have a second child . . . setting the quota at around 1.5 children per family will make the policy acceptable to the majority of peasants. Family planning will then be much easier to carry out in the rural areas.[98]

Discussion in the press is very cautious, after all, as such an exception would apply to half the families in the countryside, and it could produce the collapse of the one-child family. Moderates in the leadership who are unhappy with the severity of the present policy and the concern that it may alienate the peasant masses from both party and government are probably responsible for the fact that couples producing a second child were not dealt with too ruthlessly when the policy was first introduced. Indeed although provincial regulations now prescribe severe penalties on the birth of the second child, there are few reports of such sanctions actually being applied except against cadre families who are expected to set an example. Unless penalties for the birth of a second child are more strictly enforced than they appear to be at present, the compromise which emerges may well be that while most couples whose first child is a boy are persuaded to stop at one, many of those who have a daughter ultimately go on to try again for a son. A visitor to Maoping Brigade in a mountainous area of Zhejiang province reports that in 1982 the cadre responsible for family planning work and women's affairs admitted without embarrassment that her daughter-in-law was having a second try in just such circumstances.[99] The seeming unwillingness to impose penalties for the second births probably indicates a tacit acceptance that there will be a large number of second children where the first-born is female. Chinese demographers appear also to have moved from a preoccupation with projections based on the almost universal one-child family to an acceptance that 1.5 children per couple may be a more realistic average.[100]

THE PROBLEM OF LEADERSHIP

The role of cadres in the villages is vital to the success or failure of the one-child family programme. Obtaining and retaining their co-operation may be one of the most difficult tasks of the campaign. No programme of incentives and sanctions can succeed if the cadres are not willing to implement it, cadres are needed to carry out the time-consuming work of persuasion and indeed without their compliance the government cannot even monitor the success or failure of family planning. Yet, as we have seen, cadres have had their own problems. Their prestige and morale took a knocking when responsibility systems were introduced and the earlier forms of collective accounting with which they had been identified came under fire. Where land was contracted, the very need for cadres was challenged and in places their remuneration ceased.[101]

Anxious to retain control in the rural areas the government quickly insisted that cadres were needed and must be appropriately remunerated. Support was expressed with statements like:

With the implementation of the responsibility system, some tasks are undertaken by peasant households. This especially requires the improvement of working methods, the intensification of collective leadership and unified management and the strengthening of co-ordination work. Such being the case the work of cadres has increased rather than lightened.[102]

The number and variety of jobs listed in this statement as falling to cadres are indeed formidable. They include: assigning contract land, drawing up contracts, calculating quotas, managing farmland, forests or hills, mediating in civil disputes, collecting and looking after collective funds and administering family planning, the five-guarantees, public health and militia training.

However, the next sentence of this statement runs, 'At the same time we should pay attention to cutting down the number of personnel so as to lighten the masses' burden'. This call is echoed in many documents some of which also mention solving budgetary problems by cutting excessive stipends. A report of February 1983 in the People's Daily praised a reorganisation which had taken place in Shengqiu county, Henan province, reducing the number of team cadres from 11 823 to 4097.[103] As a result of the reform, cadre stipends and overheads annually cost the peasants 1.96 *yuan* per capita instead of 3.6 *yuan* per capita. These measures were said to have quieted peasant unrest about the expense of cadres and other areas were urged to take Shengqiu as a model. Presumably many rural cadres would feel uneasy upon reading an article like this.

If the general morale of some grass-roots cadres is low, their responsibility for family-planning work will certainly not help to raise it. Many, of course, completed their child-bearing period years ago when large families were still acceptable. Obviously it cannot be easy for an older man or woman with three, four or five children, to put pressure on a young couple to have only one. They are going to face considerable resentment. Young cadres who are starting their own families are supposed to set a good example.[104] The fiercest outcry is reserved for those cadres who fail to conform to the single-child policy and the sanctions are applied to them more rigorously than to other peasants. Cadres cannot enjoy unpopularity, yet the single-child family policy which they have to implement is unpopular, so much so indeed that family-planning workers are sometimes physically attacked. Brigade and team cadres are connected to the villages which they serve by a web of relationships. The villagers whom they must punish and reward in the course of the single-child campaign are their people, their kin, among whom they have friends and enemies. It is surely impossible that the programme can always be inplemented even-handedly without deception.

To try to ensure the compliance of cadres, they themselves are now sometimes put on a responsibility or bonus scheme under which their area is given a quota for production and a quota for reproduction. If the quotas are met the cadre gets a bonus. If not, they or their units are to be subject to punishment or 'economic sanctions'. Up to 25 per cent of their income may now depend on such bonuses.[105] The report from the Shengqiu county, Henan province, cited as a model for its reorgan-isation of the cadre system says:

> A responsibility system was devised for cadres under which rewards and penalties were based on their success in meeting six targets. The targets concerned grain, oil, cotton, tree-planting, diversified economy and family planning.[106]

An obvious disadvantage of the system is that it gives cadres an incentive to fiddle their records in order to make sure of their bonuses. It also seems likely that the lure of bonus may be responsible for some of the illegal coercion in the form, for example, of forced abortions and sterilisations frequently reported in the press. Although such practices were widely condemned in 1978 and again in 1980 and despite constant official insistence that the family-planning campaign must be implemented on the voluntary principle, it is not hard to see how the system throws up such abuses. Hard-pressed cadres are given low birth-quotas and high sterilisation and IUD-insertion quotas. They try to fulfil them but as the months pass it becomes apparent that they will fail. Reports of greater success in neighbouring provinces, counties or communes increase their concern. They worry that they may lose their promotion or even their jobs and that their salaries will be docked. They resort to desperate measures.[107]

CONCLUSIONS

In a sense the single-child family campaign is oddly at variance with the general trend of rural reform in China today. Whereas in general, individual initiative and decision-making are encouraged and the role of centralised management had diminished, in birth-planning the opposite is true. This contrast has been authoritatively recognised by a senior Party official:

> While relaxing policies there are several things localities should keep a tight grip on ... The increase in population must be strictly controlled and family planning work pursued conscientiously.[108]

In other spheres the Chinese are now emphasising the importance of patience and are striving for steady rather than high-speed growth; demographically however they are following the heroic model, attempting dramatic change in a very short period of time, through immense effort and sacrifice, a model which in the economic sphere they have rejected.

The rural responsibility system, as first introduced, worked against the single-child programme, but where the systems have now been modified to favour those who limit their families and penalise those who do not, this problem will recede. The basic obstacle to the implementation of the single-child policy in the countryside is that it requires the peasants to practise a degree of family limitation which they perceive as directly contrary to their interests. Even without all the reforms which have taken place in the rural economy, this would have been the case, although, as we have seen, the reforms here in some ways exacerbated the situation.

China's impressive achievements in family-planning work have been widely recognised. In the space of only a few years the birth rate of the world's most populous country has been brought down to a level typical of industrialised society despite the fact that the vast majority of its people are still peasants. However, it will be a long time before the success of the one-child family can be realistically assessed. In the streams of statistics issued by county, provincial and national authorities are birth rates, natural increase rates, late-marriage rates, single-child rates and multi-parity rates. Most reflect a surprising degree of success, although the figures are incomplete and may be selected to give a favourable picture.

The more important reservation is that whatever the level of success at present, the momentum must be kept up and even increased for many years to come. Every year for the next ten years, 20m young people will marry and swell the number of couples who must be persuaded to use contraception.[109] If the family-planning workers do not succeed with them, the single-child family rate could actually fall. At the same time, effort must be expended on existing single-child certificate holders, few of whom will yet be out of their thirties, to make sure they stick to their resolution and practise contraception effectively. Even city surveys indicate that a considerable proportion of certificate-holders would welcome another child if there were any relaxation of the policy.[110] This is certainly the case in the countryside. If the campaign is to succeed even partially among the peasants, there can be no let-up. Amid the reports of success there are gloomier ones of setbacks. In June 1983, Qian Xinzhong, minister in charge of the Birth Planning Commission reported that the situation in the rural areas is still serious. In 1981 alone, 5.9m babies were born into families with more than one child and 1.7m of these were born into families which had five of more children. First births made up 46.55 per cent of total births, but second births were 25.36 per cent and third and subsequent births 28.09 per cent.[111]

In comparative terms the achievements of China's family-planning campaign are remarkable. No other predominantly peasant society has lowered its birth rate so far and so fast. The human cost is great. The horror of female infanticide has reappeared in China's villages. A whole generation is being asked to give up the right to the children it wants. Millions of women undergo abortions which they would prefer not to have. The damage which this could do to the government's popularity and its support in the countryside is not yet calculable but is a factor which may inhibit the implementation of the strictest sanctions against those who defy the one-child campaign in the countryside. Against all this must be balanced the potential cost of inaction. The Chinese peasants are constantly being asked to remember these costs. So far our knowledge of peasant reaction to the single-child campaign is too patchy and inadequate to make predictions about the future with any degree of confidence.

Peasant reaction will however continue to be of enormous interest to us all, as upon it depends not only China's demographic development but her whole social, economic and political future.

NOTES AND REFERENCES

1. 1982 census results reported in *BR* no. 45, 1982. Tian Jiasheng and Li Limin, 'On Population and Education' *Renwen Zazhi*, Xi'an, October 1982, translated in JPRS, February 1983, 385.
2. Pi-chao Chen and Adrienne Kols, *'Population and Birth Planning in the People's Republic of China'*. *Population Reports*, Series J, no. 25, January–February, 1982.

3. 'Vice-Premier Chen Muhua speaks at a family planning meeting', *RMRB*, 14 February 1980, cited in Chen and Kols 'Population and Birth Planning'.
4. G. W., Barclay, *et al.*, 'A Reassessment of the Demography of Tradition-al Rural China', *Population Index* 42, 1976, 606–35.
5. Marshall Balfour, Roger Evans, Frank Notestein and Irene Tauber, *Public Health and Demography in the Far East*, Rockefeller Foundation (1950); extracts from the section on China have been reprinted in the archives section of *Population and Development Review*, vol. 6, no. 1, June 1980, 317–22.
6. Tian Xueyuan, 'A Survey of Population Growth, since 1949', in Liu Zheng *et al.* (ed.) *China's Population's Problems and Prospects* (Beijing: New World Press, 1981) 42.
7. See for example Charles H. C. Chen and Carl W. Tyler, 'Demographic Implications of Family Size Alternatives in the People's Republic of China', *The China Quarterly*, March 1982, 68.
8. Delia Davin, *Womanwork: Women and the Party in Revolutionary China.* ch. 4, (Oxford: Oxford University Press, 1976).
9. For a particularly interesting insight into the difficulties peasants had meeting school fees before the Cultural Revolution see Marianne Bastid, 'Economic Necessity and Political Ideals during the Cultural Revolu-tion', *China Quarterly*, April–June 1970.
10. The economic value of children in peasant society is a subject of controversy among experts (see Eva Mueller, 'The Economic Value of Children in Peasant Agriculture' in Ronald Ridker (ed.) *Population and Development* (Baltimore: The Johns Hopkins Press, 1977) 98–153, and Nick Eberstadt, 'Recent Declines in Fertility in LCDs, and what "Popu-lation Planners" may learn from them', *World Development* 1980, vol 8, 51–7). My remarks here are based on my impression of what Chinese peasants believe about the cost and value of their children. It is after all *belief* which determines fertility decisions.
11. Cheng Du, 'An Analysis of a Report on the Reproduction of the Rural Population', *Jingji Yanjiu*, 20 June 1982.
12. For the best discussion of the effect of virilocal marriage on women in China see Norma Diamond, 'Collectivisation, Kinship and the Study of Women in Rural China', *Bulletin of Concerned Asian Scholars*, January–March, 1975.
13. The Guangdong peasants studied by Mosher in 1979–80 believed that children were earning more than they cost by their mid-teens (Stephen W. Mosher, 'Birth Control: A View from a Chinese Village', *Asian Survey*, vol. XXII, no. 4, April 1982).
14. See the lengthy and useful discussion on the way bride-price has de-veloped in the People's Republic in William L. Parish and Martin King Whyte, *Village and Family in Contemporary China* (Chicago: University of Chicago Press, 1978).
15. Cheng Du, 'An Analysis'.
16. Zhao Liren and Zhu Chuzhu, 'A Preliminary Enquiry into the Problem of Second Births Outside the Plan'. *Renkou Yanjiu*, no. 3, 1983.
17. Liu Zheng, 'Population Planning and Demographic Theory' in Liu

Zheng *et al. China's Population: Problems and Prospects* (Beijing: New World Press, 1981) 5.

18. I lived in Beijing from 1975–6. This passage is based both on my own commune visits and the reports of other foreign residents who asked on my behalf about uxorilocal marriages when they made trips to the countryside. Living close to the cities, suburban commune members may be more receptive to new ideas on courtship and marriage. Furthermore as life in suburban communes combined some of the advantages of life in the city with more spacious conditions and a secure and ample supply of fresh food, residence in them was highly-prized. Young men from remoter, less prosperous areas and those from the cities who had been unable to get permission to stay in urban areas, may have felt that the advantages of residence in a suburban commune outweighed the shame of becoming a 'live-in son-in-law'.

19. Fei Xiaotong (Fei Hsiao-tung), *Peasant Life in China* (London: Routledge & Kegan Paul, 1939). For an interesting discussion of demographic behaviour in this village under the People's Republic, see Nancie Gonzalez, 'Household and Family in Haixiangong: A Re-examination', *China Quarterly*, March 1983.

20. Song Jian, 'Population Development – Goals and Plans', and Liu Zheng, 'Demographic Theory and Population Policy', both in Liu Zheng *et al. China's Population*, 26 and 63.

21. Marshall Belfour *et al., Public Health and Demography.* See also Jan Myrdal's, *Report from a Chinese Village* (London: Heinemann, 1965) esp. 226–7, which makes it clear that it was women, especially woman activists, who were quickest to accept birth control. Cheng Du found that the widely-observed association between education for women and a lower desired family size holds good for the Chinese countryside. Among 707 women of child-bearing age, the 42 per cent who were illiterates wanted an average of 4.8 children, the 45 per cent who had had primary school education wanted 3.05, and the 9.5 per cent who had had some secondary schooling wanted only 1.75.

22. For a study which found a strong relationship between the existence of a health clinic in a village and the village's acceptance of the 1970s birth planning campaign see, William Parish and Martin King White, *Village and Family in Contemporary China* (Chicago: Chicago University Press, 1978) 150–3.

23. The following account is based mainly on W. R. Lavely, 'China's Rural Population Statistics at the Local Level', *Population Index*, 48, 665–77 and Qian Xinjian, 'Possible Obstacles to the Realisation of the One-child Family in China', unpublished paper written for the David Owen Centre for Population Studies, Cardiff, July 1982.

24. John Gittings, 'Communes: new direction or abandonment?'. *China Now*, May/June 1982, no. 102.

25. Mosher, 'Birth Control: A View from a Chinese Village'.

26. John Gittings, 'Communes: new direction?' and the BBC 'Horizon' programme on China's One-Child Family, first broadcast 7 November 1983.

27. Qian Xinzhong, minister of the State Family Planning Commission, 'Minister Views Family Planning', Xinhua (in Chinese) 14 June 1983, translated in *Daily Report* (JPRS) 17 November 1983.
28. H. Yuan Tien, 'Sterilization Acceptance in China', *Studies in Family Planning*, vol. 13, no. 10, October 1982, 288.
29. Victor Nee, 'Post-Mao Changes in a South China Production Brigade' in Bulletin of Concerned Asian Scholars (ed.) *China from Mao to Deng* (London: Zed Press, 1983).
30. 'Guangdong to enforce sterilisation', Guangdong Provincial Service, 14 May 1983. translated in *Daily Report* 13 June 1983.
31. Information from a friend who was a family-planning worker in rural Sichaun 1977–8.
32. H. Yuan Tien, 'Sterilization Acceptance', 288–9.
33. 'There Should be No Legislation of Planned Births', RMRB, 13 September 1980.
34. See for example the text of the 6th Five Year Plan Part V, ch. 29, *SWB*, 21 December 1982 (FE/7214/C/32) and *the Open Letter of the Central Committee of the Chinese Communist Party to all Party and Youth League members* which urges support of the single-child family. (*Daily Report*, 26 September 1980).
35. The Sichuan regulations were produced in March 1979 whereas those for Shanxi were promulgated as late as 29 June 1982. At least nine other provinces produced their own regulations in the intervening three years. Some like Qinghai province have issued more than one set.
36. The commune I visited was Stonewell Commune, Guangzhou municipality; for Zhangqing Commune, near Suzhou, see Ashwani Saith, 'Economic Incentives for the One-child Family in Rural China', *China Quarterly*, September 1981.
37. 'Meeting held by the Executive Committee of the China Population Society', *RMRB*, 7 February 1983, passim.
38. 'Fujian Concerned about Planned Parenthood'. Fujian Provincial Service, 27 May 1979, translated in *China Report (JPRS)*.
39. Nee, 'Post-Mao Changes in a South China Production Brigade'.
40. This outline is based on the 'Shanxi Planned Parenthood Regulations' *Shanxi Ribao* 17 November 1982, translated in SWB, 16 December 1982 (FE/7210/B11/3). The penalties laid down in these regulations are detailed and severe. At the time of writing these are the most recent regulations to have been promulgated and presumably represent up-to-date official thinking. Other details are from the Qinghai regulations (Daily Report (China) 15 June 1982, the Sichuan regulations SWB 16 March 1979 (FE/6068/B11/9) and the Fujian regulations (see interpretation in Fujian Ribao, 3 August 1982, translated in *China Report*, 15 November 1982.
41. Shanxi Planned Parenthood Regulations, *Shanxi Ribaa* 17 November 1982.
42. See Ashwani Saith, 'Economic Incentives', China Quarterly, September 1981, 497.
43. Author's own travel notes, 1981.

44. For a recent interesting discussion of rural income inequalities see, E. B. Vermeer, 'Income Differentials in Rural China', *China Quarterly*, March, 1982.

45. For example the authors of a survey of the single-child family policy in Hefei, Anhui, believed that standardisation would assist its implementation. (The Population Research Office, Anhui University, 'A Survey of One-Child Families in Anhui Province, China', *Anhui Population*, April, 1981).

46. See for example Neijing County Party Committee regulations on rural finance no. 3: 'The amount of agricultural taxes, public welfare funds and accumulation funds levied on the peasants must remain unchanged for five years beginning 1983', Sichuan Provincial Service, 28 February 1983 translated in SWB, 11 May 1983 (FE/7279/B11/17).

47. See the Anhui survey cited in note 45. Other writers advocate still more local variation by suggesting that brigades and even teams should introduce supplementary regulations. (Xiao Sanhua, 'How to do family planning work where responsibility systems have been set up', *Renkou Yanjiu*, no. 3, 1983.) The idea that the state should provide some finance is often seen in this and other welfare contexts. See for example the idea that the state should contribute towards a pension plan for peasants (Zhao Liren and Zhu Chuzhu, 'A Preliminary Enquiry into the Problem of Second Births.)

48. Lin Fude and Zhou Qing, 'Shifang County: Family Planning', in Liu Zheng, *China's Population* 163–4.

49. This categorisation of responsibility systems is based on Greg O'Leary and Andrew Watson, 'The Responsibility System and the Future of Collective Farming', *Australian Journal of Chinese Affairs*, no. 8, 1982. I am grateful to the authors from much enlightenment about the nature of responsibility systems. Another interesting discussion of the implications of responsibility systems can be found in Barbara Hazard, 'Socialist Household Production: Some Implications of the New "Responsibility System" in China', *Bulletin of the Institute of Development Studies*, Sussex University, vol. 13, no. 4, September 1982.

50. BR, 29 April 1983, 4.

51. Xinhua report of 6 January 1983, translated in *SWB*, 18 February 1983, (FE/7261/B11/9).

52. For a much fuller discussion of household sidelines see Elisabeth J. Croll, 'The promotion of domestic sideline production in rural China, 1978–9', in Jack Gray and Gordon White (eds) *China's New Development Strategy* (London: Academic Press, 1982).

53. Ren Zhongyi, First Secretary of the Guangdong Provincial Party Committee, reported in Guangzhou Ribao, 26 December 1982, translated in *Daily Report* 12 January 1983.

54. Elisabeth Croll, 'Promotion of domestic sideline production'.

55. 'Strengthen the work of family planning', *RMRB*, 18 August 1981.

56. 'Give Play to the Leadership Role of Basic Organisation in the Countryside', *RMRB*, 19 February 1982. Similar reports are to be found and many discussions of the problems to which responsibility systems gave rise.

57. Xu Shaozhi, 'To Control Population Growth we must Emphasise "Responsibility"', *Renkou Yanjiu*, no. 4, 1982. Many different versions of the same sentiment can be found. Some such quotation crops up in every discussion of the effect of responsibility systems on family planning.
58. The prohibition on hiring labour has been relaxed, the press now contains references to the conditions under which households may hire 'assistants'. (see for example 'Anhui Regulations on Specialised Households', Anhui Provincial Service, *Daily Report*, 8 June 1983). None the less the normal way for a household to enlarge its labour force is still by increasing the number of its members.
59. 'Ningxia Meeting Discusses Rural Problems', *Ningxia Ribao*, 8 April 1982, translated in *Daily Report*, 30 April 1982.
60. For a reproduction of the census form see Elizabeth Breeze 'Counting People in China', *China Now*, July/ August 1982, 14–15.
61. See for example the local duodrama, 'Going to Meet Maternal Grandmother', in Leo Orleans (ed.) *Chinese Approaches to Family Planning* (White Plains, N.Y.: M. E. Sharpe, 1978). This is one of the many propaganda pieces aimed at the older generation.
62. See for example the letter of fifteen peasant women from Qizhen Commune, Hexian County, Anhui Province in *RMRB*, 23 February 1983. Each was the mother of between three and nine girls. The letter complains of ill-treatment from mothers-in-law and the rest of society. The women claim that they had not wished to bear so many children but were bullied into continuing to try for sons.
63. 'Call for Survey of Poor Households Enjoying the Five Guarantees', 15, Xinhua in Chinese, 15 December 1982, translated in *SWB* 24 December 1982, (FE/7217/B11/9). 'Need for Equal Emphasis on State, Collective and Individual Interests in Rural Areas', *Zhejiang Ribao*, 19 March 1983, translated in *SWB*, 31 March 1983 (FE/7296/B11/3).
64. *Marriage Law of the People's Republic of China*, article 15, Beijing: Foreign Language Press, 1982. This law came into effect 1 January 1981, but the earlier law of 1950 had also required children to support their parents.
65. Yang Fan 'Save the Baby Girls', in *Zhongguo Qingnian bao* (*China's Youth*) 9 November 1982. 'Protecting Infant Girls', *BR*, 31 January 1983. 'On the protection of baby girls', *Guangming Ribao*, 30 December 1982.
66. Based on private conversations in Beijing 1975–6. For a discussion of the prevalence of infanticide in the 1950s and 1960s see Nancie Gonzalez, 'Household and Family in Kaixiangong.
67. 'How to interpret the Census communiqué', *BR*, 29 November 1982.
68. For example the article by Yang Fan in the paper *China Youth*, claimed that the ratio was as bad as three boys to two girls in some communes.
69. These figures are taken from John S. Aird, 'The preliminary results of China's 1982 Census'. *China Quarterly*, December 1983.
70. Some of the most interesting are to be found in recent issues of the journal *Renkou Yanjiu*, for example, He Guoquan *et al.*, 'The Best Emphasis for Rural Family Planning – Lessons from a Survey in

Huaiyuan County', no. 2, 1982, Xiao Sanhua, 'How to Carry Out Family Planning After Adopting Production Responsibility Systems in Rural Areas', no. 3, 1982, Xu Shaozhi, 'To Control Population Growth we Must emphasise "Responsibility"', no. 4, 1982; Zhang Xinxia, 'One-child Families also have Possibilities for Getting Rich', no. 5, 1982. Zhu Mian, 'Agricultural Responsibility in the Work of Family Planning in the Rural Areas', no. 5, 1982. Hu Fangrong, 'The Experience of Organising the Permanent Work Team for Family Planning in Wuqushan Commune', Taojiang Co., Hunan province, no. 4, 1983.

71. See for example Xiao Sanhua, 'How to Carry Out Family Planning after Adopting Production Responsibility Systems in Rural Areas', *Renkou Yanjiu*, no. 5, 1982.

72. 'The Chinese Communist Party Central Committee issues minutes of the 1981 Rural Work Conference', Xinhua Domestic Service, 5 April 1982, translated in Daily Report, 7 April 1981.

73. See 'Shanxi Planned Parenthood Regulations', and other regulations.

74. Ibid.

75. Questions and Answers on Violators of Planned Parenthood, Fujian Ribao, 3 August 1982, translated in *China Report* 15 November 1982.

76. Xiao Sanhua 'How to Carry out Family Planning', note 64.

77. John Gittings, 'Communes: New Direction of Abandonment?' *China Now*, May/June 1982. Elizabeth Wright, 'Travel Notes from Luci Commune, Tonglu County, Zhejiang province.' I am most grateful to Ms. Wright for allowing me to use these informative notes.

78. See for example an article condemning cadres who revoked contracts in a commune in Hebei because the responsibility land had become so profitable (*China Daily*, 9 June 1983).

79. Central Committee of the Chinese Communist Party, 'Circular on Rural Work in 1984'. reported in *BR* 20 February 1984.

80. Tian Xueyuan, 'A Survey of Population growth' in Liu Zheng *et al.*, *China's Population*, 46.

81. Report in *RMRB*, 8 October 1981.

82. Parish and Whyte, *Village and Family in Contemporary China*, 150–3.

83. Eva Mueller 'The Economic Value of Children', 121–2.

84. See for example Liu Zheng, 'Population Planning and Theory', 8–10. This sort of calculation is to be found in innumerable articles on China's population.

85. 'Let's work out an account of our population, arable land and food grain', Beijing Domestic Service, 19 January 1983. translated in *Daily Report*, 25 January 1983.

86. Liu Zheng, 'Population Planning and Demographic Theory', 23.

87. See Ashwani Saith , 'Economic Incentives'. Sometimes the discrimination is in favour only of those whose single child is a daughter. For example a report from Sunjiatuan commune, Weihai city, Shandong province, describes an old people's home in which old people without sons receive a food ration and cash allowance worth 1.3 times the local per capita income. If old people who have sons become residents, their sons cover their expenses. BR, 14 February 1983 27.

88. 'Guizhou Planned Parenthood Conference Concludes', Guizhou provin-

cial service, 1 November 1982, translated in *China Report*, 30 November 1982.

89. 'The standard of supply for households entitled to the five guarantees should be at least equal to the actual standard of living of the local commune members.' (Xinhua in Chinese, 15 December 1982, translated in *SWB* 24 December 1982).

90. See Chapter 6 in this volume by Deborah Davis-Friedmann.

91. Author's travel notes from a trip to China in 1981.

92. 'Stabilise and perfect the System of Contracted Responsibilities with Payment linked to Output', editorial in the *RMRB*, 22 January 1983.

93. See for example Ashwani Saith, 'Economic Incentives', 497.

94. *Shanghai Jiefang Ribao*, 1 April 1982.

95. Tian Xueyuan, 'On the Problem of Population Aging; *RMRB*, 18 March 1980.

96. 'Shanxi Planned Parenthood Regulations,' and Fujian Provincial Regulations, Fujian Provincial Service, 5 January 1983, in *SWB* 22 January 1983 (FE/7238/B11/1).

97. 'Interview with Responsible Persons from the Guangdong Planned Parenthood Office', *H. K. Ta Kung Pao*, 6 January 1983, translated in *SWB* 22 January 1983 (FE/7238/B11/1).

98. Xu Xuehan, 'Resolutely Implement Population Policy in the Rural Areas', *RMRB*, 5 February 1982.

99. Elizabeth Wright, Travel Notes 1982, Maoping Brigade, Luci Commune, Tonglu county, Zhejiang.

100. For example a 1983 report of the State Family Planning Commission estimated that China can meet its population goal of 1200m by the end of the century if average births per woman of child-bearing age can be brought down to 1.7 by 1985 and 1.5 by 1980 (BR, 24 October 1983).

101. 'Ningxia Meeting Discusses Rural Problems', *Ningxia Ribao*, 8 April 1982, translated in *Daily Report*, 30 April 1982.

102. 'Give Play to the Leadership Role of the Rural Basic Organisations', *RMRB*, 12 February 1982.

103. 'Shengqiu County, Henan province, Reduces the Number of Rural Cadres to Lighten the Peasants' Load', *RMRB*, 4 February 1982. 'A Jilin County Acts to Reduce Peasants' Burdens', Xinhua in Chinese, 22 March 1983, in *SWB*, 25 March 1983 (FE/7291/B11/4).

104. There are numerous reports of cadres defying population policy by themselves having two or more children. For an article which stresses the importance of cadres setting an example see He Guoquan *et al.*, 'The Best Emphasis for Rural Family Planning – Lessons from Huaiyuan County', *Renkou Yanjiu*, no. 2, 1982.

105. Chen and Kols, *Population and Birth Planning*, 607.

106. 'Shengqiu County' (see note 103).

107. This discussion is mainly based on John S. Aird, 'Population Studies and Population Policy in China' *Population and Development Review*, no 1, 1982, an article which takes a very pessimistic view, and Chen and Kols *Population and Birth Planning*. For indications of official anxiety about the failure of a particular area to meet quotas see translated broadcasts from the Hainan Island radio service in *Daily Report*, 29 June 1983, and

82   *The Single-child Family Policy in the Countryside*

8 July 1983.
108. Ren Zhongyi Provincial Party Secretary of Guangdong Province, in *Guangzhou Ribao*, 26 December 1982, note 43.
109. Xu Xuehan, Resolutely Implement the Policy on Rural Population', *RMRB*, 5 February 1982, 5.
110. Anhui University, 'A Survey of the Single Child Family of West Side Hefei, Anhui Province, China', Anhui University 1980 and 'A Population Survey in the Western District of Beijing'. *Renkou Yanjiu*, no. 1, 1981.
111. 'Minister Views Family Planning', Xinhua (in Chinese) 14 June 1983, translated in *Daily Report*, 17 June 1983.

3 The Single-child Family Policy in the Cities

PENNY KANE*

It has long been recognised that family size tends to decrease in cities or urban areas earlier and more widely than it does in the countryside. Demographers often describe 'urbanisation' as a major factor in fertility decline, but that overall term covers a wide range of social and economic processes which may or may not affect the choice of individuals about the number of children to have. Definitions of the word 'urban' are not easy, and in China the difficulties are compounded by the existence of the overlapping category of suburban communes, which are generally grouped administratively within the sphere of cities and towns. Such communes are primarily agricultural but they are influenced by their proximity to a town and tend, in their fertility patterns, to reflect some of that influence, exhibiting rates which are between those of the truly urban areas, and those of the countryside. They are included in this chapter both because they thus exhibit some of the earlier changes in fertility seen in the towns, and because Chinese statistics for urban areas generally include suburban communes. The Chinese define an area as urban if it has a population of more than 2000 at least one half of which is working in non-agricultural pursuits.[1] (See also H. Yuan Tien's discussion of this definition in this volume.) It is this definition which will be used here.

Acceptance of one-child-family certificates seems to have been quite high during the early stages of the campaign, although as one would expect there were considerable variations between different cities as well as between urban and suburban districts of each city.

* I should like to thank the Department of Demography, The Australian National University, for the Visiting Fellowship which enabled me to do much of the work on which this chapter is based, and the International Planned Parenthood Federation for allowing me leave of absence to take up that fellowship.

Given the unprecedented nature of the sacrifice which Chinese parents were being asked to make in limiting their families to a single child, this high rate of compliance with the policy suggests that there were a number of existing preconditions for its success. It is with these factors, and their roles in helping to create an increasingly small family norm in urban areas, that this chapter is concerned.

URBAN FAMILY LIMITATION

There is considerable evidence for the use of fertility control methods in China dating back over 2000 years.[2] Some of the techniques involved contraceptive devices which may have been comparatively expensive: others were easily available local concoctions. The practice of traditional methods was common; a hospital in Beijing[3] reported in the 1940s that they were widely used by the poor, and factory girls had fewer children – and had them later – than other urban workers; some enjoyed a strong position in their homes without having any children at all.[4]

The pioneering demographer, Chen Da, noted the difference in birth rates between the rapidly growing city of Kunming (1939–41) and the rural areas around it.

> In contrast to these is Kunming city, where the processes of urbanisation are proceeding much faster and the influence of city life on birth rates is more clearly seen. The number of surviving children per 100 married pairs in Kunming is only 165.1, compared with 203.3 to 220.4 in the surrounding areas.[5]

Chen saw that within the city, the wealthier and higher social strata had more children than the poor. This was partly because of different survival rates, but as Chen pointed out 'those who have gone to foreign countries for a university education, though small in number, are known to have practised birth control. They therefore have the lowest birth rate of all, or 120 children per 100 married couples'. He rather implies that although less is known about modern birth control usage in other groups, some may be aware of the techniques. The implication becomes more explicit when he contrasts Kunming with Chengdu – then a very remote town – and says that in the latter modern methods of birth control are unknown.[6]

There is other evidence that in the early part of this century

questions of population growth and its effects, and of 'modern' contraceptive techniques, were being discussed among the educated urban
Chinese. Sun Yat-sen referred extensively to population issues over
the years; the fact that his views changed over time is in this context less
significant than that he had views: it was a subject being discussed.
Similarly, Chiang Kai-shek's repeated refutation of Malthusianism is
of less interest than the implication that the subject was under
discussion.[7]

Only a few women, but two and a half thousand men, made up a
crowded audience at Beijing University for Margaret Sanger on her
first visit to China in 1922. Her second, in response to a resolution
passed by the Chinese Medical Association in favour of birth control in
1935, ended as soon as it began; a side-effect of the Japanese war.[8] The
writings of Marie Stopes are mentioned by Chang Ching-sheng, Presi-
dent of an Eugenics Society in Beijing, as being available in China, in
his *Sex Histories* and contraception is taken for granted in his discussions of the *Histories* themselves.[9] It is only fair to add, though, that his
book – an early attempt at sexology – was banned in Shanghai and
Hangzhou in the 1920s. A more ambitious attempt at sexology was the
annotated translation of Havelock Ellis's *The Psychology of Sex*.
Published in 1948, it contained many footnotes and explanations
based on Chinese sources (from ancient history, diaries, novels and
poems) added by the translator Pan Guangdan to make it 'an important work on the Chinese psychology of sex'.[10]

During the late 1920s and early 1930s, various urban centres began
to establish small family planning clinics. An example was the 'Peiping
[Beijing] Committee on Maternal Health', formed in 1930 by a group
of volunteers, the majority of whom were Chinese academics or health
personnel. Though the numbers it reached with one part-time paid
case-worker were small, the Committee also published an 8000-word
Population Supplement as a section of the Sunday edition of the
Morning Post, and a monthly column entitled *Birth Control News*,
which appeared in another daily paper, *The Truth*. 'Its readers are
mainly artisans, shopkeepers and the like', reported the Committee.[11]

Simultaneously, attitudes to the family and to marriage began to
change. In the Republican period, 'influenced by social practices in
Europe and North America, the urban-educated younger generation
had begun to demand the free choice of marriage partner or the
non-intervention of parents or their parties, and the establishment of
independent households on marriage'.[12] The young were defying their
families. Although such conflicts may have been more common among

the élite in urban centres, education appears to have been an important factor, encouraging for instance, Mao Zedong [Mao Tse-tung] the son of comfortably-off peasants, to reject his arranged marriage.

Attitudes to marriage were changing among the workers, too, if less dramatically and visibly than among intellectuals. The factory girl

> has been brought in touch with modern ideas. She speaks with other women workers and sometimes even with men. She hears discussions of modern marriage and the advantages of a family without a mother-in-law. She learns that she is not legally obliged to surrender her wages to her husband or parents ... Some women workers have used their independence to escape from an impossible situation at home. And even those who do not go to such extremes are no longer the obedient peasant wives of olden times.[13]

The Chinese Medical Association had passed a resolution in favour of birth control for maternal and child health in 1936, but the circumstances of the Sino-Japanese war and the civil war precluded the establishment of services. After 1949, however, the importance of family planning as a health and welfare measure was sufficiently well accepted by policy-makers and doctors for the Ministry of Health to bring out 'Revised regulations on contraception and induced abortion' which were ratified in August 1953. The regulations were designed to widen access to birth control as part of maternal and child health care. Their immediate impact was limited, partly because of controversy within the Party about coming out officially on such a delicate issue and partly because of sheer lack of facilities.[14]

Nevertheless, the regulations did exist, and by December 1954, a conference had been held to discuss birth control and the problems of implementing a programme, and the Second Office of the State Council appointed an *ad hoc* committee to study, and submit recommendations on, ways and means of expanding family planning. An internal Party instruction, explaining official approval of birth limitation, was circulated within the membership in May 1955.

> In all probability the instruction affected only those who either had already practised contraception, or desired to do so. This group of people, however, represented . . . urban dwellers, professionals, intellectuals and Party cadres, for whom the socio-economic factors associated with the motivation to practise contraception had already existed.[15]

The family planning campaigns themselves waxed and waned in intensity in China during the 1950s and 1960s.[16] Sometimes they were overshadowed or even contradicted by other campaigns – the Great Leap Forward, for example, gave additional impetus to the idea that what China needed was more hands to take part in an economic breakthrough. Usually they suffered from their association with the linked debate over an ideology of population and the effects of population growth primarily on economic development, but the population arguments were largely over the total population – and in demographic terms that really meant China's peasants. The campaigns were also handicapped to some extent by the limitations of existing contraceptive techniques and the small number of contraceptives being manufactured, and during 1950s, by the reliance on mass media for propaganda. None of these limitations was nearly so significant in the urban areas, where facilities did exist, distribution and medical support were better, and a substantial proportion of the population was at least partially literate. In addition – because the small proportion of the urban population made it a demographic irrelevance – arguments about the value of a larger population for China, or purges of 'Malthusians' had little impact on the provision of family-planning services.

URBAN NETWORKS AND THE SPREAD OF FAMILY PLANNING

Official and ideological support for family planning – and its value in improving maternal and child health – began to be reinforced as early as 1955, with the establishment not only of services but also of informational campaigns.[17] The latter were conducted at first largely through written materials designed largely for the more literate urban dwellers. A concentration on the urban people was not out of keeping with overall Chinese policies towards the cities. The first Five Year Plan, endorsed in July 1955 by the National People's Congress, selected key cities and some provinces for development in order to improve the country's industrial performance. Among the investments to be made were social ones: 'the development of public health and medical services plays a significant role in improving people's well-being ... in developing health and medical services priority must be given to improving the work in industrial areas'.[18]

Women's organisations changed the focus of their attention from land reform to work in the towns, where, according to the first National Congress of the Women's Federation, the most urgent need was the restoration of production. Women were organised on the basis of their occupation or residence, according to circumstance, and the initial concentration on getting women to work in handicrafts or industry was quickly supplemented by welfare, hygiene and literacy activities, as it became clear that without such attention women's contribution would be limited.[19]

The development of family-planning propaganda and services was in keeping with this approach: it concentrated efforts initially in densely populated areas, such as towns and cities; on the educated sectors of the community; and on pilot projects for later expansion.[20] Examples of how the approach actually worked were reported by Pi-chao Chen.[21] In the second half of 1955, the cadres in government agencies and enterprises in the province of Hebei were the subject of a family-planning campaign. A year later, the campaign was extended to all urban dwellers, as well as to employees in industrial and mining enterprises. From 1957, the campaign was spread to the rural areas. In Hunan, by contrast, the campaign did not start in one region until 1957, when the Party committee of Ning county announced that organised efforts would initially be concentrated within cities, with villages being the last to be reached, while the persuasion campaign would be directed first to cadres and functionaries and then to the masses. One co-operative was chosen as a pilot project for an education campaign.

Given limited resources the strategy was a logical one. Urban areas were those in which it was easiest to place services, for the target population was comparatively small, there was at least some existing infrastructure and it was comparatively cheap to introduce facilities in limited geographical areas with reasonable communications.[22] There was an existing acceptance of contraception amongst the more educated people in the towns, and they might be expected to give their support to the campaign and help to spread it. As knowledge spread of the availability of family-planning services, and as those services were, from the start, closely linked with other health provisions – especially of maternal and child health care – it is probable that the number using contraception steadily grew.

FACTORS INFLUENCING URBAN ACCEPTANCE

Desire to exercise control over the number and spacing of children probably also increased with efforts to raise the status of women and to bring more of them into the workforce. Such efforts were uneven, and there was a period during 1956–7 when it seems that more women were trying to work than industry could readily absorb. Delia Davin's careful analysis of the frequently conflicting attitudes to, and pressures on, women during the 1950s nevertheless shows that the overall trend was towards a much greater involvement of women in the labour force, together with real efforts to encourage women to 'stand up' and take part in decision-making both within the family and in the wider context of society and the Party.[23]

In urban areas, again, it seems probable that these new roles for women offered greater opportunities and were taken up more swiftly. The country's industrial base – badly undermined by the war – was sufficiently reconstructed by 1955 for the first Five Year Plan to concentrate on industrial expansion: new jobs became available for the women to fill. By 1959, women workers and employees made up 18.8 per cent of all workers and employees; the increase in the number of women working was far greater than the overall increase in the total non-agricultural work force.[24]

The Women's Federation, one of the primary tasks of which was the promotion of maternal and child health, helped to spread information about such matters as contraception and at the same time gave individual women strong moral support in challenging traditional family pressures.[25]

Women no longer had to choose between working and having children. The introduction of paid maternity leave (generally fifty-six days for a worker, increased to seventy-two on medical grounds where necessary) meant she did not have to give up her job to care for the child; the introduction of creches and co-operative childcare arrangements – more successful in cities than in the country – made it possible for her to go back to work after maternity leave.[26] This, in turn, made it worthwhile for the enterprise to offer her further training and career development. With a job to go back to, childbearing ceased to be the only future for a married woman.[27]

Questioning of traditional attitudes to women's roles was intensified in the Cultural Revolution, and the slogan widely associated with the questioning of Confucian attitudes to women 'Women hold up half the sky': was increasingly taken seriously.[28] There was another upsurge in the number of working women. Few of them after the late 1950s could find jobs in the State sector, because the increase in that sector after the Revolution had resulted in a disproportionately young bureaucracy and a labour force, with little attrition from retirement.[29] Women in the cities went into (admittedly less prestigious) neighbourhood workshops or factories, or into health and welfare work. During the late 1960s there was a massive attempt to widen the basis of medical care, through the creation of ,vast numbers of barefoot doctors, low-level medical stations and other facilities. This in turn led to a considerable increase in the number of women employed in, or working part-time with, the health services, and that 'substantially increased the level of health care available to women'.[30] While it is true that the development of these additional forms of medical care ly had most impact in the countryside where previously services were sparse, their effect among the poorer or less literate sectors of urban populations should not be underestimated. Health stations in the neighbourhood, staffed by volunteer health workers from that neighbourhood, and by a barefoot doctor perhaps, took on much routine work, including the distribution of contraceptives.[31]

The effects of the Cultural Revolution on family planning – as distinct from its effects on implementation of a population policy – still require further study, and statistics either have not been released or in many instances probably do not exist, for the period 1967–9. The desire of individuals for family planning continued and although it seems that during the most intensive period of struggle, communications, supplies and organisations largely broke down, in most areas that period was comparatively shortlived.

Some women may have found that while working, the opportunities for discussion and sharing of women's problems improved their knowledge of family-planning techniques; one thing is certain, that in the years of one political campaign following another, the difficulties of combining a family with the multitudinous other tasks were formidable. An eight-hour working-day, six days a week, was supplemented by study and criticism sessions, often of great length and frequently organised to fill several evenings a week. Private household tasks were in turn supplemented by a share of the community tasks, such as street-sweeping or perhaps being responsible for some basic-level health care in the neighbourhood.

Meanwhile, an increasing number of young people, in the cities especially, were receiving schooling (see Table 3.1). This would not only have an impact on their own attitudes to family size and to contraception in due course, but meant that even where the parents in a family had no education, their children could read newspapers and propaganda to them and to others in the community including, inevitably, the discussions of the value of family limitation.

Changes in the age at marriage also influenced attitudes. The new

TABLE 3.1 *Number of female students in educational institutions, various levels and percentage of enrolment, 1949–58*

Year	Higher educational institutions		Secondary specialised schools		Secondary general schools		Primary schools	
	N	%	N	%	N	%	N	%
1949	23 000	19.8	—	—	—	—	—	—
1952	45 000	23.4	158 000	24.9	585 000	23.5	16 812 000	32.9
1957	103 000	23.3	206 000	26.5	1 935 000	30.8	22 176 000	34.5
1958	154 000	23.2	397 000	27.0	2 667 000	31.3	33 264 000	38.5

(The percentages are for the females as a percentage of all students.)

SOURCE   H. Yuan Tien, *China's Population Struggle* (Ohio State University Press, 1973).

TABLE 3.2 *Women's average age at marriage, by year of marriage and place of residence*

Year of marriage	Urban	Rural
1950–63	20.4	19.2
1964–72	22.6	21.0
1973–79	24.6	22.8

SOURCE   H. Yuan Tien, 'Age at Marriage in the People's Republic of China', *China Quarterly*, March 1983.

Marriage Law of 1950 had specified a minimum age for females of 18, and for men of 20; in practice, considerable effort was subsequently made to encourage a later actual age. It was universally agreed that the implementation of the marriage law itself was easier and quicker in urban areas and that the policy for delayed marriage worked better in cities and towns.

A recent investigation in Jiangsu province,[32] carried out by university students during the summer vacation, when they collected data for a total of 1132 couples spanning three generations, gives the figures shown in Table 3.2 for age of marriage analysed by urban and rural residence.

TABLE 3.3   *Average age at first marriage among women of child-bearing age*
(Shanghai sample)

Age at first marriage	Urban areas	Suburban areas	Overall
1950–4	20.9*	19.9**	20.4
1955–9	22.1	20.6	21.5
1960–4	23.3	21.1	22.0
1965–9	24.8	22.0	23.2
1970–4	25.5	23.2	24.2
1975–9	26.8	24.2	25.1

* According to data compiled in the Luwan District in the city proper.
** According to data compiled in the township of Chengxiang in Qingpu County in the suburban area of the city.

SOURCE   Gu Xingyan *et al.*, Shanghai: Family Planning in Liu Zheng *et al. China's Population: Problems and Prospects* (New World Press, 1981)

Another indication of the rising overall age of marriage, and the differences which continued to exist even between urban areas and their suburban communes, is provided in a study of Shanghai.[33] The actual ages of marriage in Shanghai are likely to be higher than for China overall, given the long tradition of later marriage there among the textile workers, but the trends they show, and the difference between urban and suburban areas, are probably broadly representative. (See Table 3.3).

A further factor during the 1950s which affected the numbers using contraception was the growth of the urban areas themselves. Between 1953 and 1957, the urban population grew from 71.6 to 94.4m – a rate of increase more than twice that of the rural areas. Some 8m of that additional 22.8m was attributed to immigration[34] but this figure is probably a minimum estimate. Government efforts to deal with this influx were somewhat spasmodic. Most of the increase must be attributed to national efforts to develop industry in new as well as existing urban concentrations, though some of the increase was the result of individual families drifting voluntarily to the towns, despite periodic efforts to return such people to their rural origins.

The urban workers went predominantly into State industries, with fixed retirement ages and – more importantly perhaps – pension schemes. For this sector of the Chinese population, the old fears of dependency or hardship in old age were minimised: one economic rationale for having several children (or at least for several sons) had been significantly reduced. More men than women achieved jobs in state industries; women might well be working in neighbourhood workshops or co-operatives, where benefits were considerably less; but the existence of two incomes and a pension for at least the husband created a new financial security with which to contemplate retirement.

Urban growth presented planners and the town-dwellers themselves with problems. Existing housing stock was generally extremely inadequate: provision had to be made not only to improve it but to cater for a more than 5 per cent annual growth rate: in practice, this turned out to be impossible. Communications, again historically poor, meant that getting food to the cities was difficult, and inevitably led to shortages and queues.[35] Many other still inadequate aspects of urban infrastructure – piped water, electricity, public transport, health facilities and so on – were further threatened by growth on this scale. At the official level, the first introduction of a demographic factor into urban planning came in 1955, with an article in the *People's Daily* which told city planners to match demographic expansion to economic plans and industrial construction, and argued that the city must make every effort to control population size, and prevent further influxes from the countryside.[36]

If the planners were concerned primarily with migration, rather than fertility, it is likely that the urban residents, suffering the effects of crowding in their daily lives, were also receptive to the birth control measures now being offered them. Within the increasingly crowded cities, homes themselves became more cramped. In any traditional society with high death rates, the number of generations living together – and the numbers within those generations – tended to be small. Falls in mortality, and the concomitant increases in life expectancy, which overall by 1975 was estimated to be 63.2 years for men and 66.3 for women, have meant that families have become units of several generations.[37] In the three municipalities, which are the only cities for which separate figures were calculated, life expectancy is even higher, as is shown in Table 3.4.

These longer lifespans have contributed to crowded housing conditions. Urban average living space per head actually declined from 4.5 square metres in 1952 to 3.6 square metres in 1977, as a result of lack of housing investment aggravated by population growth.[38] In principle, housing is allocated by the authorities to a young couple on their marriage, although where there are housing shortages – as there are in many of the larger cities – the couple may be forced to live for a while

TABLE 3.4   *Life expectancy at birth 1973–5*

	Male	Female
Tianjin	69.9	72
Shanghai	69.2	74.8
Beijing	68.3	70.8

SOURCE   Rong Shoude *et al.*, 'Statistical Analysis of Life Expectancy', in *Symposium of Chinese Population Science* (China Academic Publishers, 1981).

with the parents of one or other partner. Once they have achieved a home of their own, they are likely, at a later date, to have to take in a widowed parent.[39] If there are no other close relatives to take care of the parent or parents left in the rural area, the couple can bring them into their home; this despite the overall very strict controls on in-migration.[40]

The pressure on housing is widely admitted as a major – perhaps the major – problem in Chinese cities and lack of investment in this sector has been complicated by the coming to marriage age of the cohorts from earlier baby booms. The very high age of marriage in Tianjin is attributed by Lyle partly to the difficulty in securing housing – a particular problem in that city where the 1976 earthquake wrecked much of the existing stock as well.[41]

Where three generations live together in increasingly cramped conditions, the benefits of extra hands, extra help with the child and so on are possibly outweighed by the irritation of parents-in-law demanding deference and, increasingly, care. In those circumstances, too, mother-in-law's traditional yearning for grandchildren around her feet may well be muted.

By 1972, the results of widespread access to contraception, and of more than a decade of family-planning education, together with the socio-economic factors discussed above, could be seen in the birth rates of cities, in the contraceptive prevalence rates, and in small family size.[42] (See Table 3.5.) The absolute levels of crude birth rates reached by the urban population at the end of the 1970s were extremely low, even by comparison with those of industrialised nations and were in marked contrast to those of rural China (see Table 3.6).

TABLE 3.5 *Family planning indicators for China and three municipalities 1977–80*

Place and year	Late marriage rate (%)	Birth limitation rate (%)	Planned birth rate (%)	Crude birthrate (per 1000 population)
China 1978		70*		18.34
Beijing municipality 1978				12.92
city proper 1978				9.73
peri-urban counties 1978				16.72
Shanghai municipality 1979–80			80	
city proper 1978	90.0	85.0	85.0	7.4
peri-urban counties 1978	80.0	80.0	75.0	15.3
Tianjin municipality 1978	95.0	80.6		15.42
city proper 1978	96.6	88.8	88.5	10.8
suburban 1978	94.9	75.9	57.2	19.0
rural 1978	93.2	73.0	63.6	18.9

Late marriage rate: percentage of couples marrying in the year who marry at or after the ages set by the late marriage norm

Birth limitation rate: roughly, the percentage of married couples under age 50 using contraception. Use for any portion of the year is included in the numerator, and naturally infertile couples are excluded from the denominator.

Planned birth rate: percentage of couples complying with all three birth-planning norms.

* Estimate based on regression equation derived from crude birthrates and birth limitation rates in selected areas of China.

SOURCE Pi-chao Chen and Adrienne Kols, 'Population and Birth Planning in the People's Republic of China', *Population Reports*, series J, no. 25, 1982.

City families in the 1970s were generally small.[43] In Shanghai in 1978 only 10 per cent of births were of a third or subsequent child (in the city proper, the figure was less than 2 per cent). Changsha, the previous year, reported the remarkably low figure of 5 per cent of all births being third or subsequent children, while Chengdu reported 15 per cent.[44] By 1981, Beijing had reduced third order births to just over 2 per cent,[45] while Shanghai claimed that only seventeen third births occurred in the city proper that year.[46]

TABLE 3.6 *Urban and rural crude birth rates, China, 1971–78 (per 1000 population)*

	1971	1972	1973	1974	1975	1976	1977	1978
urban areas	21.9	20.1	18.1	15.1	15.3	13.6	13.9	14.0
rural areas	31.9	31.2	29.4	26.2	24.8	20.9	19.7	18.9
national average	30.7	29.9	28.1	24.9	23.1	10.0	29.0	18.3

SOURCE   Pi-chao Chen and Adrienne Kols, 'Population and Birth Planning' in the People's Republic of China, *Population Reports*, 1982.

TABLE 3.7 *Number of children and family size, Shanghai and Beijing, 1980*

Number of children	Urban Shanghai		Rural Shanghai	
	Number	percentage	Number	percentage
5	1	2	—	—
4	—	—	2	3
3	4	9	5	10
2	12	26	22	42
1	23	50	19	35
0	6	13	5	10
	46	100	52	100
	Urban Beijing		Rural Beijing	
	Number	percentage	Number	percentage
5	—	—	—	—
4	1	3	—	—
3	4	10	7	13
2	18	46	28	52
1	16	41	13	24
0	—	—	6	11
	39	100	54	100

SOURCE   Elisabeth Croll. 'The Chinese Household and Its Economy: Urban and Rural Survey Data', Queen Elizabeth House, Contemporary China Centre Resource Paper, 1980.

TABLE 3.8   *Single-child families in Shanghai and Beijing, 1890*

Age of married persons	Urban Shanghai Number percentage		Rural Shanghai Number percentage	
40–49	8	35	1	5
36–39	5	22	1	5
30–35	9	39	5	28
25–29	1	4	11	61
	23	100	18	100
	Urban Beijing Number percentage		Rural Beijing Number percentage	
40–49	4	25	—	—
36–39	2	12	1	8
30–35	10	63	5	38
25–29	—	—	7	54
	16	100	13	100

SOURCE   Elisabeth Croll, 'The Chinese Household and its Economy: Urban and Rural Survey Data', Queen Elizabeth House, Contemporary China Centre Resource Paper, 1980.

Some of the acceptance of a one-child family norm predates the policy itself. This large number of pre-existing one-child families appears to have been part of a longer-term trend. A survey carried out in urban and rural areas of Shanghai and Beijing in 1980 consisted of structured interviews with seventy-five households.[47] It elicited the number of children in each family: as can be seen in Table 3.7, the proportion of single children was high.

Even more interesting, perhaps, is Table 3.8 showing the number of single children analysed by the age of parents. As the survey noted, the figures for urban areas 'do confirm former impressions that certain urban social categories, particularly cadres and intellectuals, have tended to have one-child families in the past.'[48]

In Shanghai the proportion of single children increased steadily throughout the 1970s. Half of those women from Shanghai proper who married in 1970 had only one child.[49] It is true that Shanghai is not only an 'exemplary' city as far as birth planning is concerned, but somewhat exceptional. However, lest it be thought that such a trend applies only in the 'advanced' cities of Beijing and Shanghai, comparison can be made with a survey of single-child families carried out in the West-side district of Hefei, in the province of Anhui.[50] Among the 1000 families who had applied for a one-child certificate, half of the fathers were 36 years old or older, and 84 were over 50. Of the mothers, 267 were over the age of 35, including 6 over the age of 50. While some of these couples may have been hoping for another child before the single-child campaign was introduced, given their ages it is probable that a high proportion had already chosen to have one child in any case, and merely decided to avail themselves of the certificate, and the consequent benefits, when these were introduced.

THE ONE-CHILD FAMILY POLICY

A report of a survey of Fusuijing residential area, in the West District of Beijing, describes the local campaign for one-child families which began in early 1979, before there were any official regulations. It appears that in the previous year 19 per cent, or almost one fifth, of families with one child regarded their childbearing as completed. Within a few months of the campaign beginning, the ratio of one-child families had passed 50 per cent: before the regulations had been introduced and incentives or disincentives proffered.[51]

The larger cities were among the first to introduce local packages of incentives and disincentives for the one-child family. Tianjin, from the beginning of 1979, offered 5 *yuan* a month subsidy for health care to all single-child families to last until the child was 14. The city also promised priority in kindergarten enrolment and medical care for such families and the same housing space allowance as if they had two children.[52] Similar cash supplements were introduced by Beijing in the autumn of that year and preferential admission to schools and priority in job allocation were also promised to the single child, as well as priority in kindergartens and medical care. Beijing also decided that all urban families would be allotted housing space as if for two children, while suburban families would get private plots on the same basis. Thus the single-child family would have a bonus compared with a two-child family, while a larger one would be penalised.[53]

Shanghai introduced one-child regulations in 1979, and a supplementary set appeared in 1981.[54] The city has often been referred to as a model in implementing the one-child policy but this should not of course be attributed only to the regulations. Chinese research shows

TABLE 3.9   *Urban families with certificates as a percentage of all families with one child*

		1979	1980	1981
Beijing		70	79.4	85
Shanghai	urban	90	82	86
	suburban	75	61	
Tianjin	urban	80		
	suburban	52		
Harbin		85		
Guangzhou	urban		60	
	suburban		25	
Suzhou			95	

SOURCES   Pi-chao Chen and Adrienne Kols, 'Population and Birth Planning in the People's Republic of China', *Population Reports*, series J, no. 25, 1982; Leo Goodstadt, 'China's One-Child Family: Policy and Public Response', *Population and Development Review*, 8 (1) 1982).

that Shanghai had already achieved enviably low fertility by the end of the 1970s.[55] When the incentives were announced, they followed what was by now the familiar pattern of a 5 *yuan* health subsidy and priority in housing and the allocation of private plots, but they also included exemption from tuition fees and extras to the end of senior middle school and provision for additional maternity leave. In addition the regulations offered an extra week's leave to couples meeting the late marriage requirements, while couples who did not register a marriage and went on to have a child would have to pay the hospital fees themselves and were not entitled to full maternity-leave pay nor workpoints. Couples who had a child outside the agreed plan, especially if it was a third or subsequent child, had to pay for the hospital, the child's medical care, lost out on maternity-leave pay and might have to forfeit 10 per cent of salary or workpoints. As was mentioned earlier, such fragmentary information as is available for urban areas suggests that the take-up of one-child certificates was quite high during the initial stages of the campaign, although there are wide variations between different cities and, as one would expect, between urban and suburban districts,[56] as shown in Table 3.9.

A number of factors previously discussed as having perhaps affected urban acceptance of family planning may also have been instrumental

TABLE 3.10   *Percentage distribution of the parents of single-child families in West-side Hefei by education*

Education level	Father		Mother	
	Certificate holder	Non-holder	Certificate holder	Non-holder
College	34.5	21.7	17.7	10.0
Higher middle school	12.8	12.3	14.9	10.9
Technical school	11.5	8.4	13.4	8.4
Subtotal	58.8	42.4	46.0	29.3
Lower middle school	31.2	42.6	42.4	49.9
Upper primary school	5.7	9.9	6.3	9.9
Lower primary school	3.6	4.2	2.9	6.6
Illiterate	0.7	0.6	2.4	0.1
Others	—	0.3	—	0.2
Total	100.0	100.0	100.0	100.0

SOURCE   Anhui University, 'A Survey on Single-child Families of West-side Hefei, Anhui Province', *Anhui Population*, 1981.

in encouraging the parents to agree to stop at a single child. Some of the pressures for a small family – such as housing – have if anything intensified in recent years; other factors, such as unemployment, have added to the burdens faced by urban parents.

Figures from West-side Hefei suggest not only an increased proportion of one-child certificate holders among the better educated groups,[57] but a significant break in the pattern of acceptance when one compares those with lower middle-school education with those whose education went further. Above that level, more than half of the fathers were certificate-holders; those with lower middle-school education who had taken up the certificate were in the minority. There were also signficantly more mothers with more than lower middle-school education who had taken up the certificate, as Table 3.10 shows.

This distinction is also to be seen in Table 3.11 for the Fusuijing area of Beijing West District[58] and in Table 8.6 of Elisabeth Croll's case-study in Chapter 8 of this volume.

TABLE 3.11   *Effect of educational level on acceptance of one-child family norm in Fusuijing area of Beijing west*

	Junior high and below	High school	College	Total
Women in child-bearing age with one child	2912	713	200	3825
Women with one-child certificate	2666	678	191	3535
Certificate holders as a percentage of one-child families	91.55%	95.09%	95.50%	92.42%

SOURCE   'One-Child Family Becoming Norm in Beijing West District', *Renkou Yanjiu*, January 1981.

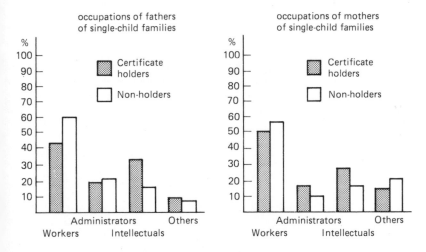

FIGURE 3.1   *Occupations of parents of single children – West-side Hefei, 1979*

SOURCE   Anhui University, 'A Survey on Single-child Families of West-side Hefei, Anhui Province', *Anhui Population*, 1982.

Education and occupation tend to be linked; the graph in Figure 3.1 for West-side Hefei suggests that administrators and intellectuals were quicker to take up certificates.[59]

Housing space was only considered in the West-side Hefei study among those families which did have a one-child certificate; the report states 'there is general tension in housing among the families surveyed. This is an important factor affecting the steadiness of thought among the parents of the certificate-holding families'.[60] Among certificate-holders the single most frequently expressed demand was that the government should do something about housing conditions and housing was the second greatest priority for the non-holders, too.

A further pressure on the housing over the past four years or so has been a growth in bride payments and a tendency for them to be spent on bulky furniture. City girls now claim that a three-piece suite is the essential accompaniment to marriage, no matter how it fits into the tiny space allocated for the couple. This has resulted from official policies for higher disposable incomes and a greater availability of consumer goods. Lyle suggests that the groom may have to pay out 2000 *yuan* on furniture[61] – from a monthly salary of perhaps 45 *yuan*.

One reason for the later age of marriage in cities may be that the costs of the marriage and establishing a household are now generally the responsibility of the young couple, rather than of the family. The savings may be augmented by small gifts in cash or in kind from kin, friends and fellow-workers, but the main burden falls on the couple.[62] Some may even begin to prefer to postpone child-bearing and its additional responsibilities for a while, in order to enjoy the luxury of being able to spend more of their combined salaries.

Life is still arduous inside the home, even if the numbers of meetings and criticism sessions which reduced free time have diminished. This is well expressed in the following account by a family-planning official:

> In cities, both husband and wife work to get enough money for the family to live on. They work six days a week, eight hours a day, plus one to two hours of travelling back and forth for those who live far from their working units. They have to do washing, cleaning, queueing for shopping, cooking etc. on their days off. Life for working couples is tiring and exhausting, and it will be more so if a couple have more children. Problems like waking up at night to feed the baby, more washing to do, not being able to go out because of young babies, nutrition, health, education and many other things all have to be dealt with. These are all time-and-energy-consuming. Conflicts may even arise between couples over taking care of children. Bringing up children is not always an easy thing to do, especially in cities where life is more hectic when both husband and wife are working.[63]

Confirmation of this description comes from a survey carried out into the off-duty activities of Shanghai's workers, the results of which were announced in 1983.[64] Household chores such as cooking, washing and commuting took an average of six hours and forty-five minutes a day. 'Moreover, the situation with women, who account for one third of the city's 4.7m workers, is even worse, as they are traditionally considered responsible for childcare.' As a result of the survey, enterprises in Shanghai are being encouraged to set up service facilities for their staff, including laundries, sewing and clothes-mending shops and repair shops for household equipment. Vegetable markets are now accepting orders, to obviate the need for queuing, and the housing departments in twelve districts arranged apartment exchanges for couples so that they could live nearer their work units. Finally, nurseries in work units are being asked to improve and extend child care provision to free mothers from the demands of a toddler. But these are very new initiatives, and in most cities a young couple's week remains extremely tiring.

Further amplification comes from Elisabeth Croll's survey of the Chinese household and its economy. In urban Shanghai and Beijing, average daily shopping time took over three quarters of an hour and half an hour respectively. Cooking took an hour and three quarters in Shanghai; an hour and twelve minutes in Beijing. Rural Shanghai and Beijing spent still more time on cooking, but in rural areas the men appeared to be more active in helping to do it. Where the household does not have a resident grandmother (and overall, 35–45 per cent of the working women had to undertake these tasks) shopping and cooking add appreciably to the length of the working day.[65]

The baby booms of the mid-1950s and mid-1960s, combined with efforts to reintegrate some of the young who had been sent to the countryside, resulted, by 1979–80, in a severe employment problem. It was one which affected cities disproportionately – partly because under-employment is easier to accommodate in the rural sector, and partly because of the return of the educated young.[66] Up to 10m young people had to be found jobs each year during that period,[67] and although most of the backlog of returnees from the countryside has now been accommodated, new employment continues to have to be found for some 5m entrants to the job market each year.[68]

Jobs in the state sector, with its coveted benefits including retirement pensions, have generally been available only through inheritance. Thus, unless both parents were lucky enough to work in state industries, they became acutely aware during the 1970s that a second child was unlikely to be able to look to the State for employment. In the late 1970s, many cities followed the examples of Beijing and Shanghai and introduced regulations which refused to guarantee employment to any child beyond the first, even where both parents worked in the state sector. Some of these regulations preceded the one-child family policy and seem to have been more of a response to employment problems than strictly designed to limit families: yet a smaller family must have been one of the effects.[69] More recently, regulations to encourage the one-child family announced by the cities specifically state that the single child will have priority in job allocation;[70] this may be designed to reduce the fears of parents that an only daughter will not get the coveted state job, because of the lingering preference of some factories for giving apprenticeships to young men.[71] In the long term, then, the urban family knows that extra children will not be much of an investment; in the short term, there seem to be few opportunities for urban children to earn. The family planning official quoted above wrote:

> In cities, children are more an economic liability than an asset. They need care, they need food, clothing and education. But they cannot provide much help to the family when they are small. In the Chinese circumstances where salaries are universally low, the average salary for working people in cities is about $25–35 a month, which is just enough for a person to live on with not much surplus. When a young couple start thinking of having a child, they must be prepared to have a lower living standard than before. When the baby is born, more expenses are involved, and the economic situation in the family becomes tighter for the couple. It will be more difficult to have another child without further decline in the living standard of the family. The cost of living in cities is much higher than in the countryside. There are few means of income generation outside wage employment, and wage increases are dwarfed by inflation. Therefore, bringing up children involves more economic difficulties for people living in the cities.[72]

Inflation, too, may have increased these difficulties and had quite an impact on the acceptance of the single-child policy. Until the late 1970s, deliberate management of the economy meant that many prices had not risen for two decades.[73] The government's decision to allow many prices to rise produced considerable shock among a population cushioned for so long. In their perception, at least, such rises more than outweighed additions to their salaries: the result was a kind of unease, a feeling that the ground was slipping from beneath their feet, which those from countries used to soaring inflation as a part of life find difficult to imagine.

Children born to urban families have also lost some of their value for their parents as a long-term investment for security in old age. Those working in the state sector are entitled to retirement pensions of 60 per cent of their previous salaries. Shanghai offers a 70 per cent of final salary pension for those who have only one child,[74] and Beijing and other cities give pensions of 100 per cent of salary to the childless.[75] In 1979 Tianjin and Beijing began to experiment with workpoint pensions for the old in suburban communes, giving such pensions initially to the childless or those who had only one child.[76] In Shanghai, suburban communes began to introduce pension schemes at around the same time, spurred on by the fact that the factory workers among them – and in suburban communes half the labour force may work in factories – were getting 60 per cent of their previous salary as pensions, so that the peasant half of the population were seen to be losing out.[77] By mid-1983, about 70 per cent of Shanghai's suburban communes had introduced pensions, their number having risen considerably in the previous six months.[78] These suburban peasant pensions are considerably lower than the factory ones but they are a start which may help to diminish the differences in family-planning acceptance between the cities proper and their suburbs.

Pensions begin to loom larger in the calculations of families not merely as they spread to more categories of worker, but as the proportion of those who have worked, and are thus eligible for a pension, increased. About 45 per cent of retired persons in the household surveys of rural Beijing and Shanghai had no pensions and were largely supported by their families.[79] All but one of these people were elderly women or housewives who had never had a formal income. The vast majority of the men and women whose daughters are now coming into marriageable age have been and are workers and are likely to be able to look forward either to a state pension or at least to reasonable savings for retirement from a second income.

Meanwhile, the immediate benefits to the individual child from reducing overall numbers are spelled out by the authorities. Shanghai, which in the 1960s had a two-shift system in schools, with a teacher: pupil ratio of 1 : 37, publicises the fact that it has managed to improve the situation considerably because of falls in the number of school-age children, as does Beijing.[80] Child-care facilities in the larger cities cater for only about one fifth of the children in the under-seven age group, which must add to the difficulties of working parents, even when there are grandparents to help.[81] Even in West-side Hefei, where 40 per cent of infants are in kindergarten, there are still complaints about the lack of qualified staff and facilities.[82] Parents there seem to be willing to reduce their families in return for a better future for those children, but they want to see visible evidence that the sacrifice is being matched by advantages for the single child.

In the absence of sufficient child-care facilities, and also to overcome the concern of some parents about entrusting a very young child – especially the precious only child – to outside care, an alternative has been to offer extended maternity leave so that the mother can look after the baby herself. A factory in Shanghai offers a year's maternity leave to single-child mothers, granting full pay and an assurance that neither their promotion prospects nor wage increases will be jeopardised as a result.[83] This experimental scheme was explained on the grounds that not all families had a grandmother living with them who could help to take care of the child; that the factory's three-shift system, and the commuting problems of its workers, made it difficult for women with babies to work; and that the baby's health was best safeguarded by its being at home with mother, rather than in a crèche picking up infections.

Shanghai's family-planning regulations in any case provide for maternity leave of up to a year for single-child mothers, on 80 per cent salary.[84] Shanxi offers four- to six-months maternity leave for a single-child mother.[85] Many individual enterprises offer similar incentives; there is six-months maternity leave at the Beijing Normal University for instance.[86]

The assumption that in cities strong family pressure is still put on the marrying couple to have more than one child may itself no longer hold good. The girls who are coming up to marriageable age now are the ones whose mothers were sterilised in the early 1960s; there exists a generation of actual, or potential grandmothers who were in the vanguard of contraceptive use. A substantial proportion, especially amongst the opinion-forming cadres and intellectuals, were themselves the parents of only one child, so that they are – or are about to be – the grandparents of a second-generation single child.

There is some evidence that traditional familial values – whether inculcated by the family or the unit – are in any case breaking down. In the wake of the Cultural Revolution, many of the young have become disillusioned with politics, and their search for alternative life-styles has been fuelled by the 'open door' policy pursued by the Chinese government since the late 1970s, which has exposed people to a far greater variety of foreign influences. Premarital pregnancy is claimed to be on the increase

The first premarital family, sex and eugenics counselling service was set up in Beijing in February 1981, with others planned to begin shortly afterwards.[87] The expressed rationale for such a move was partly to provide health check-ups for young couples to identify potential medical or genetic problems, and partly to enable those getting married to delay their child-bearing through effective contraception. But an official from the service also referred to the low level of knowledge among young people about family planning, and said that in the Xuanwu district where the hospital is situated, half of those who had abortions in the previous year had no knowledge of contraception. The implication appears to be that the service is at least partly designed to prevent premarital pregnancy. The introduction of sex education in schools is also stated to be necessary because of growing premarital sexual activity.[88]

Whether or not there has been premarital sex, a young couple who have married late and who have chosen each other may be beginning to find other satisfactions in marriage, and in their lives, than simply the family round:

> more and more workers are using their leisure time and earnings to improve their educational and technical levels, to take advantage of the mass media and to engage in creative work, sports and cultural activities. This suits the needs of modernised production and modern society. It will also influence social behaviour patterns and lead to a further decline in the population growth rate.[89]

THE FUTURE OF THE POLICY

As has already been indicated, the introduction of municipal or provincial packages of incentives during 1979 and early 1980 accelerated the trend to the one-child family dramatically. It is less clear, though, that the acceleration will be permanent. The Fusuijing survey divides those who have taken out one-child family certificates into three groups.[90] The first (about 60 per cent of the total) really only wanted one child or were at least quite happy to stop at one in the interest either of their careers and pressure of work, or of population control. A further 30 per cent were ambivalent, conforming to 'social expectations'. They were prepared to go along with the policy if it remained unchanged, in many instances, but would have a second child if there were any signs of official relaxation of policies. Others felt they could not afford a second child but if their circumstances changed they would have one – and, presumably, be willing to pay back the benefits from certification. The remaining 10 per cent felt they had been pressured to take the one-child certificate.

The survey of West-side Hefei did not ask questions in a comparable form, but interestingly, it too gathered a rather similar figure – 9 per cent – who were not at all sure they had done the right thing in accepting a one-child certificate.[91] More than half of the doubters had expected more welfare benefits or better housing than they actually got; they tended to be the poorest families and were clearly more influenced by the prospect of incentives than genuine conviction about the need for sacrifice.

There seems little reason to doubt the reliability of the trends revealed by these surveys. Obviously, the demographic success of the measures in cities will be quite considerable if most of the 60 per cent reported in Beijing as being content with the decision to stop at one child stick to their pledge. There is no way of knowing how many of the remainder will backslide, but there are indications of potential problems.

It seems very unlikely that the authorities can rapidly fulfil the pledges on housing, nurseries and so on for which those who have a one-child certificate have priority. The West-side Hefei survey indicated that even with a lower take-up of certificates, 40 per cent of those who held them had not got the improved housing for which they had hoped.[92] Those concerned with the Fusuijing study concluded:

> We must urge the departments concerned to actively support and create the right conditions for family planning and to strictly enforce the policies and regulations related to family planning. We must help the families with one child to locate day-care centres and schools for their children, to get medical care, and to find jobs and housing. We must help single-child parents resolve their domestic problems, so as to relieve them of whatever anxieties they may feel about their family life.[93]

If such measures cannot be provided, considerable resentment may build up among certificate holders.

Further grounds for dissatisfaction may arise from the differentials in incentives at the local level. West-side Hefei reported:

Take the bonus system for instance, there is no unified standard and large disparity exists between different units even within one city, the bonus standard is different from factory to factory, from factory to schools or administrative units, from state units to collective units. The people are very dissatisfied. Some of the more profitable factories or commercial enterprises provide bonuses to single-child parents amounting to as much as over 100 *yuan*, or in the form of commodities such as woollen blankets, transistor radio-sets, brocade sheets, etc. But other units, as administrative organisations, having no special funds for family planning, can only take money from the general welfare funds; bonuses are as low as 10 or 20 *yuan* or only a couple of towels, a thermos bottle, some toys, a washing basin or even nothing at all.[94]

The factory in Shanghai, already quoted as offering a year's leave to all women having their single child and taking the certificate, pointed out that this experimental incentive could not be imitated in many other Shanghai factories, such as cotton mills, where most of the workers were female: the disruption would simply be too great.[95]

In some areas, the authorities have asked units to avoid giving incentives which are wildly out of line with what others are offering. In others, units seem to have been left to their own devices. So far there has been no overall attempt to regulate incentives and disincentives provided by individual units, although some prominent policy-makers, while pointing out that a unified system would be difficult to implement because of varying local conditions, nevertheless believe that the state should have some basic requirements and limitations.[96]

In the long run, the most serious danger of the one-child family policy may result from its success in China's urban areas, compared with the level of acceptance in the countryside. Priority in education, in health care, in employment and in other areas of life for the single child is likely to widen still further the gap between the privileged town-dwellers and their rural counterparts, at least in the medium term. And the creation of an urban élite in itself may make it difficult, in the course of time, to ensure across-the-board national development.

NOTES AND REFERENCES

1. Marina Thorborg, 'Chinese Employment Policy in 1949–78 with Special Emphasis on Women in Rural Production' in *Chinese Economy post-Mao:*

A Compendium of Papers submitted to the Joint Economic Committee, vol. 1: Policy and Performance (Congress of the United States, 1978); and Hu Huanyong, *A Brief Survey of China's Population Geography* (Shanghai: Foreign Language Education Press, 1982).

2. Norman Himes, *Medical History of Contraception* (Baltimore: Williams and Wikins 1936); and H. Yuan Tien, 'Sterilisation, Oral contraception and Population control in China', *Population Studies*, vol. 27(3), 1965.
3. Olga Lang, *Chinese Family and Society* (Yale: Yale University Press, 1946).
4. Ibid.
5. Chen Da, 'Population in Modern China', *American Journal of Sociology*, 52 (1) part 2 (Chicago: Chicago University Press, 1946).
6. Ibid.
7. Pi-chao Chen, 'The Politics of Population in Communist China', PhD thesis, 1966.
8. Madeline Gray, *Margaret Sanger* (New York: Marek, 1979).
9. Chang Ching-sheng, *Sex Histories*: China's first modern treatise on sex education translated by Howard S. Levy (Yokohama: 1967).
10. Zhao Baoku, 'Sociology and Population Studies in China', paper presented at the University of Texas, September 1982.
11. *First Report of the Peiping Health Committee on Maternal Health*, July 1933.
12. Elisabeth Croll, *the Politics of Marriage in Contemporary China* (Cambridge: Cambridge University Press, 1981).
13. Lang, *Chinese Family and Society*, 1946.
14. Pi-chao Chen, 'The Politics of Population', 1966.
15. Ibid.
16. H. Yuan Tien, *China's Population Struggle* (Ohio: Ohio University Press, 1973).
17. Pi-chao Chen, 'The Politics of Population', 1966.
18. Quoted in H. Yuan Tien, *China's Population Struggle*, 1973. .
19. Delia Davin, *Woman-work: Women and the Party in Revolutionary China* (Oxford: Clarendon Press, 1976).
20. Pi-chao Chen, 'The Politics of Population', 1966.
21. Pi-chao Chen, 'China's Birth Control Action Programme 1956–64', *Population Studies*, 24 (2) 1970.
22. Chandrasekhar, S., *China's Population* (Hong Kong University Press 1960).
23. Delia Davin, *Woman-work*, 1976.
24. Ibid.
25. See for example, Jan Myrdal, *Report from a Chinese Village* (London: Heinemann, 1965); and William Hinton, 'Fanshen' *Monthly Review Press*, 1966.
26. Penny Kane, 'How Women Hold up Half the Sky', *People*, vol. 3, no. 3, 1976.
27. Delia Davin, *Woman-work*, 1976.
28. See, for example, Penny Kane, 'Population Planning in China' in T. S. Epstein and D. Jackson, *The Feasibility of Fertility Planning* (London: Pergamon, 1977).

29. Janet W. Salaff, 'Institutionalised Motivation for Fertility Limitation in China', *Population Studies*, 26 (2).
30. Phyllis Andors, '"The Four Modernizations" and Chinese Policy on Women', *Bulletin of Concerned Asian Scholars*, vol. 13(2), 1981.
31. Pi-chao Chen, 'Population and Health Policy in the People's Republic of China', occasional monograph no. 9, (Smithsonian Institution, 1976).
32. H. Yuan Tien, 'Age at Marriage in the People's Republic of China', *China Quarterly*, March 1983.
33. Gu Xinqyuan *et al.*, 'Shanghai: Family Planning', in Liu Zheng *et al.*, *China's Population: Problems and Prospects* (Beijing: New World Press, 1981).
34. Pi-chao Chen, 'The Politics of Population', 1966.
35. Ibid.
36. H. Yuan Tien, *China's Population Struggle*, 1973.
37. Rong Shoude *et al.*, 'Statistical Analysis of the Life Expectancy in the Population of China', in Institute of Population Economics (Beijing College of Economics) (ed.) *Symposium of Chinese Population Science* (Beijing: China Academic Publishers, 1981).
38. Leo F. Goodstadt, 'China's One-child Family: Policy and Public Response', *Population and Development Review*, 8 : 1, March 1982.
39. Croll, *The Politics of Marriage*, 1981.
40. Penny Kane, personal observations, 1982.
41. Katherine Ch'iu Lyle, 'Planned Birth in Tianjin', *China Quarterly*, September 1980.
42. H. Yuan Tien, *China's Population Struggle*, 1973.
43. Indeed, the remarkably low statistics for cities reported by foreigners in the early 1970s led a number of foreign demographers to disbelieve them entirely.
44. Pi-chao Chen and Adrienne Kols, 'Population and Birth Planning in the People's Republic of China', *Population Reports*, series J, no. 25, 1982.
45. Penny Kane, personal observations, 1982.
46. Ibid.
47. Elisabeth Croll, 'The Chinese Household and its Economy: Urban and Rural Survey Data', Queen Elizabeth House, *Contemporary China Centre Resource Paper*, 1980.
48. Ibid.
49. Gu Xinqyuan *et al.*, 'Shanghai: Family Planning'.
50. Anhui University, 'A Survey on Single-child Families of West-side Hefei, Anhui Province', *Anhui Population*, 1981.
51. 'One-child Family becoming Norm in Beijing West District, Beijing', *Renkou Yanjiu*, no. 1, January 1981.
52. *Xinhua*, 10 July 1979.
53. *Xinhua*, 7 November 1979.
54. Chen Mu-hua, 'Birth Planning in China' *Family Planning Perspectives*, vol. II, no. 6, 1979; and 'Shanghai Stipulates a Number of Planned Parenthood Regulations', *SWB*, 31 August 1981.
55. Gu Xingyuan *et al.*, 'Shanghai: Family Planning', in Liu Zheng *et al.*, *China's Population*.
56. Chen and Kols, 'Population and Birth Planning', 1982; Goodstadt,

'China's One-child Family', 1982, and H. Yuan Tien, 'Wan, Xi, Shao: How China Meets its Population Problem', *International Family Planning Perspectives*, 6 (2) 1980.

57. Anhui University, 'A Survey on Single-child Families', 1981.
58. *Renkou Yanjiu*, 'One-child Family becoming Norm', 1981.
59. Anhui University, 'A Survey on Single-child Families', 1981.
60. Ibid.
61. Lyle, 'Planned Birth in Tianjin', 1980.
62. Croll, *The Politics of Marriage*, 1981.
63. Qiao Xinjian, 'Possible Obstacles to the Realisation of the One-child Family', extended essay, David Owen Centre for Population Growth Studies, July 1982.
64. *Xinhua*, 21 May 1983.
65. Croll, 'The Chinese Household', 1980.
66. Hu Kaihua and Li Bingdi, 'Urban Population – Age Structure and Projections for the Future' in Liu Zheng *et al.*, *China's Population, Problems and Prospects*.
67. Li Shiyi, 'Developmental Trends in Chinese Population Growth', *Beijing Review*, January 1982.
68. Wang Shengquan, 'How the Pressure of Population Hits Chinese Life', *China Daily*, 17 February 1983.
69. Penny Kane, personal observations: and Sun Jingzhi and Li Muzhen, 'A Discussion of the Ways to Solve Beijing's Population Question' in *Symposium of Chinese Population Science* (Beijing: China Academic Publications, 1981).
70. For example, *Xinhua*, 7 November 1979; *SWB*, 31 August 1981; *SWB*, 16 December 1982.
71. *Xinhua*, 28 June 1979.
72. Qiao Xinjian, 'Possible Obstacles', 1982.
73. Peng Kuang-hsi, *Why China Has No Inflation* (Beijing: Foreign Languages Press, 1976).
74. *SWB*, 31 August 1981.
75. Penny Kane, personal observations, 1982.
76. *Xinhua*, 10 July 1979; 7 November 1979.
77. Penny Kane, 'China: New Focus on Welfare', *People*, vol. 9, no. 3, 1982.
78. *SWB*, 4 April 1983.
79. Croll, 'The Chinese Household', 1980.
80. Goodstadt, 'China's One-child Family', 1982.
81. Hu Kaihua and Li Bingdi, 'Urban Population'.
82. Anhui University, 'A Survey on Single-child Families', 1981.
83. Penny Kane, personal observations, 1982.
84. *SWB*, 31 August 1981.
85. *SWB*, 16 December 1982.
86. Penny Kane, personal observations, 1982.
87. *Xinhua*, 18 February 1981.
88. Penny Kane, personal observations, 1982.
89. Sun Jingzhi, 'Economic Development – a Major Solution to Population Problems' in Liu Zheng *et al.*, *China's Population: Problems and Prospects*.
90. *Renkou Yanjiu*, 'One -child Family becoming Norm'.

91. Anhui University, 'A Survey on Single-child Families'.
92. Ibid.
93. Ibid.
94. Ibid.
95. Penny Kane, personal observations, 1982.
96. Ibid.

4 Provincial Fertility Trends and Patterns

H. YUAN TIEN

In examining fertility trends and patterns in China, the lack of detailed sub-national statistics has restricted analyses to the national level. Generalisations at this level have inevitably neglected variations in population developments in the twenty-nine provinces, municipalities, and autonomous regions (generally referred to as provinces hereafter) that make up China. Given the size of the population, vast territory, and socio-economic differentials, documentation of recent fertility trends and patterns at the subnational level is clearly in order. Only when this has been built up will it be possible to define more precisely, and interpret more appropriately, demographic events in this most populous nation.

PROVINCIAL SOCIO-ECONOMIC DIFFERENTIALS

Population phenomena emerge in response to, and simultaneously have an impact on, socio-economic circumstances in society. Demographic events also evoke, and are shaped by, specific population policy measures. Such interrelationships are accepted at the level of theory, but do not lend themselves to easy disaggregation in practice. In China's case, the want of data has made it particularly difficult to assess the relative effect of socio-economic variables and population planning programmes. Hence, interpretations of population trends and patterns in China are often controversial. In this section various sets of recent provincial socio-economic data are assembled to place sub-national population developments in better perspective. Unfortunately, however, no systematic information about family planning programmes exists at the sub-national or provincial level. Their impact on fertility trends and patterns, therefore, can only be surmised in the present discussion.

114

At the provincial level, socio-economic differentials are clearly major. The statistics in Table 4.1, while far from exhaustive, cover some of the crucial socio-economic variables affecting fertility trends and patterns. These provide a sufficient basis for a preliminary assessment of the Chinese demographic situation.

According to the Census of 1982, some 20.6 per cent of China's population was classified as urban. There has been and still is controversy concerning the level of urbanisation in China. This most recent census count, in fact, indicates a larger than expected increase. Only 13.2 per cent of the population was previously identified as urban in 1979. Apparently, persons engaged in agriculture who resided within the city or town limits were excluded in the earlier figures. The 1982 urban classification shifted to the practice of enumerating population on the basis of place of residence. On this basis, the level of urbanisation had already reached 18.4 per cent in 1964, and showed a very small increase in the following eighteen years. Given these shifts, our present conclusions based on the available data must remain tentative.

Nevertheless, it seems clear that, in 1982 as in earlier years, there were large regional variations. In some provinces and regions, the proportion classified as urban was as low as three quarters or even half of the national level. In a number of others it was well above the average. These differing proportions should be taken into account in considering fertility trends and patterns.

Enormous variations in agricultural and industrial output also obtained, and their demographic implications should be appropriately assessed. In 1980, for instance, the total output in these two sectors exceeded 660 billion *yuan*. Apparently exclusive of tertiary production, this came to 678 *yuan* per head. However, Shanghai alone produced some 10 per cent of the total output. On the other hand Guizhou in the southwest contributed barely 1.1 per cent to the national total output. It showed a figure of 266 *yuan* per head, which was a little more than one third of the national level.

At the provincial level, differences also existed with respect to the number of newspapers and magazines in circulation. As shown in Table 4.1, for the nation as a whole there were 18.1 copies of such printed media per 100 population in 1981. In twelve provinces, the figure amounted to only about three quarters of the national average. Various other provinces reported much higher circulation figures which presumably reflected higher literacy and ability to afford 'food for thought'.

Women in China traditionally laboured in agriculture and related

TABLE 4.1 *Socio-economic variables, by province, for selected years*

Region and province	Percentage urban (1981)	Mean output (1980)	Newspapers (1981)	Women workers (1981)	Life Expectancy Male (1973–5)	Female (1973–5)
Total	20.6	Y 678	18.1	81.1	63.6	66.3
North-east						
Heilongjiang	40.5	899	27.1	159.3	69.8	71.5
Jilin	39.6	771	23.1	143.3	65.0	66.7
Liaoning	42.4	1483	34.6	189.7	68.6	70.8
North						
Hebei	13.7	583	14.2	60.6	67.1	70.2
Shanxi	21.0	604	20.3	76.0	65.3	68.0
Beijing	64.7	2824	74.0	321.6	68.3	70.8
Tianjin	68.7	2801	50.6	284.0	69.9	72.0
Shandong	19.1	630	11.7	47.5	NA	NA
Henan	14.1	407	12.2	42.5	65.1	68.8
East						
Anhui	14.3	388	13.2	50.1	64.5	66.9
Jiangsu	15.8	1023	18.2	85.1	65.1	69.3
Shanghai	58.8	5715	87.0	334.6	69.2	74.8
Zhejiang	25.7	723	17.2	77.6	66.4	70.5

	Percentage urban	Census Mean Output (Per capita)	Newspapers	Women Workers	Life Expectancy	
Central						
Hubei	17.3	661	17.5	85.7	NA	NA
Hunan	14.4	498	14.8	58.1	61.4	63.3
Jiangxi	19.4	427	13.7	63.5	62.1	64.3
South						
Fujian	21.2	467	18.1	68.5	65.2	69.4
Guangdong	18.7	543	16.8	85.8	NA	NA
Guangxi	11.8	365	14.2	50.4	NA	NA
South-west						
Guizhou	19.7	266	10.5	46.3	59.0	59.5
Sichuan	14.3	410	13.6	54.3	59.2	61.1
Yunnan	12.9	324	11.8	49.6	59.8	61.4
Xizang	9.5	328	11.7	61.1	59.5	63.2
North-west						
Nei Monggol	28.9	432	19.0	104.4	65.3	67.3
Shaanxi	19.0	506	19.1	69.9	64.0	65.2
Ningxia	22.5	516	19.2	88.1	61.9	62.7
Gansu	15.3	549	14.1	59.1	NA	NA
Qinghai	20.5	543	35.0	95.7	60.6	62.0
Xinjiang	28.4	458	28.9	162.3	61.2	63.3

NOTES: Total output in Chinese currency (Y1 = US$ 0.60 in 1979–80)

SOURCES   Percentage urban–1982 Census Mean Output (Per capita) – *Liaowang* (Outlook), No. 6, 1982, 14; *Newspapers* (Number of newspapers, magazines in circulation per 1000 population) – Computed from CHINA YEARBOOK, (1981); *Women Workers* (Number of women employed in non-agricultural occupations per 1000 females) – Computed from *China Yearbook*, (1981) *Life Expectancy* – Rong Shoude *et al.*, 'Statistical Analysis of the Life Expectancy in the People's Republic of China, 1973–75', in Office of Population Research, Beijing College of Economics, (ed.), *Symposium of Chinese Population Science*, (Beijing, 1981) 54–5.

pursuits. Part of their changing role, therefore, has to do with non-agricultural employment. Unfortunately, occupational statistics for women are extremely scarce at the provincial level. The number of women employed in non-agricultural occupations per 1000 females of all ages is available (see Table 4.1). In 1981, for the country as a whole, women so occupied reached 81.1 per 1000 females. In some instances, at the subnational level, the proportion in non-agricultural occupations markedly surpassed the national level. Women in a majority of provinces, however, lagged significantly behind. Variations in non-agricultural employment were thus considerable, and their demographic implications cannot be overlooked.

In another area of socio-economic change, salient improvement has occurred as a result of the increased availability of health and medical services. These, coupled with greater stability in food supply, led to a reduction in mortality. In the past three decades, frequent claims have been made in China for the success of these policies. For the first time, data from a retrospective mortality investigation in twenty-four provinces, municipalities and regions have made it possible to estimate provincial life expectancy at birth by sex for 1973–5. As shown in the last two columns of Table 4.1, compared with pre-1949 figures for various parts of the country, the gains in life expectancy are truly impressive and denote an overall increase of some 25–30 years. Nevertheless, in a number of instances, differences between life expectancy at birth of men and women were very small, suggesting the continuation of fairly high death rates among female infants and women. More importantly, relatively large variations in the life expectancy of both sexes between different provinces persisted: ranging in the case of men from 59 years in Guizhou to nearly 70 years in Heilongjiang, Tianjin, and Shanghai; for women, from about 60 to the low 70s. Infant mortality thus remained a real threat to the new-born and, hence, an important factor affecting fertility behaviour.

Clearly, recent data indicate large variations in socio-economic circumstances in different provinces. These variations, therefore, must be systematically examined in relation to population developments in China.

POPULATION GROWTH IN PROVINCES

In Table 4.2, provincial civilian population totals are shown for various years between 1953 and 1982. Until very recently, the demographic

TABLE 4.2   *Provincial civilian population, 1953, 1964, 1979, 1980 and 1982*
(in millions of persons)

Region and Province	1953	1964	1979	1980	1982
Total	582.60	691.22	970.74	986.74	1003.94
North-east					
Heilongjiang	11.90	20.13	31.69	31.87	32.67
Jilin	11.29	15.67	21.84	21.98	22.56
Liaoning	20.56	26.95	34.42	34.65	35.72
North					
Hebei	33.18	39.42	51.00	51.37	53.01
Shanxi	14.31	18.02	24.47	24.62	25.29
Beijing	4.59	7.60	8.70	8.79	9.23
Tianjin	4.62	6.25	7.40	7.46	7.76
Shandong	50.13	55.50	72.31	72.64	74.42
Henan	43.91	50.32	71.89	72.38	74.42
East					
Anhui	30.66	31.24	48.03	48.48	49.67
Jiangsu	38.33	44.52	58.93	59.15	60.52
Shanghai	8.81	10.82	11.32	11.39	11.86
Zhejiang	22.87	28.32	37.92	38.10	38.88
Central					
Hubei	27.79	33.71	46.32	46.59	47.80
Hunan	33.23	37.18	52.23	52.52	54.01
Jiangxi	16.77	21.07	32.29	32.50	33.18
South					
Fujian	13.14	16.76	24.80	25.03	25.87
Guangdong	34.77	40.45	56.81	57.31	59.30
Guangxi	19.56	23.20	34.70	35.04	36.42
South-west					
Guizhou	15.04	17.14	27.31	27.54	28.55
Sichuan	65.68	68.01	97.74	97.97	99.71
Yunnan	17.47	20.45	31.35	31.54	32.55
Xizang	1.27	1.25	1.83	1.84	1.89
North-west					
Nei Monggol	7.34	12.33	18.51	18.65	19.27
Shaanxi	15.88	20.77	28.07	28.19	28.90
Ningxia	1.64	2.11	3.64	3.69	3.90
Gansu	11.29	12.63	18.94	19.06	19.57
Qinghai	1.68	2.15	3.72	3.75	3.90
Xinjiang	4.87	7.27	12.56	12.70	13.08

SOURCES   Census of 1982; *1979* – H. Hu, *et al.* (eds) *Renkou Yanjiu Lunwenji* papers on population studies, (Shanghai: East China Normal University Press, 1981) 18ff. *1980* – *Liaowang* (Outlook) no. 6, (1982), 14 (Supplied by the Tabulations Section of the State Statistical Bureau – midyear population)

situation at the provincial level lacked clarity. Data shortage contributed to this state of affairs. But significant changes in provincial boundaries and administrative reorganisations accounted for much of the uncertainty. This unsatisfactory state of affairs has been more or less remedied since the 1982 Census. The provincial population figures in Table 4.2 have been adjusted on the basis of their current boundaries. Data comparability is thus no longer a serious issue.

More important is the fact that there is still no firm data base from which the relative weight of natural increase and internal migration in provincial population growth can be calculated. Post-1949 measures of industrial–urban development, as well as planned population trans-fers during the 1950s, are known to have contributed heavily to in-migration into border and inland provinces. In-migration was espe-cially pronounced in Heilongjiang, Jilin and Liaoning in the north-east, in Nei Monggol in the north, in Yunnan in the south-west and in Xinjiang, Shaanxi and Ningxia in the north-west. In all these provinces the rate of population growth ranged from nearly twice, to more than three times, that of the nation as a whole. Where such extraordinarily high rates of growth occurred (see Table 4.3) it may be assumed that internal migration was a major factor during the years 1953–64. Furthermore, between 1953 and 1964, the population growth rates of both Beijing and Tianjin exceeded the national rate by an appreciable margin, reflecting heavy in-migration. Though higher than the nation-al level, Shanghai's growth rate was probably reduced by official efforts to encourage out-migration, particularly of skilled persons, to inland provinces and regions.

In some provinces and regions, rates of population growth during 1953–64 seem to have reflected the impact of relatively heavy out-migration. Examples are Shandong and Henan Provinces, from which large numbers had gone to the north-east in the past and were sent as settlers in the 1950s. In the case of Anhui, Guizhou, Sichuan and Gansu, while internal migration undoubtedly occurred, the effect of high mortality on population growth must have remained considera-ble. Of course, under-enumeration of the population could also have distorted the growth pattern in these places.

In other provinces such as Hebei, Zhejiang, Hubei, Jiangxi, Fujian and Guangdong, however, the combined impact of reduced mortality and high fertility had already become evident by the early 1960s. A great deal more information is needed in order to establish the relative role of migration, mortality and fertility in provincial population growth before 1964. Nevertheless, it can be stressed that during those years, mortality changes were not uniform over the whole of China, but varied from province to province. Against a background of con-tinuing high fertility, population growth was more pronounced in

TABLE 4.3   *Provincial population growth, 1953–82, for specified periods (in percentages)*

Region and Province	1953–64	1964–79	1964–82	1980–82	1979–82
Total	19.4	39.6	41.9	2.2	3.9
North-east					
Heilongjiang	79.7	48.2	52.3	2.5	3.1
Jilin	58.5	22.1	26.1	2.6	3.3
Liaoning	43.5	16.7	21.1	3.1	3.8
North					
Hebei	14.2	34.6	35.6	3.2	3.9
Shanxi	27.3	34.4	38.9	2.7	3.4
Beijing	64.9	14.9	21.9	5.0	6.1
Tianjin	35.3	18.4	24.2	4.0	4.9
Shandong	10.8	30.2	34.0	2.5	2.9
Henan	14.6	42.9	47.9	2.8	3.5
East					
Anhui	1.9	53.7	59.0	2.5	3.4
Jiangsu	16.1	32.4	36.0	2.7	2.7
Shanghai	22.8	4.6	9.8	4.1	4.8
Zhejiang	23.8	33.9	37.3	2.0	2.6
Central					
Hubei	21.3	37.4	41.8	2.6	3.2
Hunan	11.9	40.5	45.3	2.8	3.4
Jiangxi	25.6	53.3	57.5	2.1	2.8
South					
Fujian	27.5	48.0	54.4	3.4	4.3
Guangdong	23.1	32.7	38.6	3.5	4.4
Guangxi	6.5	66.5	74.8	3.9	5.0
South-west					
Guizhou	14.0	59.3	66.6	3.7	4.5
Sichuan	3.5	43.8	46.7	1.8	2.0
Yunnan	41.7	52.9	58.7	3.2	3.8
Xizang	−1.6	46.4	51.2	2.7	3.3
North-west					
Nei Monggol	63.7	54.3	55.4	3.3	4.1
Shaanxi	30.8	35.1	39.1	2.5	3.0
Ningxia	31.7	68.5	80.6	5.7	7.1
Gansu	12.0	50.0	54.7	2.7	3.3
Qinghai	27.4	73.8	82.2	4.0	4.8
Xinjiang	49.3	72.8	79.9	3.0	4.1
Years in Period	(11)	(15)	(18)	(1.5)	(2.5)

SOURCE   See Table 4.2.

coastal and river provinces and municipalities: see Table 4.3. Thus it is highly probable that the efforts immediately after 1949 to control diseases and to improve living conditions resulted in an earlier and more telling decline in mortality in these provinces than in the inland regions. Apart from internal migration, the widely varying provincial population growth patterns were due, partly at least, to the leads and lags in improvements in mortality.

In contrast, between 1964 and 1979 differences between the provinces narrowed. For the country as a whole, population grew by nearly 40 per cent in fifteen years. This surge reflected more widespread mortality improvements during the entire period, together with high fertility before the 1970s.

Population planning activities in China were intensified in the early 1970s. However, until very recently, the national minorities were untouched by such programmes. Between 1964 and 1979, it appears that large mortality reductions among these groups followed an extension of health services and other improvements. Thus, not surprisingly, in almost all the inland provinces and regions in which growth rates were above the national average there were large minority groups: Guangxi, Guizhou, Yunnan, Xizang, Gansu, Qinghai, and Xinjiang.

Tianjin, Beijing and Shanghai, the three leading municipalities, all exhibited rates of growth considerably lower than the national average. Strict controls on internal migration and the transfer of the urban young to the countryside during the Cultural Revolution evidently served to reverse these cities rapid increase during earlier years. In fact, population growth in each was among the lowest in the period 1964–79.

Available data also indicate that Beijing and Shanghai were the leaders in the area of fertility reduction, as will be seen later. In demographic terms, then, the transition to low fertility as well as to low mortality was established in both municipalities far earlier than in other areas. Apart from the effect of restricting migration to these cities, and transferring young people from them, this transition was responsible for the lower rates of growth in these places after 1964.

It is notable also that in seven of the ten provinces in which the rate of growth was *higher* than the national average in 1953–64, rates *lower* than the national average were recorded after 1964. More significantly, almost all these seven provinces were maritime. Among them were Jilin, Liaoning, Jiangsu, Zhejiang, Hubei, and Guangdong. Shaanxi was the only inland province to show a similar trend in 1964–79.

Between 1979 and 1982, there were additional developments of even greater import. For the nation as a whole, the annual rate of population growth averaged about 1.6 per cent, compared with 1.6 per cent in 1953–64 and 2.7 per cent in 1964–79. If these figures are accepted at face value, differences in population growth between the provinces seem to have been further reduced during the more recent period. Lower fertility appears to have been the main reason for a lower rate of natural increase.

As previously mentioned, population planning activities had not, until very recently, extended to the national minorities. Thus, the range of trends and patterns discussed above could have resulted in part from differential policy influence. However, as mentioned previously, there were also other large socio-economic differences among the provinces, municipalities, and regions. Could, then, the apparently speedier demographic transition in some areas be accounted for, at least in part, by socio-economic change of greater range and depth?

VARIATIONS IN FERTILITY TRANSITION

Analysis of China's fertility patterns and trends at the provincial level has been hampered by shortage of data. However, as demography and population studies re-emerged in the mid-1970s after twenty years of neglect,[1] annual statistics of one type or another have been reported in scattered publications. The reconstruction of fertility patterns and trends has now become possible for a small number of provinces.

In Table 4.4, three series of such data covering most of the years after 1949 are presented, along with three other series which are either of shorter duration or have more missing figures. The series for Anhui, unlike all the others, was directly reproduced from a single source. In the case of Jiangxi, the figures represent estimates based on readings from a graph depicting vital trends. For Hunan, annual births in absolute numbers were given in the original report, but their conversion to rates required estimates by interpolation of the size of the population for intercensal years: Hunan's population grew by 11.9 per cent during the period 1953–64 and 40.5 per cent during the period 1964–79 (Table 4.3). The average rates of population increase were assumed to be 1.1 per cent and 2.7 per cent per year, respectively, for these two periods. In the case of both Beijing and Shanghai, the figures came from diverse sources.

Information on fertility therefore varies in quality. For instance, the rates for Anhui for 1949–53 are inexplicably uniform among themselves and incongruously low in relation to other figures of the 1950s. Neither, of course, is it possible to establish how representative are the various sets of data used here of the fertility patterns and trends in the country as a whole. Despite the uncertainties with respect to their

TABLE 4.4 *Crude birth rates, 1949–82, for specified provinces and municipalities*

Year	Anhui	Jiangxi	Hunan	Guangdong	Beijing	Shanghai
1949	18.1	—	—	—	19.4	—
1950	18.3	—	—	—	—	—
1951	18.3	—	—	—	—	—
1952	18.3	—	—	—	34.4	38.0
1953	18.7	—	<39.0>	—	39.6	40.4
1954	43.3	33.0	38.7	—	43.1	52.6
1955	27.8	33.0	31.6	—	43.2	41.4
1956	33.2	29.5	30.0	—	39.3	40.3
1957	29.8	39.0	34.2	—	—	—
1958	23.8	30.0	31.0	—	—	—
1959	—	29.5	24.9	—	30.7	—
1960	—	25.5	19.7	—	—	—
1961	—	20.5	12.2	—	—	28.7
1962	53.3	37.0	40.2	43	35.9	—
1963	50.7	40.0	46.8	—	43.4	30.3
1964	39.9	37.0	<42.6>	—	30.4	20.6
1965	41.8	38.0	42.5	36	23.0	—
1966	41.1	36.0	37.6	—	19.4	—
1967	40.6	34.5	42.1	—	18.2	—
1968	39.9	36.0	39.3	—	23.8	—
1969	39.3	32.5	38.1	—	22.4	—
1970	37.2	31.5	31.5	29.2	20.7	12.8
1971	35.9	30.5	29.9	29.0	18.8	12.0
1972	35.2	31.5	30.8	28.6	17.8	—
1973	29.7	35.5	30.3	27.2	15.7	—
1974	24.3	34.5	27.9	23.9	11.6	9.2
1975	22.1	34.5	27.6	21.0	9.3	9.4
1976	18.3	31.5	20.5	18.9	9.1	10.2
1977	17.9	29.5	18.8	18.6	10.2	10.8
1978	18.6	27.0	17.4	—	12.9	11.3
1981	18.7	20.4	21.1	25.0	17.6	16.4
1982	—	—	20.3	—	—	—

SOURCES   *Anhui*–Zhao Yugui, 'Anhui Province: Population Growth and Planning' in Liu Zheng *et al.*, (eds) *China's Population: Problems and Prospects* (Beijing: New World Press, 1981) 153–8. *Jiangxi*–estimates based on a graph included in Liu Junde 'On the Dynamics of the Population of Jiangxi' in Hu Huanyong *et al.*, *Renkou Yanjiu Lunwenji*, Papers in population studies (Shanghai: East China Normal University Press, 1981) 65. *Hunan*–Calculated by interpolation from annual births given in Zhou Guangfu 'One Couple Having Only One Child is the Effective Way to Shave Birth Peaks of Past Years' in special Population Issue of *Sichuan Daxue Xuebao* (Sichuan University Journal – Philosophy – Social Science Series) no. 3, 1979, 45. *Guangdong*–Obtained by Pi-chao Chen in 1978 and Pi-chao Chen and Adrienne Kols, 'Population and Birth Planning in the People's Republic of China' *Population Reports* (John Hopkins University) series 1, no. 25 (Jan–Feb. 1982, 598). Pi-chao Chen, 'The Chinese Experience,' *People*, vol. 6, no. 2, 1979, 18. *Beijing and Shanghai*–see H. Yuan Tien, 'Fertility Decline via Marital Postponement in China' *Modern* quality and representativeness however, these several sets of figures permit four tentative generalisations about the situation in China.

1. Fertility fluctuated widely, but remained high (36 per 1000 or more) in all provinces during the years before 1970 when population planning activities intensified.
2. Fertility decline set in after 1970, but progressed more slowly and less steeply in some provinces as intensified population planning activities got under way.
3. Major differences between the fertility of different provinces had already been recorded during the 1960s, but became even larger during the 1970s. On the eve of the intensified population planning efforts, it was announced that fertility in Beijing and Shanghai municipalities, the country's leading metropolitan areas, was considerably lower than in the less urbanised provinces.
4. Fertility seems to have risen somewhat during the most recent three years. This increase may have been due mainly to changes in age structure and in nuptiality.[2]

Disregarding the last point, it would seem that fertility patterns and trends in the Chinese provinces were affected by socio-economic factors to some extent. Favourable socio-economic circumstances (for example, a higher proportion of the population in towns, or higher total output per head) facilitated fertility changes in the relative absence of population planning efforts. Moreover, the impact of the population planning activities of the 1970s seems to have been different in different provinces. For instance, fertility in Anhui declined somewhat later than in either Jiangxi or Hunan. On the other hand, in Jiangxi fertility persisted at somewhat higher levels until the eve of the 1979 one-child family policy.

Of course, these leads and lags could have reflected differences in the intensity with which population planning was implemented at the provincial level. If this were true, the question arises why such differences existed. Could they have been the result of differences in socio-economic conditions which made it easier or harder for local

China, vol. 1, no. 4, October 1975, 450; Liu Zheng *et al.*, *Renkou Tongjixue* (Population Statistics) (Beijing: Chinese People's University Press, 1981) 71; and Shen Anan, 'Shanghai's Population: Structure and Analysis,' *Shehui Kexue* (Social Science) no. 6 1981, 31.

TABLE 4.5 *Rates of natural increase by province, 1978–81 (rate per 1000 population)*

Region and Province	1978	1979	1980	1981	1981*	% Change		
						1978–9	1979–80	1980–1
Total	12.1	11.7	12.2	14.55	20.91	−4.0	+2.6	+21.3
North-east								
Heilongjiang	12.2	10.14	8.6	14.84	19.79	−16.9	−15.2	+72.6
Jilin	14.3	13.89	9.65	12.35	17.67	−2.9	−30.5	+28.0
Liaoning	12.6	NA	8.71	13.21	18.53	—	—	+51.7
North								
Hebei	9.7	>10.0	9.2	17.94	23.99	+3.1	−3.0	+95.0
Shanxi	9.1	NA	NA	13.77	20.31	—	—	—
Beijing	6.8	7.71	9.0	11.77	17.55	+13.4	+16.7	+30.8
Tianjin	9.2	8.66	7.25	12.50	18.60	−5.9	−16.3	+72.4
Shandong	10.6	10.79	7.03	12.58	18.84	+4.8	−34.8	+78.9
Henan	13.4	12.88	9.53	14.63	20.64	−3.9	−26.0	+53.5
East								
Anhui	13.8	13.74	9.9	13.53	18.73	**	−27.9	+36.7
Jiangsu	9.5	8.78	6.25	12.37	18.47	−7.6	−28.8	+97.9
Shanghai	5.1	6.23	5.8	9.70	16.14	+22.2	−6.9	+67.2
Zhejiang	11.1	>10.0	4.03	11.66	17.93	−9.9	−59.7	+189.3

Central							
Hubei	10.5	NA	NA	12.84	20.17	—	—	+40.8
Hunan	10.4	NA	10.0	14.08	21.11	—	—	+52.4
Jiangxi	19.6	13.74	9.11	13.88	20.42	−29.9	−33.7	—
South							
Fujian	17.9	13.02	9.33	16.20	22.07	−27.3	−28.3	+73.6
Guangdong	14.8	>16.0	15.0	19.45	24.99	+11.9	−6.3	+29.7
Guangxi	18.3	>15.0	NA	21.64	27.28	−18.0	—	—
South-west							
Guizhou	16.0	>15.0	NA	19.41	27.89	−6.3	—	—
Sichuan	6.1	6.7	4.45	10.94	17.96	+9.8	−33.6	+145.8
Yunnan	19.2	14.6	10.25	16.76	25.36	−23.4	−29.8	+63.5
Xizang	14.2	NA	NA	21.13	31.05	—	—	—
North-west							
Nei Monggol	12.0	13.2	12.03	17.34	23.11	+10.0	−8.9	+44.1
Shaanxi	10.3	10.15	7.19	13.25	20.35	−1.5	−29.2	+84.3
Ningxia	23.0	21.99	NA	23.57	29.65	−4.8	—	—
Gansu	12.2	10.8	8.9	14.40	20.12	−11.5	−17.6	+61.8
Qinghai	19.5	18.0	NA	19.17	26.65	−7.7	—	—
Xinjiang	14.9	14.8	12.0	20.67	29.08	**	−18.9	+72.3

* Crude Birth Rate
** Less than 1.0 per cent

SOURCES *1978–1980*: Adapted from Pi-chao Chen and Adrienne Kols, 'Population and Birth Planning', 605; *1981*: Census of 1982.

officials to gain speedy and significant support from those affected at the grass-roots level? These and other related questions must be answered empirically.

Fertility patterns and trends in the Chinese provinces are far from satisfactorily documented. Annual crude birth rates are not available for most of the provinces, municipalities and regions. However, as is shown in Table 4.5 information about annual rates of natural increase for 1978–81 for most of the areas has been obtained. In addition, for 1981, provincial crude birth rates are available from the 1982 Census.

There is no way at present to test the data in Table 4.5 for accuracy or reliability. Variations in the rates for 1978 and 1979 give us a measure of confidence. While a drop of 4 per cent in the overall rate of natural increase occurred in 1978–9, changes in the provinces differed both in range and direction. The values for 1980 are probably less accurate, and tend to overstate the decline in fertility. Nationally, an increase of 2.6 per cent was recorded between 1979 and 1980. However, almost all the rates for subnational areas for 1980 showed decreases ranging from 15 per cent to more than 50 per cent. The missing data must have included figures for provinces with with higher rates of natural increase, while the reported rates for 1980 probably understated the reproductive level significantly.

Moreover, the rates of natural increase for 1981 are uniformly and substantially higher than those for 1980 and the other years. The rise in the national natural growth rates, to 14.55 per 1000 is more than 21 per cent in one year. For the provinces, municipalities, and regions, the increases are remarkably high, ranging from 40 to 75 per cent in numerous cases. Some areas have rates two or nearly three times greater than in 1980. This sudden natural increase can be partly explained by the increased number of marriages from the beginning of 1981 as the 1980 Marriage Law went into effect, permitting men and women to marry at younger ages than was encouraged in the 1970s.[3] But, as noted previously, the figures for 1980 were probably highly inaccurate.

There are, therefore weak areas in the data base for the present analysis. Nevertheless the relatively large variety and amount of socio-economic and demographic information now available permit an assessment of recent population developments in China. Specifically, in keeping with various oft-repeated generalisations in the literature, the present examination tests the negative impact of the five socio-economic variables, shown in Table 4.1, on fertility at the provincial level.

SOCIO-ECONOMIC VARIABLES AND DIFFERENTIAL NATURAL INCREASE

The correlation coefficients presented in Table 4.6 are based on the data in Tables 4.1 and 4.5. The number of pairs (N) differs mainly because of data which were missing.

Without exception, all the coefficients were negative. However, for the year 1980, the correlations between the various socio-economic

TABLE 4.6 *Linear correlation coefficients for socio-economic measures and rate of natural increase, 1978–80*

	Rate of Natural Increase				Crude Birthrate
	1978	1979	1980	1981	1981
% Urban–1979	−0.392*	−0.401	−0.251	−0.348	−0.368
(N)	(29)	(24)	(20)	(29)	(29)
d.f.	27	22	18	27	27
Total output per head–1980	−0.518**	−0.533*	−0.375	−0.467*	−0.457*
(N)	(29)	(24)	(20)	(29)	(29)
d.f.	27	22	18	27	27
Newspapers, etc. per 1000–1981	−0.425*	−0.416*	−0.194	−0.358	−0.357
(N)	(29)	(24)	(22)	(29)	(29)
d.f.	27	22	20	27	27
Women workers per 1000 females –1981	−0.426*	−0.426*	−0.122	−0.351	−0.366
(N)	(29)	(24)	(22)	(29)	(29)
	27	22	20	27	27
Life expectancy Men–1973–5	−0.492*	−0.555*	−0.042	−0.526**	−0.572**
(N)	(24)	(20)	(17)	(24)	(24)
d.f.	22	18	15	22	22
Women–1973–5	−0.538**	−0.612**	−0.130	−0.558**	−0.652**
(N)	(24)	(20)	(17)	(24)	(24)
d.f.	22	18	15	22	22

* Significant at the 0.05 level.
** Significant at the 0.01 level.

variables and natural increase were conspicuously low, as well as not statistically significant. The glaringly large drop gives another reason for discounting the provincial rates of natural increase for 1980. The correlations for the other years appear fairly consistent with one another.

Generally speaking, a rising level of urbanisation, total output per head, availability of printed media, non-agricultural employment of women or life expectancy at birth denotes deep-reaching changes in socio-economic conditions and leads to improved mortality. Thus, higher rates of natural increase would automatically result if fertility remained constant. In other words, these variables provide fairly sensitive measures of demographic transition, even when the level of fertility is indirectly quantified here by the rate of natural increase in the analysis.

Most of the correlation coefficients between natural increase and urbanisation, output per head, newspaper circulation, non-agricultural employment, and life expectancy variables were negative and statistically significant. Comparison of the correlation coefficients for 1981 (which are based on both natural increase and crude birth rates) makes clear that the impact of socio-economic change on the fertility transition can be adequately assessed on the basis of the former. Excluding the mortality component from the data (that is, employing crude birth rates as a direct measure of fertility) did not materially alter the overall picture. If anything, the present findings provide a conservative indication of the impact of socio-economic change on China's fertility transition.

Evidently, in China during the recent decades, increased urbanisation, total output per head (higher standard of living), newspaper circulation (literacy), non-agricultural employment of women (role diversification) and life expectancy at birth (lower mortality) created some of the necessary conditions for lower natural increase by way of reduced mortality and reduced fertility. Behind the reported overall reduction in the national birthrate however, fertility transition has clearly not been uniform across the country. Rates of population growth and rates of natural increase differed at the subnational level. Our findings support the view that differences between rates of natural increase in different provinces reflected differences in socio-economic conditions. While China's population planning programmes have apparently achieved successes in reducing fertility, socio-economic changes must be taken into account in interpreting China's demographic transition.

DISCUSSION

In China's recent fertility transition, both socio-economic change and population planning programmes clearly played a part. Their relative weight however cannot yet be assessed because systematic information about the latter is unavailable at the provincial level. Nevertheless, the influence of China's population planning programmes may legitimately be surmised from the data in Table 4.6.

Setting aside the coefficients for 1980 on account of their highly dubious statistical base, the relationship observed between natural increase and three of the variables was no longer statistically significant in 1981. Though remaining negative in direction, the reduced coefficients for urbanisation, newspaper circulation and non-agricultural employment of women could have reflected the further intensification of population planning activities in 1979. China's unique one-child family policy was initiated in 1979, but its widespread implementation was probably neither energetic nor extensive until after 1980. The intensified and widened application of this policy measure could well have lessened the relationship between fertility and some socio-economic variables.

More intriguing, however, is the fact that China's intensified and widened efforts have apparently not overcome the effect of some other socio-economic variables. As can be seen in Table 4.6, the negative relationship between natural increase and crude birth rates, and between total output per head and life expectancy, remained statistically significant in 1981.

One salient aspect of recent socio-economic changes in China undoubtedly relates to the markedly higher life expectancy at birth. The correlations between life expectancy at birth and natural increase were consistently larger for females than males in all the years under review. This difference must not be dismissed as being unimportant. Since the adoption of the one-child family policy, the fate of female children in various localities in China has been adversely affected. In its lead-off circular on the 1983 'New Mobilisation' for population planning, the Central Committee's Propaganda Department specifically called for the protection of infant girls, and also of women who had given birth to daughters, from social ostracism and physical cruelty at the hands of husbands, parents-in-law, or other kinfolk.[4] This appeal is echoed repeatedly and widely in official speeches, conference reports, journal articles, newspaper accounts and editorials. The frequency of female infanticide has apparently reached critical proportions in many places, as has the maltreatment of women who have borne no male offspring.[5]

Under the circumstances, the statistically significant negative relationship between the life expectancy of women and natural increase reflects far more than just an extension of, and improvement in, the health and medical services. Where a reduction in female mortality has become more pronounced, more favourable attitudes towards women and girls must also have prevailed. This is probably the explanation for the higher correlations between the life expectancies of women and rates of natural increase: attitudinal transformation, together with health and medical measures, enhanced the survival rates of females at all stages of the life cycle and increased the differences between female and male life expectancy in the anticipated direction. In provinces where attitudes had not changed, health and medical measures benefited women less and improvements in life expectancy were lower. A statistically significant negative correlation (-0.414) was found between the difference in life expectancy of men and women and the rate of natural increase for 1978. The bigger the difference (which presumably signified better treatment of females at birth and throughout life), the lower was the rate of natural increase (that is, the more advanced the fertility transition).

Presumably too, attitudinal changes benefiting women were far more prevalent in the economically better-off parts of the country. The continuing appeals for the elimination of infanticide of girl babies and maltreatment of women vividly, albeit obliquely, illustrate the slow rate of change in the rural and poorer areas. The link between success in planned reproduction and a change in traditional rural attitudes to women has been clearly recognised at the highest levels. Premier Zhao Ziyang himself chose to give space to it in his 1982 report to the National People's Congress and urged that the whole society should condemn the infanticide of girls and the abusive treatment of women who give birth to daughters.[6]

In the West, the term 'family planning programme' refers to the dissemination of contraceptive knowledge and technology so that couples can voluntarily and effectively scale down and schedule child-bearing according to personal and family circumstances. 'Controlled child-bearing,' as the term has been defined and used in China, differs in both its premises and procedures. *Population* planning, rather than family planning, correctly epitomises its rationale, objectives and implementation.

The central premise of China's government-initiated population planning policy is that the 'two kinds of production in society' (human production and material production) must be proportionately balanced in a socialist economy. In theory, then, there is a limit to reproduction, and this limit is set by the macro-economic principle of proportional growth of population and production. The objectives are to 'create ever more material wealth, improve living standards at a reasonable rate and speed up the growth of the socialist productive forces.'[7] In implementing this policy, awareness and acceptance by couples of the advantages of controlled fertility in societal terms are imperative. In fact, much of China's literature on population planning, since the early 1970s, has been couched in these terms; in notable contrast to the short-lived efforts to promote family limitation in the 1950s and 1960s, when the promotion themes emphasised the immediate beneficial effects on the health of women, mothers and children.

For the 'New Mobilisation' for population planning in 1983, further elaborations of the need to limit fertility have explicitly pointed to the negative consequences of past 'reproductive anarchy' in Chinese society.[8] Dire warnings have been issued of probable deterioriation in living standards unless China's total population is kept within the planned size of 1.2bn by the end of the century.

The urgency and importance of China's population planning programmes have been steadily and systematically reflected in the increasingly stringent norms for child-bearing and their stricter enforcement. The one-child family policy of 1979 and the concurrent introduction of rewards for compliance are the leading aspects of the programmes. More recently, penalties for non-observance have been made part and parcel of the enforcement code at the grass-roots level. China's population planning policy, therefore, extends far beyond the scope and substance of the family-planning approach to fertility reduction.

Both before and since the intensification of population planning activities, the government has consistently and energetically pushed for greater development of education and employment opportunities and for better health, medical, cultural and related services in the country as a whole and in the rural areas in particular.

The government's population planning policy does not consist of simple-minded dissemination of contraceptive information and technology. Its uniqueness and impact can be more firmly appreciated in terms of the phrase: 'a country is a family is a country'. That is, ideologically, organisationally and logistically, China's population planned programmes operate within the context of a 'welfare society'. As such planned reproduction at the household level becomes part of the affairs of the nation.

The 'induced fertility transition' of the recent past certainly deserves to be acclaimed as a population planning success. However, given the still statistically significant negative relationship between fertility, total output per head and life expectancy, it seems that Chinese couples remain very much influenced by both immediate economic conditions and longer-term need for male offspring (for old age security). Population planning programmes appear to have been more influential where economic circumstances are better, but to have been much less so where socio-economic change has lagged. Thus, the results of the population planning programmes to date cannot, and as this chapter suggests, should not, be divorced from socio-economic change, either in the past or the present.

NOTES AND REFERENCES

1. H. Yuan Tien, 'Age at Marriage in the People's Republic of China', *China Quarterly*, 93, March 1983, 90–107.
2. Ibid.
3. Ibid.
4. *RMRB*, 10 December 1982; 23 December 1982.
5. S. Li, 'The Significance of the Sex Equilibrium of the Population at Birth', *Shehui* (Society), 1982, 4, 21. Cf. also *RMRB*, 31 January 1983.
6. Zhao Ziyang, 'Report on the Sixth Five-Year Plan', *BR*, 20 December 1982.
7. Liu Zheng, 'Population Planning and Demographic Theory', in *China's Population: Problems and Prospects* (Liu Zheng *et al.* (eds) Beijing: New World Press, 1981) 16.
8. Beijing College of Economics, Office of Population Research, *Renkou Lilun* (Population Theory), Beijing, 1977. 34; H. Yuan Tien, *Population Theory in China* (New York: M. E. Sharpe, 1980).

5 Birth Control Methods and Organisation in China

PI-CHAO CHEN

The release of the preliminary results of the 1982 census and of a national 'One in one thousand' fertility survey have confirmed that a fertility decline of major proportions took place in China in the 1970s. As recently as 1968, when the fertility level reached its second highest peak since 1950, the total fertility rate was 7.025 children per woman of reproductive age. In 1971, when the government embarked on the third birth-control campaign, the total fertility rate was still a high 5.442. A decade later in 1981 it had dropped to 2.238. In other words, China had reduced its fertility level by almost 60 per cent in a decade. Such a dramatic fertility transition in a large country and in so short a time is unprecedented. This achievement is all the more impressive because China's population comprises one fifth of humankind and the transition has taken place without a profound socio-economic modernisation or a major improvement in living standards taking place prior to or during the transition period.

The fertility decline has been the result of a determined and successful birth planning programme rather than socio-economic modernisation. As the organisation of China's birth-control services is a vital part of the programme; this chapter is intended to describe its structure and evaluate its performance.

THE THREE-TIER HEALTH CARE SYSTEM

In China the contraceptive delivery system is built into the primary health care system, which in turn is based on China's administrative subdivisions. China is administratively divided into 2136 *xian* (counties) and equivalent units. These counties are in turn divided into

135

54 371 communes (now called *xiang* in some areas), 718 000 production brigades, which in turn are subdivided into 6m production teams.[1] At the lowest level of this three-tier primary health care system is the production brigade health station staffed by two to three barefoot doctors (now called village doctors in some places) whose responsibilities include sanitation, immunisation and vaccination, maternal and child health, elementary curative care and contraceptive services. The brigade health station refers serious cases to the commune health centre.

The commune health centre is financed by county and provincial subsidies, user-fees and contributions. Medical workers employed by the commune health centre include graduates of middle-level medical schools, practitioners of traditional herbal medicine and, in the economically prosperous suburban areas, graduates of medical colleges. They supervise the barefoot doctors, organise continuing in-service training for them, treat more complex cases and perform abortion and sterilisation.

At the county level there are a county hospital, a county maternal and child health hospital and a county anti-epidemic station. The county hospital is staffed mostly by graduate physicians trained either in western or traditional herbal medicine. Most are equipped with an operating room, X-ray and laboratory facilities, and some in-patient facilities. The hospital also runs continuing in-service training for the commune health staff. The county anti-epidemic station takes responsibility for disease control and supervises and provides technical support to the preventive health section of the commune health centre, which in turn supervises the barefoot doctors in carrying out preventive work. The county Maternal and Child Health hospital is responsible for the health of mothers and children throughout the county. It trains and supervises birth attendants and those female barefoot doctors who take responsibility for deliveries or other linked activities. In the last few years, increasing numbers of counties have set up their own contraceptive technical guidance institutes, under the direct leadership of the county birth planning staff office. Its responsibility includes training lower level health workers in the four operations – tubectomy, vasectomy, insertion and removal of the IUD, and induced abortion.

Today, each county unit, with an average population of 0.4 to 0.6m, is part of a health care system in which the preventive, maternal and child welfare, curative and contraceptive services are integrated, although each has its own distinct responsibilities and maintains a separate chain of command. By 1981 every county had a hospital, and the majority had a county anti-epidemic station and specialised Maternal and Child Health hospital. Over 50 000 communes had their own commune health centre; while over 90 per cent of the nation's production brigades had their own co-operative health station or similar health facility staffed by a total of 1.48m barefoot doctors.[2] (See Table 5.1) For obvious reasons, the quantity and quality of the health care service and personnel vary a great deal from one province to another, and from one place to another within each province. Generally speaking, they are of a higher standard in the provinces along the coast and in the north-east. Within any particular province, the counties and communes around the major cities tend to have better health and contraceptive services.

The birth-control delivery system has been built into the health care system so that in theory at least one barefoot doctor in every brigade health station is female. Most of the female barefoot doctors are trained in contraceptive counselling, many can insert and remove IUDs, and some are trained in the techniques of certain types of abortion such as the vacuum aspiration method. These trained barefoot doctors provide ante-natal and post-partum care, deliver babies, conduct contraceptive education and keep birth-planning records for the brigade. They are supervised in these activities by a woman cadre, who manages and co-ordinates birth-planning work within the brigade. They and the woman cadre may also arrange for the mobile sterilisation team to visit their unit, and will accompany men and women to the commune health centre for tubectomy, vasectomy, IUD insertion, or abortion. Commune health centre doctors and brigade barefoot doctors are trained and supported technically by the county birth planning technical guidance institute, a special unit funded and controlled by the county birth planning office. This office reimburses the commune or brigade from funds provided by the National Birth Planning Commission for each planned birth operation. Reimbursement is set at 5 *yuan* per sterilisation, 3 *yuan* per IUD insertion or removal. Nationally the per capita cost of these operations in the early 1980s was about 0.40 *yuan*. The integration of the contraceptive delivery system with the regionalised three-tier primary health care system has thus made China's contraceptive delivery system the largest community-based one in the world, providing contraceptive and abortion services to one fifth of humankind.

TABLE 5.1 *Health care facility and manpower, 1979–80*

All China, 1979			Rural China, Year-end 1980	
	Number	*Population per bed or worker*		*Number*
Hospital beds	1 932 000	503	County hospitals	2 377
Medical workers[a]	2 642 000	368	Beds	320 000
College-graduated physicians	395 000	2458	Anti-epidemic stations	2 093
Middle-level physicians	435 000	2232	MCH stations	1 885
Practitioners of traditional medicine	258 000	3763	Health training schools[b]	1 165
			Commune health centres	55 000
Nurses	421 000	2306	Beds	770 000
Barefoot doctors	1 575 000	616	Co-operative medical stations	630 000
			Barefoot doctors employed	1 460 000
			Health aides and birth attendants serving at the team level	3 000 000

[a] These include pharmacists and anti-epidemic workers as well as physicians and nurses.
[b] These presumably are the training schools set up by the district and county hospitals to train and retrain the barefoot doctors.

SOURCE   State Statistical Bureau, *Principal Statistical Data on the National Economy, May 1980*, and 'The rural villages of our country have established a three-tier network of health care', *Jiankang bao*, 9 July 1981.

CONTRACEPTIVE METHODS

During the 1970s, contraceptive use in China rose spectacularly. By the end of the decade China's contraceptive prevalence rate was as high as that in developed low-fertility countries. According to the one in one thousand sample fertility survey carried out in 1982, 69.46 per cent of the married women of reproductive age (aged 15–49) were contracepting.[3] By comparison, in Japan only 61 per cent of the married women aged 15–49 were practising contraception in 1976, and 69 per cent of married women aged 15–44 in the United States were contracepting in the same year.[4]

In theory, the nationwide birth control programmes have made all contraceptive methods available to married couples. In practice, for a number of reasons, the programmes have primarily promoted IUDs and sterilisations, to the extent that these now account for 85 per cent of all contraceptive use. According to the data compiled by the State Council Birth Planning Commission, as many as 50 per cent of all contraceptors in China rely on IUDs. This figure is reconfirmed by the one in one thousand sample fertility survey of 1982, which yielded exactly the same result, 50.2 per cent. In the rural areas 53 per cent of women rely on IUDs as distinct from 39 per cent in urban areas. The percentage of women using IUDs increases with the number of children. It is 18 per cent among those with one child rising to 25 per cent among those with two to three children. For women with four or more children, the figure is only 14.84 per cent, reflecting a switch to sterilisation after two or three children.

A modified Ota ring made of stainless steel is the most widely-used IUD in China. This ring has no tail and can be removed only with a fine metal hook, therefore, once inserted it cannot be removed by the woman herself. Barefoot doctors and other trained physicians are forbidden to remove IUDs without official authorisation. In the last few years the Chinese mass media have given wide publicity to a few cases in which the government prosecuted barefoot doctors or 'quacks' for removing IUDs at the request of women but without authorisation from the appropriate birth planning official. The wide publicity and the severe punishment were apparently intended to serve as a warning to others not to do the same.

Sterilisation is the second most widely-used contraceptive method in China. According to the one in one thousand sample survey, sterilised women and men accounted for 35 per cent of China's total contraceptors in 1982: of these, men accounted for 10 per cent and women for 25 per cent. In other words, of the 118.4m married women of reproductive age practising contraception, 20.87m women had had tubectomies, and a further 8.22m had husbands who were sterilised. According to one Chinese source, a total of 20.3m tubectomies and 13.8m vasectomies were performed in 1971–8; a ratio of 1.5 : 1. Since 1978, the ratio has become even more lopsided; it was 2.5 : 1 in 1982, according to the one in one thousand fertility survey. In five of China's six large administrative zones, tubectomies greatly outnumber vasectomies; the ratio ranges from 4.1 : 1 in the central south to 61 : 1 in the north-east and 68 : 1 in the north-west. The only exception is south-west, where the ratio is 0.4 : 1. The reason for this is the acceptability of vasectomy in the populous province of Sichuan, where for reasons unknown to the outsider males opt to have themselves sterilised. According to the one in one thousand fertility survey, the incidence of sterilisation increases with the number and age of children. Of all childless women or women with a single child who are practising birth control, only 2.8 per cent have had tubectomies and only 0.43 per cent of their husbands have had vasectomies. Among couples with two to three children who are practising birth control however, 25.6 per cent of the women and 1.1 per cent of the men have been sterilised. These figures rise to 41.2 per cent for women and 1.7 for men among couples with four or more children who are practising birth control. Of all women in the 20–24 age-group who are practising birth control, 6.5 per cent are either themselves sterilised or are married to men who have had vasectomies. The figure increases to 21 per cent among those aged 25–29, 39.4 per cent among those aged 30–34, 47.4 per cent among those aged 35–39, and slightly decreases to 43.2 per cent in the 40–43 age-group. (See Table 5.2) Like IUDs both vasectomy and tubectomy have achieved wider acceptance in rural areas than in urban areas. According to the one in one thousand fertility survey, whereas tubectomies and vasectomies account for 20.3 per cent and 2.8 per cent of all contraceptive use in urban areas, they account for 26.4 and 11.5 per cent respectively in the villages (See Table 5.3).

Several varieties of oral contraceptive are in use in China. The pill most widely used is a combination of 0.3mg dl-norgestrel and 0.03mg ethinyl estradiol. Other pills widely used are the low-dose oral pill No. 1, a combination of 0.625mg norethindrone and 0.035mg ethinyl estradiol, and oral pill No. 2, consisting of 1.0mg megestrol acetate and 0.035mg ethinyl estradiol. All these pills are taken daily for 22 days a cycle. In addition a visiting pill, a once-a-month pill, and monthly injections are also in limited use.

TABLE 5.2 *Contraceptive methods used by women, analysed by age groups, 1982 (percentages)*

Age	Tubectomy	Vasectomy	IUD	Pills	Condoms	Other	Subtotal
15–19	1.55	0.39	65.89	20.16	1.55	10.47	100
20–24	5.26	1.26	71.87	13.22	1.73	6.65	100
25–29	15.33	5.58	60.94	11.73	2.15	4.26	100
30–34	29.57	9.85	48.08	8.31	1.67	2.51	100
35–39	34.94	12.43	41.93	6.65	1.72	2.33	100
40–44	30.02	13.16	43.69	6.42	2.36	4.35	100
45–49	24.17	15.97	44.11	4.75	2.59	8.40	100
Total	25.39	10.00	50.16	8.44	2.00	4.01	100

SOURCE   Qian Xinzhong and Xiao Zhengyu, 'An Analysis of the One in One Thousand Sample Survey of Fertility' (Beijing: Beijing Economics College, Institute of Population, July 1983).

TABLE 5.3 *Contraceptive methods used in urban and rural areas (percentages)*

	CPR	Tubectomy	Vasectomy	IUD	Pill	Condom	Other
Total	70	25	10	50	8	2	4
Urban	74	20	3	39	19	10	9
Rural	69	26	12	53	6	1	3

SOURCE   As Table 5.2

Although hormonal contraceptives are in theory universally available, in practice they are in limited supply, most probably because of the high manufacturing cost. According to the one in one thousand fertility survey, hormonal contraceptives accounted for only 8 per cent of the contraceptive use in China in 1982, and even less in rural areas. Hormonal contraceptives account for 19 per cent of all contraceptive use in urban areas but only 6.3 per cent in rural areas. Only in two of China's administrative zones, the north-east and the north-west, does their use exceed 10 per cent of total contraceptive use. According to the one in one thousand fertility survey, their use accounts for 18.3 per cent in the north-east, and 11.7 per cent in the north-west.

As in other countries, hormonal contraceptives are used mainly to space births. Their use decreases with the age and number of children. According to the one in one thousand sample survey, their use among contracepting women aged 15–19 accounts for 20 per cent, this decreases to 13 per cent among those aged 20–24, and 12 per cent among those aged 25–29, 8 per cent among those aged 30–34, and only 7 per cent among those aged 35–39.

The use of condoms accounts for only 2 per cent of total contraceptive use in China, according to the one in one thousand sample survey. The figure for urban areas is 10 per cent of total contraceptive use whereas for rural areas it is a mere 1 per cent. The low use of condoms in China, especially in the rural areas is easy to understand given that they require ongoing distribution and that their use cannot be guaranteed.

PLANNED BIRTH PROGRAMME PERFORMANCE

During the 1970s, the major objective was reduction of fertility through later marriage, longer spacing and fewer children per couple. Programme performance was measured by the late marriage rate, the planned birth rate, the birth limitation rate, live birth rate and natural increase rate. The late marriage rate was defined as the percentage of women who get married for the first time during the calendar year and who satisfy the local norm for minimum age, which varies over time and from one place to another. Throughout the 1970s, the birth planning programmes raised the age of marriage by controlling the issue of marriage permits. The commune official in charge of civic affairs issues the permit to the young marrying couple. During the 1970s, it became increasingly difficult to obtain permission to marry if the marrying couple did not meet the minimum age requirement: usually 23 for women and 25 for men. Apparently, this practice has helped raise the age of marriage. According to the one in one thousand sample survey, in 1950 the late marriage rate (defined as percentage of women who get married after attaining 23 years of age or more) was 7.2 per cent for China as a whole and 12.5 and 6.1 per cent for the urban and rural areas respectively. By 1971, when the new campaign was initiated, the late marriage rate was 14 per cent (46 per cent in urban and 10 per cent in rural areas). By 1980, the rate had risen to 53 per cent (86 per cent in urban and 45 per cent in rural areas). Since then for a number of reasons, there has been a slight decline in the late marriage rate. In 1981 the rate was 51 per cent (79 per cent for the urban and 43 per cent for the rural areas).

The steady increase in the late marriage rate for females reflects and is consistent with the steady rise in the mean age at first marriage for females during the last three decades. According to the one in one thousand sample survey, in 1950 the mean age at first marriage for females was 18.68 for the whole country (19.41 for urban and 18.52 for rural areas). Responding to the organised programmes promoting late marriage, it continued its steady rise during the 1970s, so that by 1980 it had reached 23.05 years (25.19 for urban and 22.54 for rural areas). (See Figure 5.1.) It is clear that without this promotion the mean age at first marriage could not have risen as it has.

For years, Chinese birth planning programmes have used planned birth rate and birth limitation rates to measure programme performance. Planned birth rate is defined as the percentage of births that conform to local norms for age at marriage, spacing and parity. Since the local norms vary not only over time but also from one place to another, the statistics on planned birth rate obtained from various places are not directly comparable. During the late 1970s, the planned birth rate in many provinces was relatively high, ranging from 60 per cent in Gansu province to 90 per cent in Shanxi.[5] Birth limitation rate is defined as the percentage of all fecund married women under age 50 using a contraceptive method at some time during the year. During the late 1970s, the rate was believed to be 70 per cent for China, and was higher for most of the coastal provinces for which data were obtained by foreign visitors.[6]

Strictly speaking, the birth limitation rate is not comparable to the contraceptive prevalence rate used in most countries. Fortunately, the one in one thousand sample survey solves the problem of comparability by compiling and tabulating the contraceptive prevalence rates.

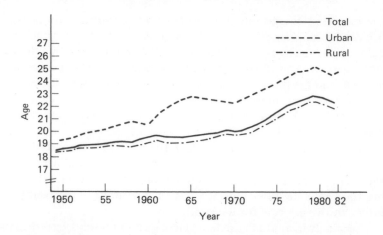

FIGURE 5.1   *Mean female age at first marriage 1950–82*

According to the survey, of the 172 788 married women aged 15–49, 120 000 were contracepting, yielding a contraceptive prevalence rate of 69.46 per cent. The rate was 74 per cent in urban areas and 69 in rural areas. The sample survey confirms that the IUD is by far the most widely-used method, accounting for 50 per cent of all contraceptive use (39 per cent in urban and 53 in rural areas). The second most popular method is tubectomy, accounting for a quarter of all contracepting couples (20 per cent in urban and 26 per cent in rural areas). Next in popularity is vasectomy, accounting for 10 per cent (3 per cent in urban and 12 per cent in rural). Hormonal contraceptives account for only 8 per cent of contraceptive use.

Until recently there has been an almost total lack of data about fertility levels and trends in China. The release of the preliminary results of the one in one thousand sample fertility survey has finally put an end to this state of affairs. (See Table 5.4 and Figure 5.2.) The result of the survey indicates that a fertility transition of major proportion took place in the 1970s, in the wake of the initiation of the campaign to persuade people to have children later, to space them and to have fewer of them. According to the survey, the total fertility rate was 5.699 children per woman of reproductive age in 1951. Between 1952 and 1957 it rose slightly, most probably because of a restoration of peace and better distribution of grain. During these years the total ferility rate fluctuated between 6.472 and 5.854, averaging 6.22.

TABLE 5.4   *Total fertility rates, 1950–81*

Year	Total	Urban	Rural
1950	5813	5001	5963
1951	5699	4719	5904
1952	6472	5521	6667
1953	6049	5402	6183
1954	6274	5723	6390
1955	6261	5665	6391
1956	5854	5333	5974
1957	6405	5943	6504
1958	5679	5253	5775
1959	4303	4172	4323
1960	4015	4057	3996
1961	3287	2982	3349
1962	6023	4789	6303
1963	7502	6207	7784
1964	6176	4395	6567
1965	6076	3749	6597
1966	6259	3104	6958
1967	5313	2905	5847
1968	6448	3872	7025
1969	5723	3299	6263
1970	5812	3267	6370
1971	5442	2882	6011
1972	4984	2637	5503
1973	4539	2387	5008
1974	4170	1982	4642
1975	3571	1782	3951
1976	3235	1608	3582
1977	2844	1574	3116
1978	2716	1551	2968
1979	2745	1373	3045
1980	2238	1147	2480
1981	2631	1390	2910

SOURCE   as Table 5.2.

During the three catastrophic years, between 1959 and 1961 (wrought by the disastrous Great Leap campaign) the total fertility rate plummeted to 4.303 in 1959, 4.015 in 1960 and to a low of 3.287 in 1961. In the wake of the food crisis the total fertility rate recovered, returning to

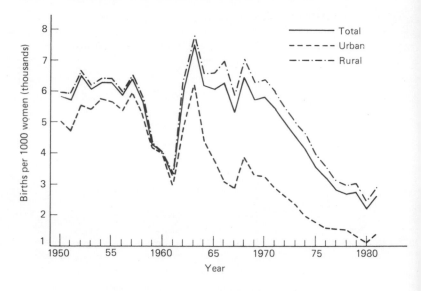

FIGURE 5.2   *Total fertility rate, 1950–81*

6.023 in 1962. It rose to a high of 7.502 in 1963; in all probability reflecting the effect of compensatory births postponed by the famine. Throughout the remainder of the decade, the total fertility rate remained at relatively high level, averaging 5.999. Except for 1967, when it declined to 5.313, probably because of the turmoil wrought by the Cultural Revolution, the total fertility rate was never below 5.7. The end of the decade saw the beginning of a precipitous fertility decline. In 1970 the total fertility rate stood at 5.812, in 1971 it was 5.442. It has since been in steady decline. It fell to 2.745 in 1979, and to 2.238 in 1980. In 1981 it rose to 2.631, through a combination of factors: the introduction of the production responsibility system and *de facto* decline of permissible age of marriage from 23 to 20 years of age. As was to be expected, fertility differential by residence persisted. In 1968, on the eve of spectacular sustained fertility decline, the total fertility rate was 3.872 in urban and 7.025 in rural areas. In 1973 the urban total fertility rate fell to 2.387. A year later it fell below replacement level, to 1.982, as compared with 4.642 in rural areas. In 1980, the total fertility rate in urban areas fell to 1.147, or twice as low as replacement level, whereas the rural total fertility rate fell to 2.480 fast approaching replacement level.

SINGLE-CHILD FAMILY

Fertility decline may also be measured by the composition of births by parity. In 1980 first parity births accounted for 39 per cent of total births nationally (73 per cent in urban areas and 36 per cent in rural areas). Second parity births accounted for 25 per cent nationally (23 per cent in urban areas and 40 per cent in rural areas). The corresponding figures for 1981 were even more striking. By then first parity births accounted for 44 per cent of total births nationally (36 per cent in urban areas and 40 per cent in rural areas). Second parity births accounted for 24 per cent (12 per cent in urban areas and 25 per cent in rural areas). Only 32 per cent of all births (2 per cent in urban areas and 35 per cent in rural areas) were of third and higher parity.

To sum up, the preliminary findings of the one in one thousand sample survey of fertility suggests that a dramatic fertility transition took place in China in the 1970s. At the beginning of the decade, the overwhelming majority of the population got married at a rather young age, did not practise contraception, and had a relatively high fertility. By the end of the decade, over half the women did not get married until they were 23 years of age or older, and 70 per cent of the married women of reproductive age were contracepting, resulting in a sharp fertility decline to something approaching that of replacement level. Furthermore, this decline was brought about by the organised birth planning programmes initiated and implemented by the government. The mix of contraceptive methods used in China suggests an interesting hypothesis: even if Chinese government had initiated the birth planning programmes and enforced the birth quota system as early as the 1950s or 1960s, it could not at that stage have achieved the same remarkable results, because of the lack of a rural health infrastructure. The three-tier integrated health service system that has provided contraceptive and abortion services to China's vast rural population was set up in the 1960s during the Cultural Revolution. Its establishment in a rudimentary form was complete only in the early 1970s, when the third birth planning campaign, for fewer, later and more spaced births, was launched. As indicated by the birth planning programme statistics and the one in one thousand sample survey, 50 per cent of China's 118m married women of reproductive age who practice contraception have opted for IUDs, another 25 per cent for tubectomies and the husbands of another 10 per cent have had vasectomies. Altogether the three highly effective methods account for 85 per cent of all contraceptive methods used. All these methods require specialised health services, local availability of trained health workers, facilities and supplies. Vasectomy and tubectomy are usually performed at the commune health centres by specially trained doctors, supervised and supported by the county hospital. IUDs are usually inserted at brigade health stations by specially trained female barefoot doctors. The brigade health stations and most of the commune health centres came into being in late 1960s and early 1970s. The commune health centre doctors and brigade barefoot doctors have been trained in special programmes organised by the birth planning offices at various administrative levels. Without this nationwide network of community-based services staffed by millions of trained personnel, China could not have raised its contraceptive prevalence rate from an undoubtedly low per centage figure to 70 per cent in the course of one decade, and therefore reduced its total fertility rate from over five to a level approaching replacement level fertility.

NOTES AND REFERENCES

1. State Statistical Bureau, *The Statistical Yearbook of China in 1981*, Beijing 1982.
2. Pi-chao Chen and Chi-hsien Tuan, 'The Primary Health Care in China: Post-1978 Development', *Social Science and Medicine*, August 1983.
3. Qian Xinzhong and Xiao Zhengyu, 'An Analysis of the One in One Thousand Sample Survey of Fertility', (Beijing: Beijing Economics College Institute of Population, July 1983). All the information from this survey used subsequently in this chapter is from the same source.
4. Dorothy L. Nortman and Ellen Hofstatter, *Population and Family Planning Programs: Compendium of Data through 1978*, (New York: The Population Council, 1980).
5. Pi-chao Chen and Adrienne Kols, 'Population and Birth Planning in the People's Republic of China', *Population Reports*, January–February 1982, series J, no. 25.
6. Ibid.

6 Old Age Security and the One-child Campaign

DEBORAH DAVIS-FRIEDMANN

THE ELDERLY AND BIRTH CONTROL

In each of the four post-1949 birth control campaigns, official and unofficial sources have claimed that elderly grandparents undermined government efforts to restrict family size by their persistent desire for many grandchildren.[1] Evidence supporting the elderly's preference for large families, particularly for large numbers of male descendants to carry on the family surname, is widely available. Conclusive proof that elderly parents actively block acceptance of the one-child ideal, however, is more difficult to find. In fact, Chinese government sources generally identify young people as the main sources of opposition and focus propaganda efforts on the young, involving the elderly only as a secondary audience.[2] The pattern of rewards and punishments used to achieve the goals of the one-child family also confirm the importance of resistance by the young rather than the old.[3] It is the salaries of the young parents that are reduced if they violate their birth-quota and it is the young couples not the grandparents who receive all bonuses and preferential treatment for compliance. Why then should there be *any* concern with the role of the elderly in the one-child campaign?

The answer is that at the root of the resistance by the young are well-founded fears about financial security and physical well-being in old age. Only when the government addresses the needs of the elderly will the young of child-bearing age willingly comply with the Chinese government's extraordinary demand that for the rest of the twentieth century all first-time mothers forego or terminate any subsequent pregnancies.

In China, old age has the same connotations of illness and dependency as it has in the West, and people have the same worries about

149

how they will cope with their reduced abilities and increased need for care. In the decades immediately prior to 1949, Chinese parents relied on the traditional coping strategy that centred on close ties with male children. Sons were instructed from their earliest years in the obligations of filial responsibility and both the extended family and the surrounding community reinforced those expectations by equating the 'good and reliable man' with the respectful and responsible son. In theory all sons were raised to be filial, but in practice elderly parents needed only one reliable son in order to survive. Large joint households with several married sons sharing responsibility for ageing parents were the privilege of the well-to-do, the exception rather than the rule. But in all classes high mortality rates among children and adolescents meant that the birth of one, or of even two sons did not necessarily guarantee parents' security in old age. Therefore, among the rich and the poor, both mothers and fathers desired at least three or four male offspring. Since 1949, parents of all social classes have continued to think of sons as the key to future prosperity and security.[4] Moreover, the Marriage Law of the People's Republic makes children legally responsible for supporting aged parents thereby reinforcing traditional practices.[5]

The advances made under the Communist Party leadership in the areas of public health and social welfare together with gains in life expectancy and expanded government services have somewhat altered traditional strategies for coping with poverty and dependency in old age. As a result of extensive efforts to inoculate the population against the most common infectious diseases and to improve the safety of drinking water, mortality rates plummeted between 1950 and 1960.[6] Nevertheless, despite extraordinary gains in life expectancy, everyday life remains uncertain. Even when average mortality rates fall dramatically, within most people's circle of acquaintances a noticeable number of infant deaths and disabling diseases still occur in childhood.[7] Consequently, even among the well-to-do there is a strong desire for more than one child as a guarantee of protection against childlessness in old-age.

Since 1949, Chinese citzens have gained many new social services. For the elderly the most dramatic have been improved access to low-cost hospital care, greater food security, and, for a few, government-financed pensions. In the first few years after Liberation, the Chinese leaders hoped to extend these benefits to all citizens, but within a short period they realized that the country was too poor, and they implemented a two-tiered system whereby employees in the 'advanced' state sector would immediately receive all the benefits (free medical care, life-time pensions after twenty years of employment, and subsidised food and housing) while employees in the 'less-advanced' collective sector relied on a combination of locally-accumulated welfare funds and the private assets of their families.[8] In 1952, 8 per cent of the workforce was in the state sector and eligible for pensions; by 1980 this had grown to 19 per cent which means that the majority of the workforce has been, and will continue to be, employed outside the state sector.[9] Therefore most elderly people have been, and will be, excluded from the government pension plan and must turn to their adult children for support in old age.

As the dichotomy between state and non-state employment conditions has solidified over the past three decades two types of family, each with its own coping strategy for old age, and therefore its own distinctive response to the single-child family policy, have developed. In rural areas where more than 85 per cent of young couples are farm labourers working outside the state sector, parents expect to guarantee survival in old age through financial dependence on a married son. They need the labour of children, both girls and boys, to run the agricultural household, and the ideal family composition is either two sons and a daughter or two sons and two daughters. In the cities, where most residents between the ages 25 and 60 are state employees with guaranteed pensions, parents do not look to their children as the main ecomomic support in old age. Children, in fact, are primarily seen as long-term dependants and the ideal urban family consists of one girl and one boy.[10] These differences between urban and rural families directly affect the intensity and pattern of young parents' resistance to the one-child policy and it is therefore useful to examine the details of old-age security separately for the urban and rural elderly.

OLD AGE SECURITY IN RURAL CHINA

From 1949 to the present, the majority of rural residents have been required to provide for their own retirement. The Labour Insurance Regulations of 1951 provided pensions for state workers but not for peasants. Subsequent revisions in 1964 extended coverage to the small minority working on state farms who in 1980, numbered only 5m out of a total agricultural workforce of 320m.[11] Since 1978 some wealthy suburban villages have implemented locally-funded retirement schemes which provide either a cash or in-kind payment worth up to 50 per cent of average income. In 1981, a Chinese source estimated that 426 000 elderly peasants were regularly collecting a monthly pension from their brigade welfare funds. This article suggested that in the future all retired people would enjoy the same financial independence and would therefore be able to accept the one-child ideal.[12]

Such official optimism about the self-sufficiency of the next generation of elderly parents is hard to justify given current (1983) economic realities. In all but the richest 10 to 20 per cent of rural communities, the costs of existing programmes for primary education and basic medical services exhaust local public surpluses. After thirty years of expansion and increased per capita levies, less than 40 per cent of rural children enter secondary school and even seriously ill rural residents who incur large hospital bills, usually cover at least 50 per cent of the medical expenses themselves.[13] Furthermore, as the basic unit of agricultural production and accountability has shifted since 1980 from a collectively organized work-team to individual farm households, rural residents may have become less willing to divert their profits into collective welfare projects and more eager to buy new houses, bicycles and even private farm machinery. Such a de-collectivisation bodes ill for any plan to increase public responsibility for the childless elderly. Moreover, since the majority of adult villagers had already successfully provided for their own old age by having several sons before the single-child family campaign was launched, only the youngest and least politically influential rural residents have any great incentive to divert scarce welfare funds into pensions.

During the 1982–3 intensification of the one-child campaign increased numbers of rural homes for old people were often presented as an alternative source of security in old age for those without support from children. By December 1982 there were over 8800 rural homes for the old, housing a total of 160 000 people, and it was planned to expand these by 20 per cent by 1985.[14] Assuming that 5 per cent of the rural population are over 60, current provision of homes for the old covers at most 0.3 per cent of the age-group – a level of provision which can hardly be expected to supply a very significant or visible alternative to the traditional pattern of reliance on adult children. More importantly, throughout the post-1949 era, these homes have been viewed by the rural elderly as solutions of last resort.[15] They provide only a minimal standard of living and require elderly residents to move in Permanently, thus taking them away from their own villages, and making the fulfilment of the Chinese wish to die at home impossible. As a result, efforts to publicise homes for the old as alternatives to family care, may intensify rather than reduce fears of impoverishment among parents of 'singletons' and thus jeopardise the campaign to encourage willing acceptance of the one-child family.

Levels of resistance and resentment are not uniformly high among all parents of one child. Parents of only daughters are less likely to comply than are those of only sons. As a summary of traditional practices suggested, it is against the preference for male offspring that the one-child campaign must fight its hardest battles. The most immediate reason why rural parents strongly prefer sons is economic.

The earnings of rural women are generally only 50–70 per cent of those of their male counterparts. They are assigned lower-paid jobs and bear heavier responsibility for unpaid housework which reduces the number of hours they can work in the paid labour force. Sons therefore can provide a higher level of support. Second, sons are also in a better position to aid their own parents because contemporary rural marriage practices favour stronger ties between parents and married sons than between parents and married daughters. Through rural China most marriages are arranged by the parents of the bride and groom, and the parents of the groom are required to pay a large bride-price. Many rural women now exercise veto power over their parents' choice, but the basic pattern of the groom's parents purchasing a daughter-in-law for their sons persists. Furthermore, in many villages, parents observe the principle of surname exogamy for brides which frequently means that the bride must come from another village. As a result the marriage of a daughter drastically reduces the opportunity for close parent–daughter ties and encourages almost all elderly parents to depend on their sons.

And finally, the preference for boys is religious. Ancestor worship has been a central rite of Chinese family life for thousands of years. In this tradition a daughter has only a marginal role, and a woman in general participates in family ceremonies as the mother of her husband's son or as the daughter-in-law of her husband's parents. Only males carry on the family line and can make the offerings that link the generations. Since 1949, the CCP has taken a firm stand against all religious organisations and has consistently tried to propagate an atheistic world view. However, except in the early years of the Cultural Revolution when youthful Red Guards entered homes to destroy family altars and ancestor tablets, the government attack on family observances in rural areas has been rather perfunctory.[16] Consequently, the importance of patrilineal descendants continues to affect thinking about ideal family size and composition, and most rural parents want at least one son to perform the rites of ancestor worship.

In the light of these several constraints on parent–daughter solidarity in adulthood, it is quite logical that rural parents whose first-born is a girl do not willingly accept the government's ideal of the one-child family. For rural parents to accept one daughter as satisfactory protection against the vicissitudes of old age, they would also need to believe that within thirty years all villagers would have pensions, and/or that daughters would be as economically powerful and residentially stable as sons. Only if these conditions were met would rural parents of a single daughter feel equal to those with a single son.

To date, government efforts either to create stronger collective welfare services or to reduce the ancient traditions of patrilocal residence and female inequality have been less than successful. Thus as young rural couples of child-bearing age survey their villages (which are the only context in which they can make meaningful judgements) they see that the families which are doing best are large ones with several grown sons and that those who are doing poorly are small and without strong male breadwinners. They see their older siblings and cousins with two or three children and they know they are not suffering from the financial responsibilities of raising several children. Under these circumstances, young couples rarely willingly accept their quota of one child, and particularly if their firstborn is a girl, they feel they are being forced to accept forty years of 'second-best'.

OLD AGE SECURITY IN URBAN CHINA

In urban China, elderly parents are far less dependent financially on their adult children than in rural areas. The 1951 Labour Insurance Regulations that provide pensions to workers in the state sector have been revised four times – in 1953, 1958, 1964 and 1978. Each revision increased the percentage of the urban labour force that became eligible, improved benefits, and reduced the number of years necessary to qualify for a minimum pension. At present women at the age of 50 and men at the age of 60 qualify for a pension amounting to 75 per cent of their last wage.[17] Those with less than twenty years employment are entitled to a smaller percentage of the last wage. But even those with only ten years' experience still get 60 per cent and in no case does the pension fall below 20 *yuan* per month – a sum that in 1982 equalled almost 30 per cent of the average wage of those in the state sector.[18] For those who have been model workers, or who participated in 'revolutionary work' before 1949, it is possible to have pensions that replace 80, 90 and even 100 per cent of last wages, and high level government officers retire with pensions that *exceed* their last wage by 5–10 per cent. In addition, all retired people continue to receive free medical care and benefit from the general food subsidies. If they lived in enterprise housing prior to retirement, they keep on their low-cost apartment.

These most recent terms of retirement are indeed very generous. For urban couples of child-bearing age therefore, the government statement that children are no longer necessary for financial security in old age is logical and credible. Furthermore, many of these young urban parents already have mothers and fathers whose pensions make them financially independent of adult children and in some cases prolong their ecomonic control over the younger generation.[19]

The high cost of child-rearing in the cities further encourages urban couples to support the ideal of a one-child family. In 1979, the government estimated that it cost 6900 *yuan* to raise a child to the age of 16 in the cities, and only 1600 *yuan* in the countryside.[20] Much of that difference can be attributed to the higher expenditures by the central government for urban health care and schools, but there are also substantial differences in the direct costs to parents.[21] Urban parents spend more than rural parents on their children's housing, food, clothing, and recreation. Moreover, unlike rural children who become economically active by the age of 10, urban children remain dependent consumers until their late teens.

A final incentive for small families in the cities is a critical housing shortage which inclines many young couples to perceive the government's one-child family ideal as coinciding with their own interests. Nevertheless, despite the obvious advantages of the policy for urban parents, the government has had to invoke tough negative sanctions in urban as well as rural areas. Moreover many urban couples still chafe under the restriction to limit themselves to one child and hope that the policy will relax before their child-bearing years are complete. The two most common reservations among urban parents are, first, a fear that a single child will be spoiled and, second, an unwillingness to accept a female singleton. Behind both these concerns remains the still more fundamental fear of a difficult and lonely old age for parents of an only child.

Since 1949, the Chinese government has consistently held families responsible for their dependent or disabled elderly members. In the cities only those without any adult children or grandchildren are eligible for government aid, and in some cases siblings, nieces and nephews are also required to provide support. As a result, by 1980 there were only 600 old-age homes in urban areas and all of these homes were restricted to the childless elderly.[22] Nursing homes or convalescent homes are even more rare and consequently adult children remain an essential part of every urban parent's long-term strategy for coping with the frailty of advanced old age.

In urban families with several children, responsibility for nursing care and household help for elderly parents falls hardest on those children with whom the parent or parents live. But siblings who do not share the home usually make financial contributions, spend their days-off visiting, and in some cases care is shared by moving the parent from one house to another. Aware that their relationship with one grown child may be better than with another, or that one child may be more able to assume the responsibility for care than another, urban parents instil a strong sense of obligation in all their children in order to reduce the risk of poor treatment by any one child. Parents with an only child therefore feel that they are not spreading their risk sufficiently. They worry that the child may predecease them or may when grown turn out to be a poor provider. They are also concerned about their only child's marriage, its financial implications and its effects on their relationship. What, for example, will happen if their child marries someone who also has total responsibility for two elderly parents? Will it be possible to ask for help if their child is already supporting two in-laws? It is considerations such as these that make urban parents (who in the short-term enjoy many advantages in restricting family size and find even second children a noticeable financial drain) anxious about the long-term wisdom of their decision. In addition, urban parents, like their rural counterparts, have a strong preference for boys that makes it difficult to accept an only daughter as willingly as an only son. As in the countryside, the preference has an economic rationale. Although many young urban men and women earn approximately the same monthly income when first employed, over their entire career men are more likely to be promoted to positions of economic and political influence than are women. Sons therefore offer parents more resources and are in a better position than daughters to help family members.

Although the preference for patrilocal residence is by no means as rigid in the cities as it is in the countryside and there is nothing comparable to the practice of village exogamy, urban parents are consistently less likely to live with daughters than with sons.[23] Fully aware that women earn less than men and fearful that daughters will join the household of their husband's parents, young urban couples still perceive daughters as a notably less secure source of support in old age than sons, and thus they only reluctantly accept the norm of the one-child family.

FUTURE PROSPECTS

In response to widespread fears about old-age security among parents of only children, the Chinese government has tried to integrate programmes for the elderly into its campaign for the one-child family. Party leaders have made public promises to expand pension benefits, guarantee current levels of aid for the childless elderly, and weaken traditional preferences for boys.[24] In the short term, these efforts have failed to convince many parents of only children that they can 'afford' to accept the one-child certificate. This has especially been the case in rural areas. For the year ending December 1981, 40 per cent of rural births were third or fourth children, and at the sixth session of the Fifth People's Congress in June 1983, Dr. Qian Xinzhong, head of the National Family Planning Commission, announced that the incidence of higher-order births in the countryside had reached critical proportions.[25] Thus five years into their twenty-year effort to guarantee the one-child norm, Chinese officials are well aware that they have failed to placate fears about old-age security and they are worried about their long-term prospects for success.

On the other hand, it is possible that the first ten years of the campaign will be the hardest. In another five years, the generation entering first marriages will have matured with the expectation that they will have only one child. Furthermore, it is possible that methods of contraception will have so improved within this period that abortion will no longer be such a common form of birth control and government officials will therefore assume a less coercive and punitive position *vis-à-vis* child-bearing women and their husbands. When primary schools are filled with only children, fears about a generation of maladjusted, selfish brats may dissipate in the face of the children's actual performance. If small families of three do indeed enjoy noticeably higher standards of living, the government's requirement that the generation born between 1954 and 1974 sacrifice for the good of the nation may seem less onerous. Perhaps even the intense preference for sons will fade as parents, grandparents, aunts and uncles invest in a particular girl-child and derive satisfaction from her growth and achievements.

Greater willingness to accept an only child (and particularly an only girl) within individual families, over the next five to ten years, however, is unlikely to create a new societal norm about ideal family size and composition. For there to be a fundamental shift of expectations, parents need to see concrete improvements in the position of childless elderly and elderly with only one daughter. They also need to be convinced that a one-child family can be as economically secure as one with several children. To achieve the first condition there will have to be significant increases in the social welfare budgets. To achieve the second condition, the government will have to break the belief in the link between large family size and high income. But during the first five years of the one-child campaign, there has been little convincing evidence of substantive change in either of these two areas. On the contrary, shifts in government policy between 1980 and 1983 moved in a diametrically different direction, decreasing social welfare expenditure, increasing the role for family in welfare functions and creating new economic incentives for households with many labourers.

In the countryside, where the birth rates are highest and resistance to accepting a single girl is greatest, new economic and welfare policies have created the greatest dissonance. Between 1980 and 1983, the de-collectivisation of agriculture that made individual households the basic unit of production became virtually universal throughout China. Households with more labourers, and in particular those with several adolescent sons, outstripped all others, providing daily reminders to the one-child families that the new wave of rural prosperity might pass them by.

Cut-backs in welfare expenditure also undermine any long-term voluntary acceptance of the one-child norm. Between December 1981 and December 1982, the number or rural households receiving welfare payments decreased by one-third[26] and in the future the government hopes to reduce the dependency on collective rural welfare funds even further by promoting income-generating activity and by stronger exhortations to work hard and be frugal. Young rural couples, however, already practise the virtues of hard work and frugality, and despite days and weeks of unstinting labour they may still find themselves at a disadvantage in comparison with the larger households. Moreover they develop their expectations of ideal family size and make plans for their own old age on the basis of what they know exists within their own village rather than on the basis of government exhortation. As a result, the current requirement that they limit themselves to one child is simply seen as a demand that they accept the risks of a very difficult old age.

A similar failure to acknowledge the real fears of young parents about their old-age security is found in the 1982–3 phase of the one-child campaign. Thus in the Shanxi regulations published in November 1982, and in public pronouncements by the national leadership in 1983, there is no sustained effort to create new forms of old-age support.[27] Instead, government sources seem uniformly to place ever greater emphasis on the need for this generation of young parents to sacrifice their private desires to the public good, or else suffer harsh punishments. This unyielding position is particularly the case in rural areas where fears about old-age security are most valid and most acute.

In urban areas, the clearest sign of government cut-backs came in summer 1983, when the retirement law was revised to eliminate the right of *ding-ti* which since 1978 had guaranteed a state job in the same workplace as the parent to one child of each retiring employee.[28] In the light of the need to raise labour productivity and cut government losses in state enterprises, the government decided that this guarantee ran counter to financial rationality. Undoubtedly from the perspective of industrial managers who need to increase control over labour supply and reduce production costs this decision is rational. For parents of only children who had looked to the *ding-ti* provision as a guarantee that in old-age their only child would be a well-paid state worker living in the same neighbourhood as themselves the reform renews old fears about security in old-age.

Despite the physical crowding and the many incentives for small families, couples who are asked to limit themselves to one child either resist or only reluctantly comply. As this paper has shown, they resent the one-child campaign because children remain an essential form of old-age insurance and in the 1980s China is too poor a country to provide a public substitute. The situation, however, is not hopeless. For the first thirty years of communist leadership and socialist transformation, Chinese families took primary responsibility for their frail and dependent members.[29] Over this period the standard of living rose and families increased their use of social services. In response to the greater affluence and security of everyday life, many couples, both rural and urban reduced their fertility. This voluntary reduction in fertility in the 1960s and early 1970s provides the foundation for future reduction. To the extent that fears about dependency in old age are one critical factor in determination of ideal family size, all government efforts that display sincere commitment to the elderly will increase compliance with the one-child goal and all failures to address this underlying need will perpetuate high levels of resistance.

NOTES AND REFERENCES

1. *Women of China*, no. 8, 1962, translated in JPRS no. 16, 12 December 1962, 697. Jack Chen, *A Year in Upper Felicity*, (London: Macmillan, 1973) and D. Davis-Friedmann, interviews in Hong Kong with twenty-seven former residents of China.
2. Li Caiying, 'Benefits of Having Only One Child', *Zhongguo nongminbao*, 2 May 1982. 'We Must Do Birth Planning Work Well', ibid, 4 January 1983 and 'Enjoy Young Girls', ibid, 11 February 1983. Liu Xing, 'Protecting Infant Girls', *Beijing Review* (BR), 31 January 1983. 'Eliminate the Thought of Preferring Boys Over Girls', *RMRB*, 7 April 1983 and Mei Hongjuan, 'The Case of Killing One's Own Baby Daughter', *Shehui*, Februaury 1983.
3. 'Some Regulations of Shanxi Provincial People's Government on Planned Parenthood', 17 November 1982, translated in *Survey of World Broadcasts (SW8)* 16 December 1982, B11/3–9.
4. Yan Keqing, 'Problems and Prospects in Population Planning', *China Reconstructs*, June 1983. Deborah Davis-Friedmann, *Long Lives: Chinese Elderly and the Communist Revolution* (Harvard: Harvard University Press 1983).
5. 'China's Marriage Law', *B R*, 10 March 1981.
6. Judith Bannister and Samuel Preston, 'Mortality in China', *Population and Development Review*, March 1981, 'Beijing Residents Enjoy a Longer Life', *BR*, 9 September 1979, 'Facts and Figures', *BR*, 17 August 1981, 'For the Healthy Growth of China's 300 million Children', *BR*, 3 May 1982 and Wang Weizhi, 'A Preliminary Analysis of the Age Structure of China's Population Since Liberation', *Renkou Yanjiu*, no. 4, 1981.
7. Hao Hongshen, 'A Comparative Analysis of the Child-bearing of Women of Different Generations in Yanqing County, Beijing', *Renkou Yanjiu*, no. 2, 1983.
8. Deborah Davis-Friedmann, 'Essential Services in Rural China', in Richard Lonsdale (ed.) *Essential Services in Rural Areas*, (Westview Pess, 1984).
9. Ren Tao, 'Population and Employment', *BR*, 28 March 1983.
10. Yan Keqing, 'Problems and Prospects in Population Planning'.
11. Lillian Liu, 'Mandatory Retirement and Other Reforms Pose New Challenges for Chinese Government', *Aging and Work*, no. 6, 1982.
12. 'Peasants Enjoy Pensions', *BR*, 4 October 1982.
13. Davis-Friedmann, 'Essential Services'.
14. 'Nationally there are Over 8800 Old-age Homes', *RMRB*, 10 December 1982.
15. Deborah Davis-Friedmann, 'Welfare Practices in Rural China', *World Development*, No. 6: 609–619 and *Long Lives*.
16. Deborah Davis-Friedmann, *Long Lives*,
17. *Finance Regulations for those working in State and Central Units* (Beijing: Finance Ministry, 1979). Davis-Friedmann, *Long Lives*; 'Essential Services'; and 'Chinese Retirement: Policy and Practice' in Zena Blau (ed.) *Current Perspectives on Aging and the Life Struggle* (Greenwich, Connecticut: JA1 Press, 1984).
18. In 1982, the average wage in the urban state sector was 66 yuan per month. *Fujian Ribao*, 26 September 1983, translated in *Foreign Broadcast Information Service*, 4 October 1983.
19. Davis-Friedmann, *Long Lives*,
20. Chen Muhua, 'To Realise the Four Modernisations it is Necessary to Control Population Growth', *RMRB*, 11 August 1979.
21. Davis-Friedmann, 'Chinese Retirement.
22. Lillian Liu, 'Mandatory Retirement'.
23. Davis-Friedmann, *Long Lives*.
24. Zhao Ziyang, 'Report on Sixth Five-year Plan', *BR*, 20 December 1982. Liu Xing, 'Protecting Infant Girls', *BR*, 31 January 1983.'Peasants Enjoy Pensions', *BR*, 4 October 1984. 'Rural Elderly', *BR*, 29 November 1982. Chen Si-ya, 'Five-

guarantee Elderly in the Capital Agree Socialism is Good', *Jiankang Bao*, 12 December 1982.

25. Yan Keqing, 'Problems and Prospects in Population Planning', and 'Severely Restrict Second Births', *RMRB*, 15 June 1983.

26. Joint Circular from the State Economic Committee, Ministry of Civil Affairs, Ministry of Finance, Agricultural Bank of China and eight other central ministries, 18 December 1982, *Xinhua News*, translated in *SWB*, 31 December 1982, B11/5.

27. *Shanxi planned parenthood regulations*; Yan Keqing, 'Problems and Prospects' and 'Severely Restrict Second Births', *RMRB*, 15 June 1983.

28. 'Sincerely Rectify the Work on Employing Sons and Daughters', *RMRB*, 9 September 1983.

29. Davis-Friedmann, *Long Lives*, and 'Essential Services'.

7 The State and Fertility Motivation in Singapore and China

JANET W. SALAFF

Unprecedentedly rapid population growth rates in developing nations threaten to derail programmes to industrialise. The first industial nations had developed in the absence of massive public health measures. Death rates were high and the great cities did not reproduce themselves. In contrast, today the new nations have sewage systems, clean water, improved transportation systems to move food and end famines quickly, and prophylactic drugs to head off major epidemic diseases. These environmental sanitation and public health measures reduce death rates in the developing nations below those of the now industrialised nations in an earlier era.[1] Families in the early stages of development view children as productive assets. In agrarian and early industrial settings the household exercises autonomy and control over its labour. In labour-intensive agricultural settings small children can play a productive role.[2] Even in newly-industrialising cities the lack of a 'living wage' for adults requires family members to combine their incomes.[3] In both settings youngsters provide help around the home and will later give support to their elders.

In developing nations today wage-earners rarely earn enough to support their households without contributions from their offspring. Yet without prior fertility reduction, it is difficult for states to raise capital for industry or social services to replace what the household provides for its members. Several states seek to resolve this dilemma through the public sector, manipulating basic social services to provide incentives to induce families to lower their size. They forge new social institutions, a set of social norms, and a new way of thinking to promote small families.[4] The state is the only body with power and scope to attempt these ambitious projects. These states hope that these measures reduce population growth quickly, allowing the economy to pick up momentum. Families that have limited their size can then benefit from the expanded school system, new jobs for their children, and pensions for themselves.

This agenda requires family size to drop before the economy expands enough to give concrete benefits to the small family. The historically unprecedented measures to reduce family size taken by China and Singapore are the subjects of this chapter.

CHINESE POPULATION POLICY

China experienced a sharp dip in its crude death rate from 13.1 in 1955 to 9.6 per 1000 people in 1965, and to 6.9 in 1977. Great changes in the economy and society led to a drop in the crude birth rate from 39.0 per 1000 people in 1965 to 17.3 in 1977.[5] Population growth between 1955 and 1977 was hence rapid. China moreover fears a rise in the crude birth rate when the large cohorts born in the mid-1960s enter their reproductive years in the 1980s. China desires to reach zero population growth quickly and even a negative population growth has been discussed.[6] It expects that a reduced population growth rate will put less pressure on services and require a lower rate of economic growth to reach full employment and raise living standards.

A systematic effort to restructure social services to reduce fertility ensued. Starting in 1979 a series of stringent economic and political measures to encourage families to limit themselves to a single child was introduced.[7] In the rural areas, production brigades withdrew existing subsidies to large families such as the right of large needy households to buy grain and borrow money at low cost. In urban areas public housing is no longer offered first to large families. The new anti-natalist measures support rural one-child families by giving them priority access to scarce social services, such as health, education, pensions and old age homes, and cash bonuses. In the cities, employment, housing, and education are promised first to parents of one child. As all of these are in short supply, large families are thus left at a disadvantage.

Where the central and local governments control job placement and major capital investment, it is easier for them to follow through. At first rural one-child families were granted larger private plots. With the introduction of the responsibility systems, however, many villages contract out former team land to local households to till. These systems give rise to a major conflict in economic and population policies by enlarging families' perceived need for labour, especially that of strong sons.[8]

The state is forging a family that depends less on collective sources of income and more on the market. It may be wondered whether state officials were aware of the rural need for labour power under the responsibility systems. But it is also possible that some leaders believe that the new family form can be consistent with the new rural economic measures. For by calculating profits and losses parents are expected to see clearly the reasons for bearing small families. In such a calculation, the outcome will not always be anti-natalist, since households face a range of economic environments. In areas dependent on labour intensive units, families with more hands believe they can raise their living standards. They may decide to bear more children to do so. Or they may enter other arrangements, such as taking on or exchanging labour, or living in a complex household to enlarge the labour pool. In areas where the cash is available, earnings will be invested in agricultural machinery,[9] thus mechanisation may reduce the need for families to obtain more labour power. Families which are more fully involved in cash economies may be most open to the new family policies. They may be able to assess, as if on a ledger, the costs of bearing many children and find them excessive. A new state ideology promotes such analyses of family economic behaviour. Units hold study sessions to convince parents that large families will be costly to them and to the nation. They stress the deprivations that parents with several small children bring upon themselves and their offspring. Such an ideology attributes poverty to a family's excess fertility. This line of reasoning links poverty to high fertility.

A report on Dayi County, Sichuan province, describes the attempt to convince parents to reduce their family size to one child.[10] The study showed that while 20 per cent of the peasants fully supported a single-child norm, nearly as many actively opposed it. In public meetings cadres analysed the current incomes of families of different sizes to show that households with a high dependency ratio earned less than those with few children. Peasant parents were concerned as to whether households with numerous children would become prosperous ahead of others once the babies had grown up. They were reminded that although grown sons earn workpoints, their parents have to find them wives, send betrothal gifts and build and furnish housing for them, all of which requires a lot of money. The whole family has to save for a son's marriage, and for two or three sons, the expenditure is even greater. This argument only partly deals with the issue of household income and expenses, for parents expect the costs of the marriage of a son to be cancelled by the funds brought in when a daughter marries, and grown children's earnings are in fact needed for family survival.

Dayi cadres also argued that it was easier to improve the quality of their children in smaller families. They quoted the example of a particular commune member whose single daughter was well-cared for. People called her 'Little Darling'. When this child was five years old, a second one was born, and household chores increased. There was no time to look after the children. The elder child got lice, but no-one did anything about it. 'Little Darling' turned into a 'Louse Nest'. Such moral tales blame parents for bearing more children than they can devote time to in the rural household faced with numerous daily tasks.

In the past, village and working class parents balanced the losses they accrued in the early stages of the family cycle when they had many dependants, against later gains when their grown children earned income. They entered social exchanges with neighbours and kin, borrowed from the collective and postponed celebrations. They expected to repay these exchanges and make up for their frugality at a later stage. This cyclical model of the household economy is followed by the working poor in many nations.[11] Now parents are warned not to go into debt at the outset of their family cycle. They are urged to live within their means at all times. This line of reasoning which attributes poverty to the family's lack of foresight is common in developed nations, especially among the urban middle classes.[12] It is clearly a prescriptive model for the Chinese poor, rather than a description of how families live. Considerable changes in the family as an institution would be required to realise it.

The Chinese further argue that the single-child family is in the interests of the nation and the collective. The leadership stresses that the welfare and solidarity of rural production teams and urban work groups are threatened by families who do not comply. Thus the leadership relies on group control to bring pressure on reluctant families so that they do not jeopardise the material well-being of the rest. Such social pressures and even coercion play a major role in the short-term implementation of the restrictive single child-policy in China.[13]

It is not yet possible to assess the effects of the single-child incentives and disincentives in China. Families in better-off units may respond more positively than those in below-average settings. The leadership in rural regions does not everywhere comply with the state policies, and some accept a two-child family. Only a series of detailed case-studies from a wide range of areas can help us learn how people respond to the policy and these are not yet available. We can, however, look to a South-east Asian state which has strong links with China and also has strong state intervention to reduce fertility.

SINGAPORE'S POPULATION POLICY

The Singapore government aims towards zero population growth to ease the shift from labour- to capital-intensive production, a key developmental goal. The crude birth rate in Singapore was a high 40 per 1000 population before 1960. By 1969 the crude birth rate had dropped to 21.8. But the large post-World War Two cohorts entering their reproductive years raised the crude birth rate again to 22.3 in 1970, and a further rise was feared in the 1980s.[14] In 1973, while recognising that its development programme had already lowered the crude birth rate, the government passed a series of measures further to reduce family size to two children and speed the decline in population growth.

The Singapore government has set a goal of a two-child family as a social norm and in 1969–70 it introduced a series of disincentives which actively discourage larger families by means of social and economic penalties. These measures, known as the 'social disincentives against higher order births', withdrew eased access to key social services such as public housing for large, needy families, which had been based on social assistance guidelines. The disincentives make it more costly or difficult for parents whose births exceed the two-child norm to obtain quality education, maternity care and benefits, and income tax deductions. There are also a number of financial incentives to encourage sterilisation.[15]

In the relatively free market economy of Singapore, the state cannot manipulate hiring and firing to penalise families which exceed the norms in the family planning policy. It cannot deny jobs to parents with many offspring. The government can use its leverage over the unions to penalise working women with large families. Multiparous women cannot obtain paid maternity leave. This is the sole direct labour force sanction that is used to enforce family planning goals. The ideological back-up to the measures stressed the importance to the nation of a low rate of population growth. The mass media promoted the idea that numerous children were inconsistent with an industrial way of life. A sense of crisis permeated these media presentations, in which large families and overpopulation were identified as a threat to the limited material resources of the city-state. Social services especially would suffer if population growth continued at a high rate. In the words of the Prime Minister, a system of disincentives is needed:

> so that the irresponsible, the social delinquents do not believe that all they have to do is to produce their children and the government then owes them and their children sufficient food, medicine, housing, education, and jobs. . . . Until the less educated themselves concentrate their limited resources on one or two to give their children the maximum chance to climb up the educational ladder, their children will always be at the bottom of the economic scale.[16]

The government does not rely on community pressure to implement these policies, but rather manipulates the costs and benefits of having children. In addition its new ideology contains a set of interrelated assumptions which link saving money and planning for the future with contraceptive use. This new model that links parents' family size to the their living standard blames poverty upon the inability to plan and justifies the economic class system.[17] The ideology gains credibility from the many middle-class families with only two children who are prosperous. Using them as an example, the state argues that family prosperity depends on each family taking responsibility for reducing its own size. This will enable them to afford higher quality education, health care and housing, and to devote more time to each child. Thus their children's lives will improve.

This ideology that explains the socially mobile family in terms of its small size is convincing to many urban Singaporeans, especially the affluent working- and middle-classes. However, there is an alternative explanation of the link between poverty and family size which is seldom publicly disclosed. Poor families need many members to promote their household economy. They exchange services and money, and many believe that a family with several children is better off than a small family. The following discussion shows why better-off families adhere to the state ideology which predicts that economic improvement will flow from foresight and self control, while poorer families insist that their poverty requires more children to make do.

The Data

This study draws upon case data on 100 young Chinese parents from a range of social classes studied from 1974 to 1976 (referred to as Phase 1). A panel of 45 of these couples was again studied in 1981 (Phase 2). The key distinction in the sample is between the poorest and ordinary working-class couples, or Group I, and the affluent working-class and middle-class, or Group II. Couples were ranked according to scores derived from their joint parental occupational status, and couples' income, educational attainment, and occupational status.[18]

Singapore parents in the sample based their decisions about family size on (i) the economic costs of raising children; (ii) the time women must spend with their children; (iii) pressures from kin; and (iv) state sanctions against higher order births.

'Intended family size' of the panel couples refers to the number of children they decided to have in Phase 1, taking into account the ages and sexes of the children they had borne, their expected economic situation and pressures of kin. Table 7.1 shows that the actual fertility of the panel in Phase 2 fell below their intentions in Phase 1. Not a single one of the parents followed up had borne more children than had been their intention in Phase 1. Many bore fewer, and nearly all said that they had completed their child-bearing.

Both Groups lowered their family size goals. Nevertheless, in Group I families with four children are more numerous than families with two. *Group II* parents increasingly stress the two-child family, their modal family size.

Economic Costs of Raising Children

Most Group I parents hold jobs without career ladders and want several children to aid the family economy. Those on family farms with their sons to labour beside them and their daughters to help in the home. Wage-earners without property are anxious to ensure themselves support in their old age. They expect further that their children will need to help each other look for work or exchange goods and services.[19] Structured extra-familial job-finding and training are not available to poorly-educated men when they enter the workforce and they look to close personal relationships for such help.

The short-term costs of raising children, providing their food, clothing, and housing, are the main obstacles to having larger

TABLE 7.1   *Intended and actual family sizes of panel couples: Singapore study*
(Percentages)

Number of children	Phase 1. – Intentions			Phase 2 – Actual size		
	Group I	Group II	Total	Group I	Group II	Total
2	7	18	11	32	47	38
3	43	65	51	29	47	36
4+	50	18	38	39	6	27
	—	—	—	—	—	—
Total*	100	101	100	100	100	101
Actual number	(28)	(17)	(45)	(28)	(17)	(45)
Average number of children	3.4	3.0	3.3	3.1	2.6	2.9

* Percentages may not total 100 because of rounding up.

families.[20] Longer-term educational costs of children rarely enter into child-bearing decisions. Children of both sexes can help their family and kin groups and couples are likely to continue to have children until they had both sons and daughters.[21] They frequently bear many children in the process.

An example is homemaker Ho Geok Hio, married to Kee Keng, a truck driver in the construction industry. They lived with Kee Keng's sister after marriage and got help with their daily chores. Then the Hos with two children rented a flat and soon had a third child, a boy like the first two. Geok Hio had always wanted a daughter, and her mother supported her ambition.

Geok Hio feels that her life is similar to that of women in the senior generation and although she lives apart from kin, she holds views in common with them. Geok Hio plans to educate the children in Chinese family tradition and according to ascribed sex roles as her elders had done. Her large family goal is clearly related to low educational standard for the children.

Sons should enter technical jobs, and a daughter should have some skills, too. Seamstress training is better than hairdresser training, because a woman will end up with kids and a family, and with her sewing skills she can work part time at home.

What are your expectations for your children in future years?

Her answer reveals a life intertwined with children. She expects the same will be true of her children in coming years.

> If my children have nice jobs with good salaries, they should contribute some money to us. As to whether they will live with us in the future, it's up to them. Of course, I'd like to live with my children. If my daughters-in-law are smart, they'll realise that it is much better with a mother-in-law around to help them. They can go out and leave the kids with me.

Since she pines for a girl, Geok Hio concedes that it would not be problematic to have another child, despite its lower entrance priority to a quality primary school under the disincentives.

> Of course, if the government had announced there would be no school at all for the fourth child, we wouldn't dare think of having a fourth. If the fourth child turns out to be a girl, she could be trained in certain skills without much schooling. But if that child is a son, how can he get on in the world without education?

She feels confined to her home with three youngsters in her care and no women from the wider family circle to help her. Without a network of close kin to reduce her child-care burdens, she claims she cannot follow a schedule. In Phase 1 she spoke of entering the factory, but in Phase 2 all she can manage is to do seaming as outwork. This, too, reinforces her desire for a large family size.

In Phase 1 Geok Hio described her family planning indecision as due to her desire for a daughter. In addition, because of her heavy homemaking tasks, she cannot take time out for a tubal ligation.

> I did not practise birth control until I was pregnant with my third son. Because of our child-care and financial problems, I tried to abort by eating a lot of green pineapples and drinking dark beer. (This folk prescription is said to cool the system and encourage spontaneous abortion.) But I had no success. I did this without telling my mother or mother-in-law who would have opposed an abortion. I then decided to have the third baby, and probably to ligate afterwards. In the end I never signed the ligation form because the third turned out to be a boy and because I could not find anyone to look after the two

children at home for me if I stayed extra days in the hospital. Also, you need a good long period of rest after coming home from such an operation, and that's impossible in my situation.

The interviewer asked, *'Do you know there's a new way of ligation? The operation takes only twenty minutes and all you need is a couple of days' rest at home. Would you consider such a ligation in the near future, or do you still plan to try once more to get a girl?'*

It's not worthwhile to have a ligation now after we paid $100 for the birth. If I wanted a ligation, I should have had it when giving birth to my third child, so I could save the delivery fee. Now I'd rather wait until our living condition improves and then try once more for a daughter, and avoid the childbirth charge as well.

Geok Hio's effort to negotiate for government health services is typical of the conditional approach of Group I parents who wish for large families. They prefer to ligate when they are already hospitalised and thus effect a money-saving bargain. Geok Hio with three sons was not, however, ready to limit her family:

It's nice to have children of both sexes. It's like picking up different things out of a bag. If you keep picking, you might eventually get what you want!

Because of the limited frame of reference imposed by their short-term cost consideration, Group I parents like these use gambling analogies to justify having another child.[22] They often chance the next child in the hope it will be of the desired sex. Kee Keng supports his wife's hope for a daughter, so long as they postpone it until he can afford to feed, clothe, and house another. Soon after the third birth, Kee Keng changed construction firms and received a raise. He then felt that if his work remained steady, he would be able to support four children.

After her third birth, Geok Hio started oral contraception, but turned to the rhythm method after suffering from the side effects of the pill. She soon became pregnant. In Phase 2 she reported:

I had not really intended to become pregnant. I was very happy it was at last a girl. This girl is a lucky prize!

Still she does not ligate, repeating that she lacks in-laws to help her run the house:

After a ligation you need to rest completely. Even during my confinement, I had to cook, wash, do the housework, and send the boys to school. How can I afford to ligate and lie in bed all day long? I have a friend who ligated and became very weak as a result. She has to go to the doctor's now and then. I have to run the whole show here. If I should fall sick, who is going to look after my kids?

Your husband can help, can't he?'

If I die from ligation, my poor kids will be very pitiful. I have no intention to have any more. If I'm 'caught' the next time, it will be an abortion for sure.

Geok Hio refers to lack of kin help as her reason for not ligating. Her world contains no complex set of ties to others that might broaden her views and provide alternatives to having children. Such a setting supports high fertility.

Nevertheless, the Ho family's plans reflect the socio-economic changes over the past decade. Geok Hio considered abortion at two points in her pregnancy history. She sees her family as 'small' in comparison with that of her parents, and spaced her fourth child. She has stopped far short of the biological maximum in response to the short-term costs of bearing children.

People who own family businesses which are inherited by sons also tend to have large families. The head of the three-generation Yeo family whose firm packages and sells charcoal briquets for open-burner cooking will have no pension. The firm does not keep modern business ledgers, and the household budget is merged with the enter-prise accounts. In Phase 1 our respondents Wee Leng and his wife Seong Chee, their three young daughters and an infant son lived in the two-room flat owned by the elder Yeos. Mother Yeo urged Seong Chee to bear a second son. To ensure the fifth child, on Seong Chee's fourth delivery in 1975, Mother Yeo placed her in a private maternity home with flexible visiting hours, instead of the Kandang Kerbau Maternity Hospital. The older woman feared that the Kandang Ker-bau government medical staff would put pressure on Seong Chee to ligate after the birth. The older woman hovered over Seong Chee's bed to forestall an operation.

Seong Chee became pregnant again between Phase I and Phase II and decided to have the baby at Kandang Kerbau Hospital and to ligate afterwards. Mother Yeo acquiesced, and Seong Chee ligated after her fifth child, another girl, was born. This case shows the great pressures the elders exert on fertility decisions where the family all participate in a family business and the extent to which they may resist disincentive measures. But their final decision to ligate on the fifth birth is an acknowledgement of the impact of the measures on their lives.

Other parents do not directly use their children's productive labour. But because poverty limits their options, they are enmeshed in mutual ties to survive and therefore desire large families. Beh Jin Wee, an unskilled labourer in Phase I was frequently out of work, and his wife Kit Poon, an electronics assemblist, had four children. Kit Poon revealed her impoverished childhood:

My mother lived a pitiful life after my father took a second wife. I believe she didn't have enough food to eat and may have starved to death. She died when I was 3 years old. I was adopted then by a widow with a 17-year-old son, who treated me as if I were her own daughter. Her son didn't have a regular job, and ran some kind of 'protection service'. I met my husband through him. But Stepbrother tried to prevent us from seeing each other. I insisted, and was sent away at age 16.

Kit Poon moved in with Jin Wee, became pregnant and they registered their marriage. They lived with Jin Wee's father. Until her fourth child was born, Kit Poon was a homemaker who spent much of her time with her friends and neighbours and her adopted mother. She had her babies at a young age when she did not expect to work. She had limited schooling and few work opportunities. Full-time employment became attractive to her only in the early 1970s after the birth of her fourth child by which time there was considerable demand for semi-skilled women workers. Kit Poon entered a factory and her work there affected her subsequent child-bearing, although she already had a large family.

I didn't practise birth control before giving birth to my fourth child. But since I breastfed my children, I didn't get pregnant very soon after each child. However, after giving birth to my fourth, I started taking pills because I was then working full-time at National Semiconductor and wasn't able to nurse the baby. I gave her to my stepmother to care for while I was on the job.

Shift work tends to upset routines and Kit Poon skipped several days of birth control pills:

> I got pregnant again by accident. Since I worked full-time and Stepmother was too old to look after another child for me, I decided to get rid of the fifth baby, and I had a ligation after the abortion.

By the time of the second set of interviews, Jin Wee had been imprisoned on a drugs charge, and after he was released he rarely came home. Kit Poon was compelled to take up a job as a bar hostess. Despite her own limited schooling, she now earns more than she did as an electronics worker and therefore no longer believes that her children need much education. Throughout these years Kit Poon's youngest daughter continued to be fostered out to the Stepmother, and Kit Poon often visits them.

Parents like these, who earn low wages, favour large families because they do not believe that they can provide any better education for two children than for four. They expect that these children will assist them later in times of need. Moreover, child-care arrangements like fostering among kin reduce the burden for such parents.[23] Indeed, Kit Poon ended her child-bearing only when Stepmother's care was no longer forthcoming for a newborn child. Nevertheless, Kit Poon is not totally fatalistic. She employs a wide variety of methods to ease her lot, including contraception, abortion, lengthy breastfeeding, ligation and fostering-out. But her difficult economic circumstances do not encourage long-term planning and she ceased child-bearing only after a large family.

The few working-class couples who, in Phase 1, intended to have a small family, were exceptional. They had relatively good jobs, higher than average schooling and strong marriage bonds. These factors helped them to assess the future costs of a medium or large family and limited the pro-natalist pressure from their kin. By Phase 2, however, these couples were joined by other two-child parents who originally wished for three children, and reduced their intended family size to two. All have at least one son and can meet family obligations to bear a male and support the household economy. The new possibilities of buying their own home and consumer goods are attractive and compete with a third baby. They focus on their current earning power. The future costs of improving their children's training or their higher education rarely enter their calculations.

In contrast, Group II parents were on career ladders from the outset.

They expect their wages to improve along with the expansion of the Singapore economy. They have wider social contacts and depend little on close kin or neighbours to obtain work. Their greater resources allow them to buy a home early on and they can also make long-term plans for their children's higher education. The women who work earn a good wage, while those who leave their jobs devote themselves to preparing their children to do well at school and in life.

An example is Yeo Sek Hong, a primary school teacher married to Kim Lwee, who was in Phase I, a low-paid factory worker, and at the time of Phase 2, a housewife. In phase I, the Yeos had one daughter, and Sek Hong explained that two children were enough. He could not budget for the higher education needed if there were more. Sek Hong identified his aim to improve the quality of his children in keeping with the needs of his family and the Republic.

When I was still in high school, I came to believe that a person should stay single if his income is not sufficient to support two people, and that a couple should not have any children until its income is sufficient. Then when children come along, you have to think about their proper upbringing. I often tell my wife that actually one child is enough, but I think we will probably have a second child.

'Suppose you were earning $2000 a month, how many children would you then like to have?' 'I'd still want two.' *'Why not more than two?'*

With more income, but not more children, I'd be able to give our children better quality care and upbringing. Besides, people should not only think about what they are able to afford, but we also should think about the conditions and situation of Singapore when we decide how many children we want.

The Yeos discuss their future plans with each other. Kim Lwee told us how their discussions help them plan for the future:

My husband tells me about his work, and I also confide in him, especially when I have a problem. We talk about the child, improvements to our house, and other things. Once you become an adult and raise a family, you especially have to think about its interests. You must plan every action carefully and think through all the possible consequences beforehand.

By Phase 2 Sek Hong was increasingly feeling the limitations of being a school teacher, compared with his school mates who chose business careers which gave them expanding economic opportunities. This feeling of relative disadvantage had confirmed his two-child resolve. A son was born in 1978, and the couple stated they would have no more children. Kim Lwee has not ligated, because she had heard of a friend who ligated but became pregnant afterwards. Nor does she take contraceptive pills, to which she claims an allergy. The couple use condoms effectively. Their two child family reflects their plans for the future and their commitment to improve the lives of their children.

The Time Women Devote to Children

Where families need to expand their earnings, it is not surprising that women find new uses for their time other than bearing an additional child. Three forms of women's labour compete with child-bearing – full-time wage labour, part-time wage labour and the unpaid care and training of their children to upgrade their place in the industrial order.

Large families and continuous full-time labour force participation are completely incompatible.[24] Since married women with children in Phase 1 had to earn enough to reimberse kin for their support, the women in the panel who worked continuously during their child-bearing years earned above-average female wages. By Phase 2, as the wages of the blue-collar working women with secure jobs rose further, they determined to remain in employment to improve their family livelihood. By Phase 2 they were receiving less support in child-rearing from kin. Fourteen Group I and II panel informants who had entered the labour force before marriage were still employed in Phase 1 when they had one or two children and remained at work through Phase 2. In Phase 1 three of these women intended to have a fourth child, however by Phase 2, they foresaw that a fourth child would entail unacceptable investments of time. All had lost convenient child-care arrangements when close relatives withdrew from former care-giving roles. Each bore one fewer child than originally intended for financial reasons. Thus, in both Groups, women who retained their solid jobs throughout marriage and motherhood had lower fertility than the sample as a whole. By Phase 2 these women workers had an average of 2.6 children and there were no large families among them.

A number of women joined the full-time workforce only after their children were of school age. Two had worked before marriage and had long planned to return to work. They kept their family size small and by Phase 2 had successfully realised their plan. Like these woman, the school teacher's wife, Yeo Kim Lwee left her low-paid factory job after Phase 1 to care for her newborn second child. She regrets having left work, bemoans her newly circumscribed role and hopes eventually to return to the labour force when both children reach primary school age. As a result, she will not have a third child:

> Two children are enough. I want to go out, and even watching kids is a burden. I'm glad that my mother-in-law now allows me and my husband to decide on our family size.

In contrast, a number of women with limited schooling had large families at a young age when they had few work opportunities. Full-time employment became attractive to them only in the years 1974–80. Their children were older and by then there was considerable demand in the Republic for unskilled assembly-line workers. Full-time employment meant they could not have additional children. Thus, Beh Kit Poon underwent an abortion and tubal ligation on her fifth pregnancy in order to remain in her factory job.

Part-time labour is the refuge of lower-class women who lack alternative wage-earning means, and in this study is not closely associated with small families. Many women left the labour force upon marriage or motherhood because they earned too little to make the necessary arrangements worthwhile. These women often set large family-size goals based on their limited future horizons. Several later took up part-time work. For example, Ho Geok Hio, mother of four, became a low-paid home seamstress in Phase 2. These Phase 1 women, who worked or seamed at home for very little money, had little to lose by bearing and rearing additional children. In a minority of cases, even part-time work was important enough to family income to persuade women in Group 1 to reduce their intended family size.

Better educated Group II parents emphasise training their children at home to improve their place in the competitive school system. Several women devote much time to rearing their children and improving their skills and a number of mothers had left wage work entirely by Phase 2 to devote themselves to this goal. This form of unpaid women's labour competes with having more children, since each child absorbs large amounts of time.[25]

Kin Influence on Childbearing Decisions

Since kin perform important economic and social support roles they can also exert influence on the number and timing of children of our respondents. 53 per cent of the panel couples reported such influence in their decision to contracept, abort, ligate or bear an additional child. In three-quarters of these families, kin exerted pressure in favour of more children. Class differences are marked. Table 7.2 shows the influence of kin on child-bearing decisions.

Because of their economic dependence upon their kin, fully 64 per cent of Group I parents reported kin influence over their child-bearing decisions. Young parents who are part of family enterprises, such as farms or stores, are most likely to heed their elder's desire for more offspring. Their marriages are contracted in the interests of the kin-group and to ensure that property is passed on, and child-bearing decisions accord with the wishes of the family group. An example is the three-generation family of Yeo Wee Long whose store packages and sells charcoal briquets for open-fire cooking. In Phase 1 the Yeos lived in a two-room flat owned by the senior generation. Mother Yeo desired two grandsons and her daughter-in-law Seong Chee gave birth to five children before Mother Yeo allowed her to ligate. In Phase 2 although the junior couple had moved to a separate flat purchased with the proceeds of the store the whole family continued to have a single budget. Understandably, Seong Chee shares her parents-in-law's view that more sons were needed.

Group I couples who are not part of such a close-knit economic group may still require support from kin and are thus influenced by kin in a wide range of matters, including fertility decisions. Structured extra-familial job-finding and training channels were less available to poorly-educated men when they entered the workforce and this paucity of institutional resources has continued for many. Moreover

TABLE 7.2   *Influence of kin over childbearing in panel families*
(number of couples)

	Influence	No influence
Group I	18*	10
Group II	6**	11

* Pro-natalist influence, 15 couples; anti-natalist influence, 3 couples.
** Pro-natalist influence, 4 couples; anti-natalist influence, 2 couples.

the limited education of Group I youths fitted them only for unskilled jobs without career mobility. Their limited education and experience had not exposed them to alternative influences and they were therefore more likely to accept traditional customs and concepts of the family system. Sharply segregated marital roles meant that Group I husbands and wives were less likely to share friends in common and they were thus more open to influence from the elder generation. Finally, when kin provide material help and especially when they live together or near by, they can exert greater pressure for more grandchildren.

Where no property was involved, the elders had often loosened their hold by the second set of interviews in Phase 2. Fewer of the young couples were living with their parents and the distance between kin reduced the amount of help offered. Moreover some Group I workers could for the first time command higher wages and steady work. In the absence of obligations to kin, and with greater prosperity, their original intentions of having another child were modified.

In all, 30 per cent of Group I panel couples decided upon their family size with no reference at all to the wishes of their kin. Pressures to follow the child-bearing norms of elders were weakest where the grandparents lacked the will, the resources or the energy to provide continuous material assistance to young parents. Couples are subject to the influence of two sets of parents who might have differing views of the importance of more grandchildren. The emotional links between some respondents and either set of parents will vary. Finally, by 1981 and Phase 2, after eight years of Singapore's new industrialisation policy, many elders themselves had become reconciled to fewer grandchildren so long as there was a son.

Couples are stronger in their resolve to disregard the wishes of kin when they most keenly feel the cost of a large family. They establish sufficient work independence to take into account the costs of raising children themselves. Wives who work throughout their marriage see in an additional birth an unacceptable investment of time, especially since many have lost convenient child-care helpers. Those couples who planned small families from the outset have strong marriage bonds and friends whom they share in common.

We see these factors in the case of San Man, an electronics assemblist. Her husband Far Ehr, was a van driver for a government health clinic at the time of Phase 1, and had risen by his own efforts to become a foreman in a transnational corporation plastics factory by the time of Phase 2. Far Ehr's father, had died when he was a child, and his mother, a factory worker, had him fostered by kin. Although old Mrs Lim wants her daughter-in-law, San Man, to bear a third child, the couple ignore her views. They are able to do this because they already have a son, and old Mrs Lim had not been able to help them much since they had moved out of her home. In any case, as he had been fostered out, Far Ehr's obligations and ties with his mother are weak. However this is an exceptional case.

In contrast, 65 per cent of Group II's couples decided at the outset upon their family size, independently of wider kin views, even though most of them in Phase I had resided or interacted closely with their kinfolk. They helped to care for their aging parents and even when the couples moved away from their family homes they continued to provide financial and practical support. Singapore is small in area and respondents frequently travel in private cars and taxis to visit their relatives. However, despite this contact between Group II partners and their parents, their enhanced socio-economic opportunities facilitate a degree of autonomy.

The relatively firm economic standing of Group II respondents reduced their need for the help of kin. The networks which they used for job-seeking contained secondary and even post-secondary school classmates from comfortably-off backgrounds. These people also broaden their employment opportunities by adult education in technical courses. Husbands and wives in this group often shared their leisure time with each other and friends outside the web of neighbours and kin. This strengthened their marriage bond and inclines them to plan for their future together which in itself weakens their links with kin. As a result, the majority of Group II panel couples made their family-size decisions apart from their wider kin circles.

A typical example of this group is Yeo Seok Hong, a primary school teacher and his wife Kim Lui, a factory worker in Phase 1. At that time the Yeos had one daughter and wanted another child. They lived with Seok Hong's mother, who was already looking after her daughter's child. She was therefore too busy to care for her son's child who had to be fostered by Kim Lui's mother in a nearby housing estate. The elder Mrs Yeo urged the couple to have three children, but as she did not provide any concrete help, the couple disregarded her. Their small-family decision and their conviction that it is their own business have been reinforced by their personal circumstances.

Earlier in their marriages more couples in Group II than in Group I enjoyed this sort of independence. However, the expansion of the

economy and downward extension of social services over the intervening period has conferred similar independence on Group I couples,
with predictable results for their fertility.

State Sanctions Against Higher Order Births

Singapore parents were urged to make their family-size decisions in
the context of the needs of the nation and the response of many of
those interviewed in Phase I indicated that many did so.[26] When asked
their opinions of the disincentives, 72 of the 100 couples in the initial
survey of Phase 1 approved without reservation and many of the
remainder expressed qualified approval.[27]

By the time of Phase 2, couples' reactions to the disincentives clearly
varied by their class standing. A few had not been affected by the
measures, while others were strongly influenced by them, even feeling
themselves to have been somewhat coerced. For the third segment, the
vast majority of the panel, the measures appeared to be among the
factors which had determined their family size. Each of these three sets
of responses will be discussed below.

Family-size Goals Set Without Regard to the Policies

Some young parents desired small or medium families and based their
reproductive decisions on their earning power and opportunities for
material betterment. These couples are upwardly mobile, relatively
well-educated and expect economic advancement. They claimed to
have taken little account of disincentives when deciding upon their
family size.

The upwardly mobile couple, Lim Far Ehr and his wife San Man,
denied that they had been influenced by the disincentives. Far Ehr
thought two children were sufficient.

*'Why? Has your preference anything to do with the government's
policy?'*

Very little. We have thought clearly about our own interests. There's
no use having too many children when you don't have the money to
bring them up properly. It's no good if you have to give them to other
people.

This couple believed that most others also set their family size without reference to the disincentives. *'Do you think the measures have an effect on other people?'* San Man replied:

> If people think straight they will limit the size of their family. Others just won't care. [As for the measure on school admissions] a woman I know said, 'I have nothing much to do at home. I can just as well take my child to another school further away than the one we'd like'. [As for the measures on higher accouchement fees with each parity] someone else I know gave away their second child for money to pay the medical fees. So, really, this measure won't seriously affect families who don't care.

Primary school teacher Yeo Seok Hong also firmly decided upon a two-child family:

> Yes I know those policies. They are made by the government to encourage people to stop at two children. I began hearing about family planning and birth control in 1960 when the government advised people to practice family planning. Like a missionary urging people to believe in God. But the policies issued in 1973 are written into the laws. This time the missionary is telling people that they must go further and become Christians.

'Do these policies have any effect on the number of children you would like to have?'

> I don't think so. To decide how many children we should have, we must first think about our own ability and then consider the conditions of our living environment, like population growth, inflation, and adequate living space.

'Do you think that these policies influence the decisions of your colleagues?'

> Most of my married colleagues on the school staff have stopped at two children. My opinion is that these policies may be more effective for people with a lower income, like working-class people. Actually, I think these policies are only 'negative'. The 'positive' method is education. Let all the parents know the situation we are in and they will understand that they should not have too many children. Let's

get rid of the old idea that 'many children is a blessing'. You see, my mother thinks that we should have three or four children. I have been trying to convince my mother that two are enough ane even that the filial piety of daughters is sometimes stronger than that of sons.

Coercion and Family Limitation

People whose family circumstances brought them under heavy pressure to bear sons felt strongly that the disincentives were coercive. An example of the overriding desire for sons is that of Yeo Seong Chee who bore five children before she accepted ligation. Her mother-in-law had insisted that she kept trying for sons and the entire family felt that the Singapore population policy was designed to force them to limit their family size against their wishes. They totally ignored state sanctions, but few couples found the policies so unacceptable, although other Group I families also referred to the government's family-planning policies as 'laws' that they had somehow to circumvent or manipulate.

The Disincentives as Added Support

The majority of our informants felt that existing material circumstances would have required them to limit their families, and the disincentives reinforced their decision. Some of them experienced conflicting desires about family size. Figuring among them are parents from insecure backgrounds who wish for larger families but settle for fewer children mainly because of economic costs, including those imposed by the disincentives. They seek in the measures support for decisions reached on economic grounds.

Truck driver Ho Kee Keng did not initially accept the government's family limitation policies because his wife Geok Hio wanted a daughter. When she was delivered of her third son, she refused to be ligated despite urging from the hospital staff. The couple were aware that their views did not accord with the government's policies, which they saw as a form of interference with their family plans. Because of their felt desire for a daughter, they were determined to go their own way and have a fourth child when they could support it.

Geok Hio told us that she became pregnant, 'by accident'. She then insisted that an abortion 'would be cruel' and carried her fourth child to term. Happily the infant was the girl she wanted and only then did she decide to limit her family size. Caught between Geok Hio's intent to try again for her daughter and the birth-control pressures on the family, Kee Keng mused gloomily:

> I have read in the newspapers about people starving to death because of the population explosion. So it's better not to have too many kids. But still, people always want children, and they probably will always have several of them.

'What do you think of the population disincentives then? Will they be effective?

> They are the government, we are the people. If they pass laws, they will carry out these laws, whether we like it or not, or we'll get fined. So, what else can we say about their family planning policies?

'Were you influenced by the government's family planning policies in setting your family size?'

> A little, but the main reasons we have limited our family size are the child-care problems and our low income.

The Hos, like other Group 1 couples, feel in the main that their material circumstances required them to limit their families, and see the government disincentives as, at most, reinforcement. They take responsibility for their family-size decisions, and even if they accede to state pressures, they take credit for having done the right thing.

A number of Group II couples see the measures as added support for their plans for the future. Thus, two Group II couples had tubal ligations after their second birth to improve the chance for their children to enter a reputed elementary school.

The study shows that most parents integrate the population control measures into family-life plans that are mainly determined by their economic position. State policies are effective where they seem appropriate to parents with skills and aspirations. State population policies have interacted with the economic costs of raising children, the time women must spend with their children, and reduced kin pressures to lower family-size goals for the more affluent and mobile parents. They have had far less influence on the poorer parents left behind.

POPULATION POLICIES – CHINA AND SINGAPORE

The Singapore social disincentive package can be compared with measures to support the single-child family policy in China since both manipulate the key social services. Both states developed their policies in response to a feared rise in the crude birth rate when the large cohorts born during earlier periods of high fertility would enter their reproductive years. China not only wished to reach zero population growth, but to do so within a short time and therefore introduced a more restrictive set of population measures. Singapore was willing to allow population growth to stabilise over a longer period, and thus accepted a more gradual decline.

Both states initially removed social welfare type subsidies to large and needy families. These were more extensive in China, and their removal, in a society with a low living standard, must have meant some hardship. In both nations the state controls the crucial services needed in daily life and this together with state hegemony over the civil service and party bureaucracy enables it to implement anti-natalist policies. But the two states differ in the extent of their control over manpower deployment and capital investment. In the 1970s China introduced a large range of small-family incentives but as China expands the role of the market in the economy, her power to enforce population measures may attenuate and reach the lower level of enforcement of Singapore.

Both nations stress the collective benefits of zero population growth. But China's productive system depends on organised small-group efforts, whereas that of Singapore does not. Hence China's population policies use the work group and the political group to bring social pressure and even coercive pressure to bear in the implementation of the restrictive single-child policies. In Singapore the policies are less restrictive, less stringency is therefore necessary, and in any case there are fewer opportunities to apply group pressure.

The ideology of development in both nations today stresses that families which wish to advance economically must control their fertility. It is expected that fertility limitation will lead to an improved standard of living; in contrast, too many children will leave families in poverty. Both states have developed a model of the household that attributes a family's social station to its culture or behaviour, and takes little account of the institutional structures in which the family economy operates.[28] In Singapore this correlation is only accepted by parents in better-off households. The determinants of Singapore family-size may also operate in China. Parents who feel that children will be very costly over a long period will rapidly reduce their family-size aspirations. Other parents who believe that these costs are short term and will be outweighed by later gains will react differently to the population policies. These families probably predominate in the poorer rural areas under the decentralised household production system.

Women's labour-force participation in urban wage-work has been difficult to combine with large families in China, but in rural areas women could combine mothering with remunerative work to a far greater extent. The new economic policies may substantially change this, although much more needs to be known about the effects of the new economic policies on family roles. One study has noted that as collectives are disbanded, some women work in greater isolation than before.[29] This isolation may increase the time taken to perform household tasks and in caring for children in rural China. Where wage-earning opportunities for women are greater as in the more developed areas, then it would profit women to reduce their family size.

It is hard to imagine grandparents – especially in rural areas in China – contenting themselves with a single female grandchild who can neither continue the family line nor support them in their old age. They must therefore bring strong pressure upon young couples to have at least one son. In Singapore also these pressures are very strong.

NOTES AND REFERENCES

1. Rene Dubois, *The Mirage of Health* (New York: Doubleday Anchors, 1961); Kingsley Davis, 'The Urbanisation of the Human Population', *Scientific American*, 213 (September 1965) 40–53.
2. M. Mamdani, *The Myth of Population Control* (New York: Monthly Review Press, 1972); H. Leibenstein, *Economic Backwardness and Economic Growth* (New York: Wiley, 1957) 147–75.
3. Jane Humphries, 'Class Struggle and the Persistence of the Working-class Family', *Cambridge Journal of Economics*, 1977, 1, 241–58.
4. Henry P. David, 'Incentives, Reproductive Behaviour, and Integrated Community Development in Asia', *Studies in Family Planning*, 13, no. 5, May 1982, 159–73.
5. Ansley J. Coale, 'Population Trends, Population Policy and Population Studies in China', *Population and Development Review*, 7, no. 1, March 1981, 85–97.
6. A number of scientific articles in the Chinese press of 1979 through 1981 describe results of population projections based on different assumptions

of birth and death rates, designed to arrive at a 'rational population plan'. See, for example, Zhuang Bingjin *et al.*, 'Projection of Population of Three Counties in Zhejiang Province', *Renkou Yanjiu* (Population Research) no. 3, 1981, 32–7. Zhuang *et al.*, propose an average 1.5 children per family which they project to a national population figure of 1.2b in 2020. Others expect universal adoption of the single-child family will lower the total population size below the current 1b people. See Charles H. D. Chen and Carl W. Tyler, 'Demographic Implications of Family Size Alternatives in the People's Republic of China', *The China Quarterly*, 89, March 1982, 65–73.

7. Pi-chao Chen, and A. Kols, 'Population and Birth Planning in the People's Republic of China', *Population Report*, no. 25, X, J–577–J–618; Pi-chao Chen, 'China's Birth Planning Program', in R. J. Lapham and R. A. Bulatao (eds) *Research on the Population of China: Proceedings of a Workshop* (Washington, DC: National Academy Press, 1981) 78–90; Victor Nee, 'Post- Mao Changes in a South China Production Brigade', *Bulletin of Concerned Asian Scholars*, 11, 1979, 51–63; The Population Research Office, Anhui University, 'A Survey of One-Child Families in Anhui Province, China', *Studies in Family Planning*, 13, 1982, 216–21.

8. Elisabeth J. Croll, 'Production Versus Reproduction: A Threat to China's Development Strategy', *World Development*, 11, no. 6, 1983, 467–81.

9. Cf. the county studied by Norma Diamond, 'Model Villages and Village Realities', *Modern China*, 9, no. 2, April, 1983, 163–81.

10. W. H. Wu, *et al.*, 'How Do Peasants View the Idea of a Married Couple Having Only One Child? – A Survey Done in Dayi County, Sichuan Province', *Renkou Yanjiu*, 4, 1981, 45–6.

11. Cf. Jane Humphries, 'Class Struggle'.

12. Geoffrey Hawthorne, *The Sociology of Fertility* (London: Collier-Macmillan, Ltd, 1970) 60–5; for an excellent analysis of the ideology of sexual restraint that developed amoung the late Victorians, see Peter Cominos, 'Late Victorian Respectability', *International Review of Social History*, 7, nos. 1 and 2, 1963, 18–48, 216–50.

13. Survey of World Broadcasts (*SWB*) May 29, 1980; (FE/6431/B11/11); *SWB*, January 29, 1982 (FE/6943/B11/8).

14. Ministry of Health, *Population and Trends* (Singapore: author, 1988) 11; Economic Statistics of Singapore, 1980, 43; Chen-tung Chang, *Fertility Transition in Singapore* (Singapore: Singapore University Press, 1974) 4, 20.

15. Peter S. J. Chen and James T. Fawcett (eds) *Public Policy and Population Change in Singapore* (New York: Population Council, 1979).

16. Lee Kuan Yew, Parliamentary Debates, Republic of Singapore, Official Report. First Session of the Second Parliament, 1969, vol. 29, col. 322, cited in George G. Thomson and T. E. Smith, 'Singapore: Family Planning in an Urban Environment'. Pp. 217–55 in T. E. Smith (ed.) *The Politics of Family Planning in the Third World* (London: Allen & Unwin, Ltd, 1973) cited at p. 249.

17. See William Ryan, *Blaming the Victim* (New York: Vintage, 1976); Cominos, 'Late Victorian Respectability'.

18. We contacted our sample when the wives were aged 20 to 30, with at least one child, through factory rosters and district maternal and child health clinics. Each Singapore mother is registered in the clinic that serves her district, and we drew respondents' names from clinic records in settlements from a range of social classes. Our study sample consists of a series of quotas for husbands' occupations to coincide roughly with the socio-economic structure of the populace as shown in the 1970 census. Husbands held farm, menial, average and above average working-class, white-collar, entrepreneurial and professional jobs. Phase 2 couples contained a similar mix of men from a range of occupations. In Phase 1 we oversampled working wives to obtain enough numbers for analysis: half the sample of women worked for wages outside the home full-time, and an additional number worked in their homes for a wage.

    The scoring procedure that we used to divide our couples into socio-economic status Groups I and II is more fully described in Janet W. Salaff, 'Marriage Relationships as a Resource: Singapore Chinese Families'. Pp. 159–94 in S. Greenblatt, A. Wilson, and D. Wilson (eds) *Social Interaction in Chinese Society* (New York: Praeger, 1982).

19. On exchanges between kin see Carol Stack, *All Our Kin*, (New York: Harper & Row, 1970).

20. We distinguish between the short- and long-term economic costs of children. Short-term costs refer to immediate costs of feeding, clothing and housing children. Historically, short-term costs increased in the West when family labour could not be productively employed on behalf of the household, and goods and services were purchased in the market in lieu of exchanging them between families. Peter H. Lindert, *Fertility and Scarcity in America* (Princeton: Princeton University Press, 1978).

21. Nancy E. Williamson, *Sons or Daughters* (Beverly Hills: Sage, 1976).

22. Lack of a long-term career ladder leads men to stress luck in their work lives, and they will often chance sexual relations without expecting a birth, or a birth hoping for a child of the right sex. Lee Rainwater, *Family Design: Marital Sexuality, Family Size and Contraception* (Chicago: Aldine, 1965); Janet Askham, *Fertility and Deprivation* (Cambridge: Cambridge University Press, 1975).

23. Ester N. Goody, 'Forms of Pro-Parenthood: The Sharing and Substitution of Parental Roles'. Pp. 311–45 in Jack Goody (ed.) *Kinship* (Harmondsworth: Penguin, 1971) – Goody shows how sharing the rights of parenthood by kin can influence family-size decisions; Elena Yu and William T. Liu, *Fertility and Kinship in the Philippines* (Notre Dame: Notre Dame Press, 1980) find fostering leads to high fertility in the Philippines.

24. Stanley Kupinsky (ed.) *The Fertility of Working Women: An International Synthesis of Research* (New York: Praeger, 1977). The evolution of increased opportunity costs in bearing children in the West is traced in Louise Tilly and Joan Scott, *Women, Work and the Family* (New York: Holt, Rinehart & Winston, 1978).

25. Judith Blake, 'Family Size and the Quality of Children', *Demography*, 18, no. 4, November 1981, 421–42.

26. We asked couples 'Do You Believe that Singapore is overpopulated?' If

one partner disagreed the couple was recorded as disagreeing; 'no opinion' means that neither partner had an opinion. The answers of the panel
respondents when met in Phase 1 are as follows (shown as percentages):

	Group I	Group II
Yes, overpopulated	64	76
No, not overpopulated	14	0
No opinion	21	24
	99* (28)	100 (17)

* percentages may not total 100% due to rounding in this and the following table.

27. Views of the disincentives as expressed by the panel couples in Phase 1 to
this question are as follows (also shown as percentages):

	Group I	Group II
Approve without reservation	29	59
Approve with reservation	50	24
Disapprove	14	18
No opinion	7	0
	100 (28)	101 (17)

28. Cf. Ryan, *Blaming the Victim.*
29. Mary Sheridan, 'Women of the Sties', to appear in Mary Sheridan and
Janet W. Salaff (eds) *Lives: Chinese Working Women* (Bloomington:
Indiana University Press, in press).

8 The Single-child Family in Beijing: A First-hand Report

ELISABETH CROLL*

Beijing the capital city of China located in the north-east of the country, is a municipality which covers an area of 16 000 square kilometres and includes not only the ten urban districts of the city proper, but also nine adjacent counties made up of a number of small satellite towns and large suburban communes. In 1978 the municipality's population was 8 490 000, or double its 1949 population of 4 140 000.[1] It is estimated that three-quarters of this rise can be accounted for by natural increase as distinct from migration[2] and that much of this natural increase occurred during the decades between 1953 and 1963 when the birth rate was rising fast and was higher than for China as a whole (see Table 8.1). After 1963 the birth rate showed a substantial decline which coincided with the more extensive and radical birth control campaigns.

By the end of the 1970s and the introduction of the single-child family policy, the birth rate had already dropped to a low 10–12 per cent, and a new birth pattern was in evidence, in which couples had two children in the first five or six years after marriage and thereafter practised birth control.

The average birth rate between 1950 and 1963 in Beijing was 36.5 per 1000 compared with an average of 14.09 per 1000 between 1971 and 1978. To examine what this lower birth rate meant in more

* The documentary research, the interviews in China and the writing of this paper were all made possible by a generous grant from The Leverhulme Trust. The author would particularly like to thank the All-China Women's Federation for inviting her to visit Beijing in the summer of 1983 and for the opportunities they provided for research and for interviews on the single-child family programme.

190

TABLE 8.1   *Birth rate in Beijing and in China as a whole 1949–78*

	Beijing			China		
Year	Birth Rate %	Death Rate %	Natural Growth %	Birth Rate %	Death Rate %	Natural Growth %
1949	19.40	11.90	7.50	36.00	20.00	16.00
1950	36.30	14.60	21.60	37.00	18.00	19.00
1954	40.87	8.60	32.30	38.00	13.20	24.80
1957	42.10	8.20	33.90	34.00	10.80	23.20
1963	43.41	8.10	35.30	43.60	10.10	33.50
1964	30.40	8.00	22.30	39.30	11.50	27.80
1967	18.16	5.03	13.03	34.10	8.40	25.70
1968	23.75	6.74	17.01	35.80	8.30	27.50
1969	22.36	7.37	14.99	34.30	8.10	26.20
1971	18.82	6.40	12.42	30.70	7.30	23.40
1976	9.06	6.53	2.53	20.01	7.29	12.72
1977	10.23	6.21	4.02	19.03	6.91	12.12
1978	12.92	6.12	6.80	18.34	6.29	12.00

SOURCE   Based on Personal Communication, State Family Planning Commission, 1983.

detailed terms of family size and birth patterns immediately prior to the introduction of the single-child family programme, a survey of more than 8000 women was carried out by the Beijing Municipal Family Planning Committee in a number of urban and rural communities in Beijing in December 1981.[3] The aim of the survey was to elicit information about women of all age-groups, and even allowing for any faults in the methodology, it reveals certain trends and patterns in more detail than previous collections of material. As Table 8.2 illustrates, the sharp decline in the birth rate in Beijing in the early 1960s was also reflected in the decrease in the average number of children born to each of the 8299 women surveyed.

The birth control policies of the 1960s based on later marriage, fewer and spaced children, not only affected the average number of children born per couple, but also effected a rise in the age of marriage, and the age at which the first birth occurred.

As Table 8.3 demonstrates, the average age at marriage has gradually risen except for the 51-year old age group which can be explained by the special conditions obtaining after 1949. The sharp rise in age at marriage for the 41-year old age group probably directly reflected the

TABLE 8.2   *Average number of children born to each woman*

Year of birth	Age of woman	Fertile years (rough estimate)	Beijing	Urban	Rural
1914	67 (800)*	1930s	5.10	4.52	5.66
1920	61 (1078)	1940s	5.17	4.50	5.95
1930	51 (2030)	1950s	4.59	3.89	5.80
1940	41 (2174)	1960s	2.91	2.33	3.75
1946	35 (2217)	1970s	2.13	1.59	2.58

* Figures in brackets refer to number of women surveyed in each age-group.

TABLE 8.3   *Average age at marriage and average age at first birth*

Age of Woman (1981)	Average age at Marriage			Average age at first Birth		
	Beijing	Urban	Rural	Beijing	Urban	Rural
69	19.57	20.28	18.18	22.37	22.79	21.98
61	19.78	20.94	18.45	22.64	23.68	21.50
51	19.65	20.44	18.28	22.30	22.88	21.30
41	22.17	23.12	20.84	23.96	24.86	22.66
35	23.36	24.61	22.37	24.78	26.06	23.76

results of the campaign to raise the age of marriage in the 1960s. However, although the age at marriage had risen, the age at first birth had not risen concomitantly, suggesting that the gap between marriage and childbirth had been gradually shortened (see Table 8.4).

What emerges from a study of the different age groups is that by the 1970s couples were marrying later, having their first child soon after marriage and the period of their child-bearing was much shorter with fewer births now taking place outside the age range of 20 to 30 years. Table 8.5 shows that the three age groups of 67-, 61- and 51-year olds had the longest periods of child-bearing and their birth rate for all fertile years was high. In comparison, the 41- and 35-year old age-group had a shorter child-bearing period concentrated between the ages of 20 and 29, which again suggested the pattern of one or two births followed by the long-term practice of contraception.

One of the most important background factors to any understanding

TABLE 8.4   *Gap between age at marriage and birth of first child* (in years)

Age group (1981)	Municipality	Urban	Rural
67	2.30	2.34	2.26
61	2.31	2.30	2.33
51	2.17	2.10	2.28
41	1.62	1.62	1.62
35	1.35	1.41	1.30

TABLE 8.5   *Child birth patterns by age of mother*

Age of mother at birth of each child ever born	Women of different age groups (in thousands) (1981)				
	67	61	51	41	35
Under 15	3.8	1.9	0.5	0.0	0.0
15–19	81.0	76.8	75.0	36.1	17.2
20–24	241.0	230.4	263.1	199.0	148.0
25–29	222.0	252.3	277.6	215.8	191.3
30–34	212.0	244.0	207.6	112.4	68.3
35–39	171.3	165.5	74.7	18.1	10.4
40–44	83.3	59.9	17.0	0.6	—
45–49	10.3	5.2	1.1	—	—
	5107.5	5172.5	4580.3	2910.3	2134.9

of the birth rate in Beijing is the higher concentration of cadres and intellectuals in this capital city than in almost any other single location in China with perhaps the possible exception of Shanghai. A high proportion of households will have members who have some form of post-primary or higher education and are employed in government enterprises, in the professions or in large factory complexes. For the municipality as a whole, studies of birth patterns show a closer relationship between educational level and number of children than any other single factor including income, both in the city and country, and among the younger age groups (see Table 8.6). The average number of children for the 35-year old age group with post-primary education lies between 1.0 and 2.2 children.

Interestingly even before the introduction of the single-child family policy, a proportion of child-bearing women had only one child. In the

TABLE 8.6   *Educational level and number of children per woman*

Educational level	Municipality	Average Urban	Rural	41 years (1981)	35 years (1981)
University	1.90	1.90	2.00	1.73	1.35
Upper middle school	1.95	1.91	2.67	2.04	1.48
Lower middle school	2.41	2.28	2.64	2.64	2.02
Primary school	3.28	3.30	3.26	3.23	2.55
Basic literary	4.46	4.40	4.52	3.72	2.70
Illiterate	5.22	4.74	5.50	4.12	3.01
Average	3.62	3.00	4.27		

TABLE 8.7   *Percentage of only children in different age groups*

Age of mother (1981)	One Child Total	Urban	Rural
67	6.05	8.24	3.93
61	4.75	6.79	2.49
51	3.00	3.88	1.50
41	7.22	11.53	1.46
35	19.32	38.07	4.44

older age groups the proportion of women with one child, approximately 5 per cent, probably reflects the survival rates of children and the high incidence of infant mortality rather than any single factor. However, in the 1960s when first, family-spacing, and later, two children, were encouraged and child mortality rates were low in Beijing, more than 10 per cent of women in the 41-year old age group had one child. At the time of the introduction of the single-child family policy, when the present 35 to 41 year group would have been at an age when most child-bearing might have been expected to have ceased, a substantial number had only had one child. (see Table 8.7).

This confirms previous first-hand observations and some survey data which have both given the impression that there was a significant trend among urban-educated cadres and intellectuals to limit their families to one child before the single-child family policy had even been thought of.

THE SINGLE-CHILD FAMILY POLICY

Although the substantial and overall decline in Beijing's birth rate between 1963 and 1978 was both recognised and applauded, by 1979 the municipal authorities were once again clearly expressing anxieties about both the projected future birth rate of Beijing and the effectiveness of the previous birth control campaigns. In February 1979 they began to question seriously and openly whether the lower birth rates in Beijing were not still too high, given the scale of population projections for the municipality. In 1978 a total of 15 per cent of births in the suburban and rural communes of the municipality were still of third (or more) children and newspaper reports suggested that the numbers of higher order births were due to two sets of reasons.[4] The first were to do with the traditional values attached to sons and maintaining the family line which still exerted a great deal of influence particularly on the family size of peasant couples, although the phenomenon of giving birth until a son appeared was not confined to the countryside and occurred even among Party members and cadres of the city. The second set of reasons was to do with perceptions of ideal family size and individual family plans which still failed to recognise and take into account the gravity of the national population problem and ignored the population projections of the future.

In Beijing, the high birth rate between 1950 and 1964 meant that by 1980 persons under thirty years of age accounted for 58.8 per cent of the municipality's population.[5] Already in 1977–8 the birth rate was beginning to rise again and it was expected to rise further over the next fifteen years as more and more young people reached marriage- and child-bearing-age (see Table 8.8).

With projections such as these, it was plainly going to be difficult to

TABLE 8.8   *Number of couples expected to be married 1977–84*

Year	Number of couples
1977	69 000
1978	88 000
1979	130 000
1980–84	900 000*

* (average = 225 000 per year)

SOURCE   Beijing Ribao, 9 September 1980.

keep Beijing's population below the 10m mark and to aim for the national target of a population growth rate of 5 per 1000. Even if birth rates could be maintained at present levels, the city's population would still register a net increase of approximately one million persons by the end of this century.

In 1979 Beijing municipality was one of the first to take up and implement the single-child family policy. By mid-1979 there were reports of couples pledging to have no more than one child, of women textile workers and People's Liberation Army cadres receiving their single-child family certificates.[6] In November 1979 Beijing municipality embarked on a family-planning campaign combining education and an experimental system of incentives and disincentives to persuade the population to reduce the number of third children and to increase the number of one-child families:

> A one-child one-family campaign aimed at the city dwellers and surburban peasants starts this month as has a system of incentives for peasants to have only one child.[7]

Beijing parents who undertook to have only one child were to receive an annual subsidy of 60 *yuan* and a certificate entitling their only child to preferential access to nurseries and kindergartens, priority in medical care and preferential entry to schools and in job allocation A one-child family was also to be entitled to additional housing space and private plots if the family lived in the countryside. Both the subsidy and the certificate were to be withdrawn should the couple later decide to have a second child. After her first birth, a certificated mother was to be allowed six months paid leave instead of the standard fifty-six days, but if she had a third birth although she was allowed fifty-six days unpaid leave, but she would have to return any pay received during the first maternity leave. As early as 16 August 1979 the municipal authorities in Beijing and Tianjin had published further penalties to be exercised against those ignoring the new family-planning policies, so that if a third child was born in a family the parents were to lose 10 per cent of their annual income until the child reached 14 years (a fourth child was to cost 15 per cent and a fifth child 20 per cent).[8] Families with two children were not to be penalised but neither were they to be rewarded.

At the time of this first campaign, the municipality anticipated that if every couple had no more than two children and 90 per cent of wage earners and 70 per cent of peasant families had only one child, then

Beijing's natural population growth would go down to about 5 per 1000 by 1985. To examine the early years of the implementation of this campaign and the initial response of city dwellers and suburban peasants in Beijing and its immediate environs, interviews with municipal and local level family-planning workers were undertaken in July 1983.

THE BEIJING MUNICIPAL FAMILY PLANNING COMMISSION

The Beijing Municipal Family Planning Commission is one of twenty-nine provincial and municipal commissions responsible for family planning for the largest areas of administration, either the province or the municipality and which are directly accountable to the State Family Planning Commission. In Beijing the Municipal Commission heads an elaborate structure for family planning encompassing the ten urban districts and nine rural counties and subdivided administratively as shown in Figure 8.1.

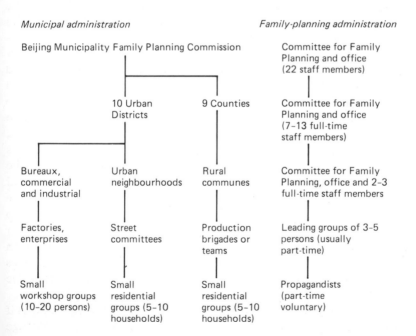

FIGURE 8.1   *Family planning in Beijing municipality*

The Beijing Family Planning Commission is headed by a committee made up of municipal leaders and officials together with representatives from its constituent urban districts and counties plus delegates from the family planning office of the municipality. The family planning commission has an administrative office staff of twenty-two full-time workers who are divided into three departments responsible for propaganda, planning and liaison work. The propaganda department is mainly concerned with presenting and popularising the single-child family policy among the population of Beijing. Its primary task is to publicise and acquaint the population with the reasons for introducing and implementing the policy and the single-child family regulations. At the end of 1982 a new set of regulations tightening the single-child family policy had been introduced which not only called for all workers, cadres and residents in both town and country to have only one child, but also clarified many of the conditions under which a second child was allowed.

In the city, a second child was permitted only if the first child had been born with a congenital defect, if either partner of a second marriage had not previously had a child or if a woman who had been diagnosed as sterile and had adopted a child then became pregnant. In the countryside around Beijing there were three additional exemptions to the single-child rule. A second pregnancy was to be permitted where both mother and father were themselves only children, where the husband had moved into his wife's household or where only one brother was fertile. Additionally, in scattered patches in five mountainous countries located at the extremities of the municipality where eking out a livelihood is still considered to be very difficult, two births per couple were to be permitted. No other second or higher order pregnancies were supposed to proceed to term and if they did so they were to be termed 'out-of-plan' births, and the parents were to be penalised. Offenders had then to meet all the maternity expenses themselves, no benefits were available to these mothers during maternity leave, both parents were to have 10 per cent of their monthly salary or annual income deducted for seven years (fourteen years for a third birth) and their bonuses were to be stopped for one year.

The planning department was responsible for keeping the records and compiling the statistics for family planning for the whole municipality and for setting the goals for each administrative level during the coming year. Table 8.9 which gives the figures it supplied for the previous four years shows that the birth rate had been rising steadily despite the introduction of the single-child family policy. This rise was

TABLE 8.9   *Birth rates and natural increase in Beijing, 1979–82*

Date	Number of births	Birth rate	Number of deaths	Death rate	Natural increase	Natural rate of increase
1979	118 006	13.66	51 140	5.92	66 866	7.74
1980	136 814	15.56	55 347	6.29	81 467	9.27
1981	151 225	16.92	53 809	6.02	97 416	10.90
1982	182 196	20.04	51 646	5.68	130 550	14.36

largely due to the expanded numbers of young people reaching marriageable age, for, as Table 8.10 shows, there had bee a dramatic decline in the number of second and third births per couple. By 1982 they represented just more than 10 per cent of all births (see Table 8.10).

The number of couples with one child who had taken out single-child family certificates had been over 80 per cent throughout the entire municipality since 1980. There is a marked contrast between the urban and rural acceptance rates for most of the four years, although the rise in the rural acceptance rate in 1982 may suggest that the gap will be progressively narrowed (see Table 8.11).

Family planning workers thought that the most difficult year in the implementation of the new policy had been between 1979 and 1980 when the population was suddenly asked to accept the new model of family size as one child, not two children. They also thought that two children, preferably a boy and a girl, remained the ideal of most young couples.

The planning department tabulated and analysed the figures for every administrative level within the municipality, but it was the liaison department which was mainly responsible for supervising the implementation of the single-child family policy in the districts, towns and suburbs and the commercial bureaux. It monitored their response to the policy and acted as a channel of communication to which local units could report their problems and generally ask for advice and help in implementing the policy. These might be on the technical side to do with contraceptive delivery or on the counselling side, resolving awkward individual cases which arose from time to time. One of the tasks of the liaison department is to act as an arbiter in deciding cases in which second births were allowed. The problem of remarriage seems to have been particularly complicated and has led to some difficulties

TABLE 8.10   *Numbers of first, second, third parity births in Beijing 1979–82*

	Average percentage of births			
	Municipality		Town	Country
	Number	Percentage	Percentage	Percentage
1979				
First births	74 697.8	63.30	74.65	55.15
Second births	33 041.7	28.00	24.48	30.52
Third births	10 266.5	8.70	0.90	14.32
Total	118 006.0	100.00	100.03	99.99
1980				
First births	102 336.9	74.8	87.47	62.21
Second births	30 235.9	22.1	11.38	32.27
Third births	4 241.2	3.1	0.16	5.87
Total	136 814.0	100.0	99.01	100.35
1981				
First births	130 909	86.57		
Second births	17 040	11.27		
Third births	3 276	2.16		
Total	151 225	100.00		
1982				
First births	159 258	87.4		
Second births	19 513	10.7		
Third births	3 425	1.9		
Total	182 196	100.00		

TABLE 8.11   *Percentage of certificated single-child families, Beijing*

Date	Municipality	Urban	Rural
1979	52.70	69.94	22.44
1980	83.44	92.73	64.99
1981	85.00	94.65	64.80
1982	86.23	98.41	74.18

in interpreting the regulations, especially in cases where one partner already has two children while the other partner has none and is determined that they should be permitted to have a child. How should family-planning workers respond in such a situation? Recently the liaison department has dealt with the case of a man who had been persecuted during the Cultural Revolution and had been separated from his wife and two children. He had now remarried and although he already had two children he was now granted permission to have another child. In another 'exceptional case', a couple whose boy aged 10 years had drowned was given permission for 'the sake of the mother's health and sanity of mind' even though there was a second child in the family. In yet another type of case, not unexceptional, which had been referred to the liaison department in recent months, a father of two children remarried and only after his marriage did his new wife learn of the existence of his children and that she herself was therefore not permitted to have any children.

To obtain a more detailed impression of how the policy is implemented at the lower administrative levels and the common problems which face those directly implementing the new policy in the local community, interviews were conducted with family planning workers in the residential lanes, factories and communes of Beijing and its environs.

THE URBAN NEIGHBOURHOOD

To obtain complementary data within one administrative segment of Beijing, interviews were conducted with family planning personnel at each administrative level in a direct line of responsibility, from the Western district and the West Chang'an neighbourhood to the Lianzi Street or Lane Committee (see Figure 8.2). The Western district itself has a population of 740 000, of whom 114 000 are women of child-bearing age. The committee responsible for family planning in its 250 000 households is made up of twenty-three persons who include both Party and government leaders of the district, representatives from its constituent neighbourhoods and medical and educational personnel. An office of eight persons supervises the implementation of the single-child family policy and, like the Municipal Family Planning Commission it is divided into departments responsible for propaganda, planning and liaison work.

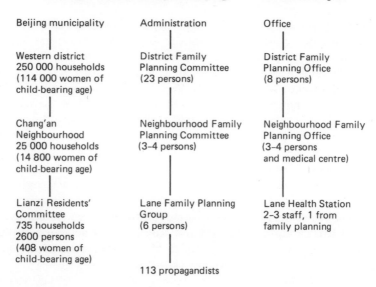

FIGURE 8.2   *The family planning organisation in the Western District*

In the district, 99.8 per cent or 96 800 of the 97 000 fertile married women used contraceptives and 59 000 had one child. Of these 58 667 or 99.1 per cent were certificated (see Table 8.12).

As in Beijing, the percentage of single-child family certificates issued rose sharply in 1980 and the single-child family certificate rate in the Western district has consistently been 1–2 per cent higher than the average for all the urban districts of the city proper. Again as for Beijing as a whole, the birth rate has risen despite the rise in number of single-child certificates issued and despite the decline in second and third order births (see table 8.13) Over the four years, third order births all of which are now out of plan have declined from a low 0.18 per cent to an even lower 0.01 per cent. In 1982 there had been 145 second births, about half of which (73), were in-the-plan births and the remaining 72 were out-of-plan. By the first half of 1983 a mere half of one per cent of births were second order births and only ten of these were out-of-plan.

Most of the out-of-plan births occurred in households where the first child was a daughter, although in some instances the parents of a son proceeded to have a second child in order to provide a sibling and some companionship for their first-born. The one out-of-plan third birth in 1982 was to a couple who had both been married before and were

TABLE 8.12   *Western district single-child family rates*

Date	Natural growth per 1000		Single-child family rate	
	Western district	Beijing	Western district	Beijing
1979	4.54	7.74	72.18	69.94
1980	7.31	9.27	94.10	92.73
1981	9.51	10.00	96.80	94.65
1982	12.76	14.36	99.10	98.41

TABLE 8.13   *Western district birth order of infants born 1979–82*

Date	First births	Second births	Third births
1979	77.68	22.14	0.18
1980	89.6	10.29	0.12
1981	98.2	1.77	0.05
1982*	98.91	1.08	0.01
1983 (first half)	99.45	0.55	

* Figures were also gained for 1982 for the South-western district which show that the Western district was not extremely successful. In 1982 there were 11 087 births, of which 11 035 (99.6 per cent) were first born, 12 (0.1 per cent) were second born in-the-plan, 30 (0.27 per cent) were second born out-of-plan, and one (0.03 per cent) was a third born.

determined to have a son of their own despite the fact that they each had a daughter from their previous marriage. A rough estimate of in-the-plan second births suggested that the majority, 50 per cent, occurred in second marriages, 40 per cent were allowed because of congenital defects in the first child and 10 per cent were to parents of a minority nationality still permitted to have more than one child.

Like the municipal family-planning workers, those at the district level thought that the most difficult phase of their work had occurred in the first year between 1979 and 1980 when couples who had begun to accept the two-child family were suddenly required to be content with one child. Interestingly a study of this first phase in the process of persuasion of the Fusuijing neighbourhood of the Western district was undertaken in July 1980 by an investigation team of family-planning workers from the Western district, the Beijing municipality and the Beijing College of Economics.[9] Early in 1979 the family-planning committee for the district first introduced the single-child family policy and thereafter they conducted an extensive campaign which began by:

> conducting demographic seminars and propaganda campaigns to educate the public, by meeting with each and every married couple who already had one child, by posting on street bulletin boards the names of those pledging to have no more than one child, by writing to their employers informing them of their decision and by sponsoring neighbourhood meetings to exchange experiences on the advantages of having one child.

By September 1979 before any incentives were offered, the proportion of those with one child who were prepared to limit themselves to that one child had risen from 19.03 per cent in 1978 to 53.12 per cent. By the end of that year, and shortly after the regulations, rewards and penalties were instituted, the number of one-child families certified rose to 67.47 per cent.

In early 1980, there were to be further campaigns to increase the percentage of single-child families, but first a study was organised to identify the reasons why more than 30 per cent of those with one child had not yet accepted or committed themselves to the policy. The reasons were found to be several: some women, their husbands and especially grandparents, wanted a second child, or more specifically a son, in the family. If the continuation of the family line was weak or insecure, the birth of an only daughter or even an only son caused anxiety and fears which were not easily placated. Misunderstandings about the aim of the policy and its implications for family size and the future abounded, hence the family-planning committee decided to educate and adopt a 'gentle approach' towards the reluctant rather than penalise them immediately. Thus in early 1980:

> the chairpersons of the various residents' associations, health workers and family planning promoters each went to work at an ideological level on a certain number of uncertified women in their neighbourhood. Long hours and setbacks were of no concern to them. They would hold heart-to-heart talks with these women to try to make them see the light. If it was their elders who refused to co-operate they would go to work on their elders. If the women had personal problems, they would come to their aid. For example, they helped place twenty-four children in day-care centres and provided

care for twenty-six old people. They also worked hand in hand with the women's work units in providing ideological guidance to uncommitted women and in finding solutions to their domestic problems.

Enlisting the co-operation of uncertificated families with one child proved to be quite a problem but as a result of this intensive campaign lasting six months, the number of women with one child born before 1980 who has signed the certificate by June 1980 had reached 3139 out of 3332, or 94.21 per cent. Of those 493 new mothers whose baby had been born in the first half of 1980, 396, or 80.32 per cent, had taken out the certificate by June, altogether the number of one-child families certificated by that date amounted to 3535 of the 3825 eligible, or 92.42 per cent. A study of those who were certificated show that the number of one-child families was higher among the older mothers of one child, families with sons, mothers with a higher education and cadres and intellectuals, than among workers. Of the women certificated, family-planning investigators estimated that 60 per cent of the certificated families had been happy to accept the limit of one child, 30 per cent had only taken out the certificate because of social and political pressures and 10 per cent were very reluctant but in the end after much persuasion had accepted the policy.

A similar investigation into the causes of refusal of 185 women who had not yet signed the certificate showed that the majority feared that their one child would be emotionally disadvantaged without siblings, or hoped for a son. Of these, 106 had daughters, and although only twelve specifically mentioned this as a reason, the investigators thought that it was one of the main causes for refusal. Many also mentioned that state policies were themselves unpredictable and might therefore again be subject to changes, and they thought that the five yuan subsidy was insignificant, certainly not enough to warrant signing away one's rights to have a second child. Interestingly, seven women were bargaining for better housing conditions or job prospects and had refused to sign the certificate until their demands were met (see Table 8.14).

The office workers of the Western district family planning committee interviewed two years later thought that if a couple were to persist in having an out-of-plan child there was little they could do to prevent the pregnancy proceeding to term, and that in these cases the penalties did not seem to be a deterrent since most of the offending couples had already calculated that they could afford to lose 10 per cent of their salaries over the next seven years.

TABLE 8.14   *Primary reasons for refusal to sign the single-child family certificate*

Primary Reason Given	Number	Percentage
Future change in policy	27	14.6
Wanted second child	79	42.7
Wanted boy	12	6.5
Fears for survival of child	21	11.4
Demanding better conditions	7	3.8
First child handicapped	22	11.9
Cases of remarriage	2	1.0
Not yet applied for certificate*	15	8.1
Total	185	100.0

* Most of these were women who worked away from home and who had not yet had time to apply locally for the certificate.

SOURCE   'One-child family becoming norm in Beijing West District' *Renkou Yanjiu* (Population Research), no. 1., January 1981, 29–34.

The West Chang'an neighbourhood is one of ten urban neighbourhoods which make up the Western district. It is made up of 25 000 households with a population of 90 000, of which 14 800 women are of child-bearing age. As in the district, there is a family-planning committee made up of the leaders of the urban neighbourhood, medical personnel and those concerned with propaganda and education, while an office of four persons supervises, guides and effects the implementation of the policy in the forty street or lane committees. It is these street or lane committees which are responsible for the actual implementation of the single-child family policy. Lianzi street committee is made up of 735 households and 2600 people, of which 408 are women of child-bearing age. A 'leading group' of six persons is responsible for family planning and these include the head and deputy-head of the street committee, a medical worker from the health centre, a member from the public security bureau, the head of the local women's organisation and a representative from the street committee office. Their main task is to investigate, study and encourage the implementation of family planning policies in their administrative area and identify difficulties and problems. Each member of the Committee heads a small sub-group made up of representatives of family-planning workers or propagandists and responsible for one hundred or so households. The main task of the family planning committees has been to present the case for limiting the population, to solicit support for the policy and to aid the propagandists who are personally responsible for promoting family planning within each household.

As in the city, the most difficult year for the Street Committee had been the first year between late 1979 and 1980. The new policy had been introduced initially among the cadres and family-planning workers of the neighbourhood and only afterwards among the neighbourhood residents. The new policy had then been carefully explained against the background of the national demographic projections and population problems at numerous meetings and additional meetings had been held for the elderly who had proved the most difficult to convince at the early meetings. Members of the family-planning committee had then personally visited each household to explain the policy, the new regulations and what they meant in practical terms. During the first year the incentives and disincentives had been introduced in the neighbourhood, and after this the family-planning workers reported that it had become easier to persuade couples to stop at one child. In 1983 the Lianzi street committee had a 100 per cent success rate in persuading parents to take out a single-child family certificate (see Table 8.15). This street committee was more successful than the urban neighbourhood as a whole where there were still ten out-of-plan births.

The propagandist interviewed was one of 113 propagandists responsible for achieving these results within the street committee. They were part-time voluntary workers who had been selected by the street residents' committee and trained by the local health centre. One of the

TABLE 8.15   *Single-child family rate in an urban neighbourhood*

Date	West district	West Chang'an urban neighbourhood	Lianzi street committee
1979	72.18	60.5	70
1980			
Jan–June	94.1	91.8	—
June–Dec.		95.5	—
1981			
Jan.–June	96.8	96.09	96.8
June–Dec.		97.15	98.42
1982	99.1	99.3	100

propagandists interviewed had attended two short training courses run by the local health centre each of which had lasted for a fortnight. The training had consisted of lectures on the policies of family planning and on the technical side of contraception and basic hygiene. She had also been taught how to present the policies to the households assigned to her, how to counsel both the women and other family members and what problems she was likely to encounter in her work as the immediate point of contact between the women in her care and the family planning administrative hierarchy.

Now that she was trained, one elderly and kindly woman, who was herself the mother of two children, was responsible for five courtyards concealed behind the grey walls of a single lane which contained twenty-two households with seventy persons. Of these only twelve were women of child-bearing age, and her main work among these twelve was to keep the records of their family plans, contraceptive use (see Table 8.16) and monthly cycles and generally maintain close contact with them. When a young woman from any of her households registered for marriage, she, as the propagandist, received a card from the neighbourhood office which detailed the woman's date of birth, date of marriage, occupation and residence, contraception and her place on the local birth plan or the date beyond which she was permitted to become pregnant. The card is thereafter kept in the Lane Health Station and kept up to date by the propagandist who periodically consults and updates it. The propagandist checks the regularity of the woman's monthly cycle, her contraception and for any signs of

TABLE 8.16   *Contraceptive use in Lianzi street committee*

Contraception	Number of women in lane	Number of women in one group
IUD	126	4
Sterilisation	55	1
Barrier	61	2
Pill	78	5
Others	9	
Pregnant	15	
Waiting to get pregnant	54	
Breastfeeding	10	
Total	408	12

pregnancy. Anything out of the ordinary will be reported to the health station. If a woman is pregnant with permission then the propagandist will keep an eye on her up to and after the birth, all the while preparing her to accept the new policy and sign the single-child family certificate.

Since this propagandist like most of her colleagues, resides so near to the women for whom she is responsible, she is in frequent informal doorstep contact with them, especially in the summer. Once a month she talks to them to check that their contraceptive measures are successful, that they are aware of the policy and regulations and to inform them of any new policy developments. Every three months or so she makes a more comprehensive check and investigation and files a report on the women assigned to her and on any problems she has in implementing the policy.

Of the group of twelve women in her care, four have two children, one has three children and the seven with one child are all in possession of single-child certificates. These latter seven are the 'target' women of her group and the ones over whom she keeps a more careful check. Soon after the introduction of the new single-child family policy she had had to work hard to persuade grandparents and parents that one child was sufficient and that a girl was as good as a boy. Among her seven single-child families, five had daughters so she thought her work had been much more difficult than that of many of her colleagues. Members of the older generation had often been very reluctant to receive her and were cold and indifferent to her and her cause. Only very gradually had she won their confidence and persuaded them to accept the policy. Although those with one child had successfully signed the certificate, she still took every opportunity in the courtyards in the evenings to point out that one child could fulfil all the purposes of having children and to cite examples where daughters were better than sons in looking after the elderly.

TWO FACTORIES

In the cities, large state factories and other institutions have their own family planning networks which are directly responsible to the Commercial Bureaux of the municipality or city (see Figure 8.1). The factory workshop, a place of work rather than residence, thus becomes the basis of a closely-monitored organisation which in the last four years has elicited a large measure of support for the single-child family policy among factory workers. The certification rates in the State factory complexes are of the same high order as the nearby urban neighbourhoods.

The Capital Iron and Steel Company

The Capital Iron and Steel Company is a large factory complex located between the Western Hills and the city of Beijing. It was founded more than fifty years ago, and in 1982 a workforce of 70 000 processed iron ore and produced iron and steel plates and tubes. More than 70 per cent of the labour force were male workers, and of the 20 000 women, all but the 2000 of them who were technical, management and health cadres, were workers in the various factories, workshops and mills which made up the company. Approximately 30 per cent of the work force were of child-bearing age (see Table 8.17). The family planning administrative network followed closely the structure of the company (see Figure 8.3).

TABLE 8.17   *Fertility status of Capital Iron and Steel labour force*

	Number	Percentage
Not yet married	13 833	20
Married and of child-bearing age	20 890	30
Over 40	34 571	50
Total	69 294	100

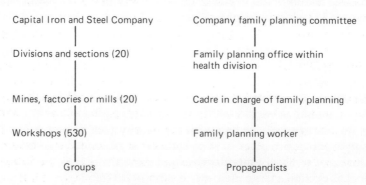

FIGURE 8.3   *Family planning structure of the Iron and Steel Company*

Family planning personnel also co-operated closely with Company cadres, the trade unions, and women workers' welfare committees for family planning and the single-child family programme was reckoned to be as important a priority as production in the company program- me. The large Capital Iron and Steel Factory was known as a model factory on the production side, and in family planning it had aimed for the same recognition. The single-child family programme had been introduced into the company in 1979, and four years later by 1983, a total of 23 387 (91.4 per cent) of the 25 582 workers with one child had received the single-child family certificate. To obtain further data on the implementation of the single-child family programme within the large factory complex, a family-planning office worker and a prop- agandist from one of its component factories were interviewed.

One plant in this factory had a woman cadre who supervised family planning in its seven constituent workshops, each of which also has its own family-planning worker. Within each workshop there were ten or so groups made up of ten to thirty persons. There were 75 groups in all, each the responsibility of a propagandist. Of the 1800 workers, 80 per cent were male so the groups were frequently mixed, and fifty-seven of the seventy-five propagandists in this factory were men. All the propagandists were married and had children. Most were in their late twenties or thirties and had one child, although a few had two or more children. The cadre responsible for family planning in the factory was herself 41 years old and had three children. After she had been chosen by the factory leaders and approved by the workers, she had been sent on a training course run by the company family planning office to study the single-child family policy and the regulations, and to learn how to persuade and counsel the workers to accept the policy. She in turn was responsible for training the seventy-five propagandists within her factory and in this way she passed on what she had learned.

The main tasks of the propagandists were to collect and organise materials to publicise and acquaint their groups with the family- planning policies, to keep their records, to supervise their contracep- tion and to establish friendly and relaxed relations with each member. The aim of the factory was to persuade every young couple to accept a certificate within a few days of the birth of their first child. In 1979, around 50 per cent of those with one child had signed a certificate, but within a year the percentage had reached the high nineties. There were very few second babies born either in or outside the plan (see Table 8.18).

The family-planning workers in this plant thought that they had

TABLE 8.18   *Births to workers in the factory plant, 1979–82*

Date	Total number of births	Number of first birth	Percentage of first birth	Number of second births
1979	100	98	97.90	2
1980	97	94	95.74	3
1981	166	164	98.25	2
1982	162	161	99.37	1

achieved a measure of success because the factory workers had a high level of political consciousness and could see the advantages of limiting family size to one child, both for themselves as parents and for the country. Apparently what particularly attracted them was the chance of enjoying a higher standard of living, the advantages they could now provide for their only child and their own opportunities to pursue further education, acquire new skills and give more time and energy to their work and studies. To further their appreciation of such opportunities, the factory leaders had encouraged this younger generation to compare their lives with those of the older generation and assume a direct connection between a high number of children, a lower standard of living and a lesser ability to acquire skills and further their education. The family-planning workers thought that it was the factory workers' own recognition of these advantages, rather than any system of incentives and disincentives which persuaded couples to sign the certificate. All those who did sign the certificate received the monthly subsidy of 5 *yuan* and paid 3 *yuan* less per month for a factory nursery place and lesser sums for other educational and medical facilities. Although it was a wealthy state factory with many fringe benefits for the workers, the rewards for a single-child family seemed low. Only a very few workers in the large factory complex had been penalised for out-of-plan second births in the past in that they were not eligible for nomination as model workers and were barred from promotion. Generally, though, the incentives and disincentives were thought to have become progressively less important as the policy was accepted throughout the company.

The majority of couples were now persuaded to sign the certificate within a few days of the first birth, but in 1982, ten of the 162 couples with new-born children had delayed signing the certificate. Most of these couples were reluctant because they thought an only child would have a lonely life especially in later years and old age. The family-planning workers thought that the birth of a daughter – a problem in the countryside – caused less concern in the factories or in the cities generally because urban parents frequently maintained closer ties with their daughter and indeed regarded girls as better caretakers in their old age. Moreover, most of the workers in this factory could look forward to a pension and therefore were more likely to be financially independent in their old age. Although the family-planning workers thought that the new socio-economic and political equality of woman had done much to reduce the belief in male superiority, it did however remain a problem. The company conducted some education on the equality of sons and daughters each year on the grounds that many of the parents of their workers were rural migrants or indeed were still resident in the villages and therefore exerted pressure on their sons and daughters to continue to try for a son. However, a newspaper report of April 1983 suggested that the problem of preference for sons may have been more substantial. It was a report of a legal case in which a 33-year old male worker from the Capital Iron and Steel Company had beaten his wife, maltreated his infant daughter and subsequently deserted and refused to maintain them, so furious was he at the birth of a daughter.[10]

Despite the reluctance of these ten couples, family-planning workers were able to persuade all of them to sign the certificate within two months of the birth of their first child. Thus, the factory as a whole was able to maintain its model status in both production and reproduction. According to family-planning workers, the implementation of the single-child family programme had become much easier during the past two years, but they did also add that if it was easier now than in the past and easier in the cities than in the countryside, it was still difficult to implement in the city factories.

The Beijing Woollen Mill

The Beijing Woollen Mill is a much newer factory which was founded in 1958 and is one of a large number of textile factory complexes located in the capital. Its 2800 workers and staff, spin, weave and dye wools and annually produce a total of more than 3m metres of worsted materials, 60 per cent of which are now exported. The factory is divided into four workshops, each of which is responsible for a separate process, and within each workshop there are four work shifts, each comprising a division of 100 or so workers. These divisions are

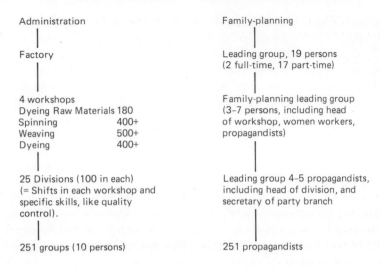

FIGURE 8.4   *Family planning in the Beijing Woollen Mill*

each subdivided into ten groups of ten persons (see Figure 8.4). 60 per cent of the workforce and about half the seventy-eight technicians and engineers are women. The average age of the workforce is 30 years, so just under half are unmarried while 1500 workers (526 men and 974 women) are married and of child-bearing age. Their contraception plans are the particular responsibility of the family-planning network, the structure of which closely follows the organisation of the factory (see Figure 8.4).

The family-planning workers divide their work into three components each coinciding with a stage in the life-cycle of the worker. First they begin by encouraging late marriage among the young single workers who once they have reached an appropriate age and chosen a prospective partner are encouraged to have a pre-marital medical check-up. Late marriage is defined in this factory as more than 23 years old for females and 25 years for males. All the young workers in the factory were reported to follow this recommendation, but they did not all avail themselves of the pre-marital check. The recent emphasis placed on this check-up as a part of the single-child family policy in the interests of raising the quality of the only child has not proved popular, and in the capital city as a whole few couples have been persuaded to have such physical examinations.

Second, the family-planning workers were responsible for arranging

TABLE 8.19 *Family planning in the Beijing Woollen Mill*

Sterilised	394 (236 = women)
Barrier methods	414
IUD	348
Pills	131
Injections	47
Pregnant, awaiting abortion	166
Total	1500

for, distributing and checking on the contraception of the married workers. In the factory all those in the child-bearing ages were practising birth control the most popular measures being sterilisation, barrier methods or the IUD (see Table 8.19). Of those sterilised, 60 per cent, (236 of the 394) are women.

The third area of their work and the more recent addition to it, is to implement the single-child policy. In the last four years, the family-planning personnel had regarded this goal as the most important and they have conducted a number of campaigns within the factory to publicise the policy and persuade the workers to accept it. There were numerous lectures and posters advocating the single-child family. One poster demonstrated the number of births per day and per hour in the world and in China, and wall charts in many workshops illustrated the family plans of the workers there for all to see. For instance, a chart in the quality control workshop showed the number of workers, women of child-bearing age, the form of contraception, numbers of first, second and third children born to workers in the workshop and the birth plans for the present and coming year. It showed that indeed there was a 100 per cent contraceptive use rate and no second or third births in the last few years. It also showed that there had been seven abortions, and on enquiries, three were reported to be the result of a failed IUD, one a failed injection and three were performed because the pregnancy had apparently come too early and interfered with studies or could not yet be afforded financially.

In this factory there were a number of financial incentives associated with family planning and the single-child family certificate. In addition to receiving the benefits outlined in the municipal regulations, the single children of workers in this factory also received extra medical check-ups, additional care and presents. Mothers of single children had the right to six months maternity leave or eighty-six days and a maternity bonus of 100 *yuan,* and if they consented to be sterilised or use the IUD, they received the sums of 100 *yuan* and 20 *yuan* respectively. The Beijing Woollen Factory paid very generous subsidies and bonuses out of its welfare fund which the factory could afford to pay since its profits were substantial. Up to a few years ago a considerable amount of the welfare fund was spent on new housing for workers and on subsidising large families with several children who suffered some hardship. Now funds were no longer needed for these purposes and were instead allocated to single-child families. Up to this year, the factory had spent 11m *yuan* on subsidies and rewards which still amounted only to 3 per cent of the total welfare budget. This year the sum had risen to 30m *yuan,* (10 per cent of the budget) because of the new maternity bonus of 100 *yuan* awarded to those who returned to work early after eighty-six days rather than the six months allowed. The factory estimated that the extra profits accumulated as a result of the shortened maternity leave would soon more than pay for the extra subsidy of 100 *yuan.*

The factory had a high response rate to the single-child family policy. All but one of the births since 1980 was the first and all new parents had been certificated. The one birth in 1982 which was not a first birth occurred where a young bachelor in the factory married and had a child although his new wife already had two children by a previous marriage. (see Table 8.20). Of those in the factory with one child all but one was certificated. In this single case, the one child was seven years old and not well, therefore the parents had so far refused to take out a certificate. For the others, the average length of time between the birth of the first child and its certification was estimated to be one month. The family-planning workers of the factory thought that their success was mainly due to the number of educational programmes, the general levels of political consciousness of factory workers

TABLE 8.20   *Single-child certificates in the Beijing Woollen Mill*

Date	Number of one-child families	Number of one-child families certificated	Percentage certificated
1979	127	115	90.6
1980	57	57	100.0
1981	54	54	100.0
1982	68	67	98.5

and the fact that as certification had become increasingly 'normal' it had affected the expectations of young couples so that now they approached the birth of their first child on the assumption that it was also to be their last. Nevertheless they also thought that the acceptance of the policy had not come easily, especially for those parents of daughters who lived near members of the older generation or whose family line was now at an end. The most difficult case in the factory so far had concerned a male worker, who, like his only brother, had fathered a daughter. Because both this worker and his wife were of peasant background and great pressure had also been put on them by their own parents to have another child, the propagandist in the factory had to visit their home several times before they could be persuaded to sign a certificate.

One propagandist interviewed was in charge of one of the four groups into which the quality control division of sixty-two workers was divided. She had been selected by the division and factory leaders and had attended training classes run by the mill for one day each month. She was one of the senior propagandists and had been elected by her colleagues to join the leading group in charge of family planning at division level. In her own group of eighteen workers, sixteen were women, and two were men. Six of the group were as yet unmarried (see Table 8.21). Part of her job was therefore to persuade them to get married late, but she had found that most got married as soon as they reached 23 and 25 years the first ages within the late marriage category, because they were so anxious that if they left it any longer, they would find it might be too difficult to find a suitable partner.

The fact that there were three married workers with no children seemed to require some explanation. One of them was thirty years old and although she had been married for four years, she had delayed her

TABLE 8.21   *Family planning details of propagandists group, Beijing Woollen Mill*

Class of Women	Number of Children	Contraception
Unmarried	6	—
Married, no children	3	—
Married, one child	2	IUD, barrier method
Married, two children	7	3 sterilised 4 barrier methods
Total	18	

pregnancy because her husband was not well. Another woman of 26 years who was married in February, had already become pregnant, but she later had an abortion. Apparently, she felt that it had occurred too early and that it was too soon to have a baby, given that her husband was still a new graduate. The third woman worker had been married in April and as yet had not become pregnant. All married workers, either childless or with one child, were to be persuaded to stop at one. This propagandist had not so far found too many difficulties in achieving this goal for both the workers with one child had given birth to sons – a factor which she thought had made her task easier. If a couple had a daughter, or if one partner had recently come from the countryside, then her job would have been much more difficult. The rest of her family-planning work was mainly delivering and checking the contraception of the members of her group. She held no formal meetings for her group that were entirely devoted to family planning, but at each monthly production meeting, she put family planning on the agenda for a report and discussion. She talked with the women individually many times, and at least once a month, she formally checked on their monthly cycles, distributed contraceptives and generally kept an eye on their health. The head and chief engineer of the Company, who is a well-known national model woman-worker, thought that this new attention to the health of the women workers, the increased care for them during their pregnancy and longer maternity leave were all improvements which had come about as a result of the single-child family policy. She thought that now that there were fewer children in the nurseries and kindergartens attached to the factory, the care of the young had also improved. She concluded that women workers could now see these advantages for themselves and that being limited to one child, they were able to give more time to their own work and study and improve the material standards of their own and their children's lives.

TWO COMMUNES

To gauge some effects of the single-child family policy in the countryside, interviews were conducted in two suburban communes located in the rural environs of the capital city, Beijing. Both communes visited are rich in resources, labour power and commercial opportunities, hence their achievements in implementing the single-child family policy may well reflect their privileged position in rural China.

Evergreen Commune

In Evergreen Commune, on the edge of the city proper, the majority of the peasant population resident in its 13 000 households that make up large and small villages, work in the fields cultivating vegetables and producing grains and undertake domestic sidelines such as raising pigs, chickens and ducks. The women of the commune had been fully acquainted with and educated in family planning policies, and every woman of child-bearing age had been assigned to a propagandist who recorded the details of her reproductive cycles, supplied her contraceptives and kept a close watch on her attitudes towards the policy. The propagandist was part of a well-developed family-planning network which was fully integrated into the administrative hierarchy of the commune itself (see Table 8.22).

TABLE 8.22 *Organisation of Evergreen Commune family-planning network committees responsible for policy*

	Committees responsible for policy	Office responsible for implementation
Commune level	Family planning committee (9 persons). Vice-Director of Commune, vice-directors of Women's Federation, Youth League, Propaganda Department, representatives from the Family Planning Office and Production brigades	Family Planning Office (2 full-time workers)
Production brigade	Family-planning leading group composed of 9 production brigade officers as for commune	Health and hygiene station workers
Production team	Officer in charge of family planning/women's deputy head of production team and representatives of propagandists	Women's head of production team and propagandists

While the administrative committees were responsible for implementing the policy and adapting national recommendations to suit local conditions, it was the family-planning office of the commune which publicised and administered the programme throughout the commune. The commune office kept a record of every woman of child-bearing age which listed details of their child-bearing and contraceptive histories. It was responsible for ordering and distributing contraceptives and for implementing and checking the quotas or the 'three percentages' of those contracepting, those giving birth and those signing the single-child family certificates. The commune office sponsors periodic campaigns and education in family-planning policies and supervises the work of the production brigade clinics and production team leaders in implementing the policy. Once a month it holds meetings for those in charge of production brigade and production team family planning in order to check on the implementation of the policy and consider any problems which may have arisen. It is also responsible for selecting and training the propagandists who work within each production team and who are the direct contact with the women of child-bearing age and take responsibility for their family plans.

The single-child family policy had been introduced into the commune towards the end of 1979, where until that time the two-child policy had been in operation. Family-planning workers thought that the transition from the two-child to the one-child policy had been a very difficult one to manage. In 1979 they had publicised the new regulations and then organised Party leaders and cadres to study the relevant documents so that they could take the lead and set an example to others. Once the first group of women was ready to receive their certificates, a large public ceremony had been held to acknowledge their acceptance publicly. Soon every young couple in the commune was being asked to sign the single-child family certificate after the birth of their first child. To encourage them, the commune in conformity with general policy introduced a system of rewards and penalties by which all the single-child families in the commune received the sum of 5 *yuan* each month, free medical and nursery care and a higher-than-average grain ration. Conversely, those who had not got permission to conceive and had given birth to an 'out-of-plan' baby, had to pay for all the welfare, medical and educational expenses themselves. In these circumstances parents lost their bonus for between ten and fourteen years and a portion of their pension rights, and, if they were field workers, their production quotas had been adjusted in the last year or so, so that they had to supply greater amounts to the State. In addition – and perhaps this was the severest penalty – all members of the production team or work unit of the offending couple had 10 *yuan* deducted from their wages. Family-planning workers regarded this as the most effective sanction as few couples were prepared to risk the wrath of their fellow-workers and neighbours. The family-planning workers at the production brigade and team level were also rewarded and penalised themselves by 5 – 10 *yuan* according to both the number of out-of-plan births and late terminations in their administrative areas.

The commune was very proud of its record in achieving a 100 per cent contracepting rate among couples with one or two children and a 99 per cent single-child certificate rate among those with one child (see Table 8.23). In the commune there was a total of 9451 women of child-bearing age, of whom 40 per cent, (4247) had one child; of these 4216 (99.3 per cent) had signed the single-child family certificate. The number of couples with single-child family certificates had remained at more than 90 per cent since 1980.

In 1982 there had been a total of 1033 births of which only 17 were second parity births and one was third parity. Three of the second-order births and the third birth were out-of-plan births. The out-of-plan second births had occurred because the first child had been a daughter and the couples wanted a son. Two of their number had had girls the second time round so had apparently not in fact achieved their objective. The case of the third-order birth was unusual in that the woman concerned already had a boy and a girl, but she had hidden her pregnancy right up to the ninth month because she was afraid that she would be pressurised into having an abortion. She gave birth to her third child and then had it adopted by another couple in the commune who were believed to be infertile. In the first six months of 1983, there had been 790 births (compared with 1033 for the whole of 1982) of which 12 had been second-order ones but only one of these was

TABLE 8.23 *Percentage of families with one child who are certificated (Evergreen Commune)*

1979	75.6
1980	94.5
1981	97.8
1982	99.3

out-of-plan. Despite the quantity of single-child certificates issued, the numbers of young couples reaching marriageable age was increasing year by year, so that the commune birth rate was still a high 23.07 per 1000 in 1982 – far above the target for the commune of 10 per 1000.

Although the women of the commune appeared to accept the new policy in terms of the national good and future prosperity, family-planning workers were not so sanguine about its general acceptance. They thought that though peasant women might accept the policy, they did not follow it willingly and enormous effort had to be expended to maintain the high rate of certification. Thus the propagandist played a crucial role in determining women's response to the policy. In the commune there were 640 propagandists who were responsible for the 9451 women of child-bearing age, which meant on average each one was responsible for about 14 households. Propagandists were predominantly women in their thirties who had completed their child-bearing and who had some education. They had to be popular with their neighbours and fellow-workers and have the ability to persuade without antagonising those for whom they were responsible. Their training consisted of attendance at periodic short courses on the theory of population and the reasons for family-planning programmes; the techniques, effectiveness and side-effects of available contraceptives and finally, the importance and methods of keeping accurate records for the women in their care. These short courses were run either by the commune family planning office or hospital or by health personnel in the production brigade clinics. In each production team, the propagandists themselves met once a month to report on their work and to discuss any new changes in policy or problems which they might have in implementing the policy. The most common problem raised by the propagandists in June 1983 was how to convince those whose first child had been a girl to accept certification. Hence peasant parents and grandparents of daughters were identified as the main target for their attention for the remainder of the year.

One propagandist who was interviewed at length about her responsibilities and the women for whom she cared was a bright young woman in her mid-thirties who had just one 8-year-old boy. She had readily accepted the policy of the one-child and she had received one of the first single-child family certificates issued in the commune. She had completed primary school and was a worker in the construction industry where, for the past six to seven years, she had been propagandist for thirty workers in a construction team. During that time she had attended a number of short day courses to learn about family-planning policy and the practical side of the work. Now she attended a commune meeting once a year when family-planning policies and goals for the past year were reviewed and those for the next year discussed. Once a month she met other propagandists from the fifteen teams of the construction company to discuss their work. Each propagandist reported the number and circumstances of the women who were pregnant and of those who posed special problems requiring more attention.

In her team of thirty women, twenty-five were of child-bearing age; five had two or more children before 1979, fourteen now had one child and five were due to have their first child in 1983. Another birth was due early in 1984. To ensure that there were no out-of-plan births among the women of her team, she listed the monthly cycles of all her women and the results of her twice-monthly checks in an exercise book. Her notes detailed the type of contraceptive for each woman and, where appropriate, the dates on which it had last been checked and was due to be next checked. In fact all the women in her group used the IUD, thus she had to arrange for examinations to be made every three to four months. She also constantly reminded women of the family-planning policy and their responsibility to limit their familes to one child. This took great care and tact and she tried to begin the process of persuasion as soon as a woman became pregnant for the first time, so that by the birth of the first child the parents were already expecting to sign the certificate. It had not been easy to persuade couples to stop at two and persuading couples to accept one child had been even more difficult. The couples who required the most persuasion were always those who had no son, and in her group, nine of the fourteen women with one child had given birth to daughters. One of her women had refused even to accept contraceptives for more than a year after the birth of her daughter.

She had not only to persuade the parents, but also the grandparents who were often especially adamant in their desire for a second child and above all, a boy. The other factor which made her work difficult was the overall rise in standard of living which meant that many couples could now afford to have, and indeed wanted to have, a second child. She thought that if conditions allowed, 75 per cent would have a second child, because they could afford it and because they thought that two children were really no more trouble than one. Probably 25 per cent were quite happy with one, mainly because they were keen to study and work and felt that a second child would need more energy, time and money than they had available.

The Women's Federation in the commune had also recently investigated a number of problems which affected women's rights and interests. In particular they had been asked by the National Women's Federation to investigate and document any cases of female infanticide or discrimination against female infants and cases of physical maltreatment of mothers and daughters. They reported that their investigation had shown no cases of female infanticide or serious maltreatment of women in the commune. They thought this was probably because of their favourable economic situation and the high living standards and the fact that women could and frequently did earn more than the men of the family. However, their investigation did reveal that there were lesser forms of discrimination against the female infant and they had reported on them to the commune members to draw attention to the problem. These included the contrast in celebrations between the positive welcome accorded to the birth of a son and the discrimination against daughters. While the birth of a son might be the occasion of much rejoicing among the kin with the mother enjoying special foods and the son much fuss, there have been occasions when disappointed relatives have left hospital immediately on hearing that the expected baby was a girl. Grandparents were particularly likely to show their disappointment, and there had been instances where the grandmother had taken a little time to be reconciled sufficiently to order milk for the baby girl and food for the mother. Frequently, however, the women leaders thought that the birth of a baby girl had not so much caused the subsequent deterioration in familial relations as exacerbated existing tensions which in turn were the product of poor marital relations or the results of problems of economic management. Although cases of prejudice and discrimination were rather in the minority in this suburban commune, the Women's Federation had conducted an educational campaign to improve attitudes towards daughters and show that they could participate in economic and political activities to their own and to their families' advantage. Very importantly the Federation had also tried to change post-marital residence patterns by encouraging grooms to settle in their bride's households, but so far few had done so.

Beijing Farm

Beijing Farm is also located some 25 kilometres from central Beijing, although it differs from the Evergreen Commune in that a larger proportion of its cultivable land is devoted to grain rather than vegetables and it also incorporates a substantial number of dairy units. The population of the commune is some 40 000 and the majority of peasants in the commune divide their time between agricultural field work or raising animals and domestic sidelines. The implementation of the single-child family policy in the commune was the responsibility of a committee composed of five to seven persons including the deputy secretary of the Commune Party Committee, the leaders of women's work and the propaganda department, and the three full-time workers from the commune family-planning office. The committee examined and set the birth quotas, arranged for educational work and periodic propaganda campaigns while the family-planning office was responsible for implementing its decisions and keeping records.

Each of the thirty-six production brigades had a leading group of three to seven persons consisting of the leader in charge of women's affairs (who was also responsible for family planning within the brigade) the deputy secretary of the brigade Party Committee and some production team representatives. Their main task was to educate, implement quotas and keep records for the production brigade. In the production team, the cadre responsible for women's work was in charge of family planning and the propagandists were responsible for the family plans of individual women. These part-time voluntary workers organised educational meetings for women of child-bearing age and reported on the circumstances of their women to higher administrative levels. As in the first commune, the hospital and local clinics played a major role in training the propagandists, distributing contraceptives and carrying out basic health care.

The single-child family policy had been introduced into the commune in 1979, and by the following year a system of rewards and penalties was in operation. In this commune, single-child families initially received a one-off cash bonus in addition to the normal monthly subsidies, an adult grain ration, and free medical and educational facilities until the child reached the age of 14 years. In 1981, the cash bonus was abolished and the cash subsidy reduced to 100 *yuan* a year in line with the amount paid elsewhere. This reduction in subsidies was thought to be responsible for the decline in numbers certificated in 1981 (see Table 8.24). Production quotas were also adjusted to the advantage of households if they took out a certificate and to the disadvantage of a household if a birth was out-of-plan, and subsequently in 1982 the cash penalties for an out-of-plan birth had been raised to deter couples from deciding to have a second child. In July 1983 these fines had been further increased to a staggering 3500 *yuan* in order to take account of the sharp rise in incomes in the

TABLE 8.24   *Number of single-child families 1979–82*

Year	Number of families with one child	Number certificated	Percentage certificated
Beijing Farm			
1979	900	366	40.7
1980	1600	1131	70.7
1981	1920	1196	62.3
1982	2589	2517	97.2
One production brigade			
1979	3	3	100.0
1980	30	17	57.0
1981	61	44	72.0
1982	91	91	100.0

commune. All those responsible for implementing the policy were also rewarded according to the numbers of certificated births and penalised according to the number of out-of-plan births.

The response to the policy had been much more gradual and there had been a higher number of out-of-plan births than in the Evergreen Commune and most other urban and suburban communities for which figures are available. However, by 1982, only 3 per cent of the couples with one child still remained uncertificated and these couples were motivated by a continuing preference for boys, fears that the single child might not survive, the continuing resistance of the older generation to the policy and the hope that the policy would soon change.

The decline in numbers certificated in 1981 and the rise in 1982 was thought to relate to the differences in levels of subsidies available to single-child families. However the decline in numbers certificated in 1981 is not associated with a rise in the number of second births (see Table 8.25) which suggests that couples were not proceeding with a second pregnancy but adopting a 'wait and see' attitude.

For 1982, there were twenty-three second parity births within the plan, seventeen or eighteen of which had been allowed because the firstborn had some congenital disease. The remainder were the result of either second marriages in which one partner had no children or uxorilocal marriages in which the husband had moved into his wife's household and therefore qualified for a second birth. Of the twenty

TABLE 8.25   *Number of first births 1979–82, Beijing Farm*

	1979	1980	1981	1982
Number of first births	351	418	579	693
Number of second births (in-plan)	188	173	10	23
Number of second births (out-of-plan)			23	20
Total number of births	549	591	612	736
Percentage of first births	64	71	94.6	94.1

out-of-plan births, in all but one case, the firstborn had been a girl and the parents were determined to have a boy. In the single case where the firstborn was a son, the parents felt that a family was not complete without a second child. According to the leaders of the commune there was a marked difference in the speed with which parents of boys and girls signed the single-child family certificate. Those who had girls took much more persuasion to accept the policy and in one case, a family had to be visited many, many times before they could be persuaded to sign the certificate. Overall they estimated that about 60 per cent of the peasant parents voluntarily accepted the policy, about 30 per cent were prepared, or could be persuaded, to go along with it and another 10 per cent were opposed to it. Interestingly, in the commune hospital there had been 609 terminations of pregnancy in 1982, of which 70 per cent were said to result from 'failed' contraception and 30 per cent were due to 'out-of-plan' pregnancies. Of those defined as 'out-of-plan' and terminated, 30 per cent of the parents already had two children, 30–40 per cent had one child, and 5–6 per cent had occurred among the unmarried.

In one production brigade of fifty-four households, the family-planning group was made up of the leader of the production brigade, the leader in charge of women's work and representatives of the propagandists. There were nine propagandists in the production brigade, each of whom was responsible for five or so households, and the remaining nine households, all defined as 'difficult', had been allocated to the care of Party members. In the past few years in this production brigade, there had been no out-of-plan births, and this achievement was attributed to the political consciousness of the brigade leaders and the enormous effort that had been made to explain the policy to the parents via the official broadcasting system and as the result of frequent meetings and visits to individual households. The result was that most people had come to accept the policy, although a few 'difficult households' had taken some persuading. The leader of the production brigade was responsible for three of these 'difficult' households. In one case the parents had given birth to a daughter, and the father was one of three brothers, of whom the oldest was dumb and had no wife, and the younger brother was not yet married. The parents wanted to give their baby girl to the eldest brother so that they could have another child, hopefully a boy. This was not within the rules, so the propagandist had initially tried to persuade the couple. However they persisted in their refusal. Responsibility for the case was then assumed by the leader of the production brigade who exercised more pressure on the wife at home and contacted the husband's place of work, so that pressure could be applied to him too. Eventually they had given way and signed. In the second case, the reluctant parents were related to the production brigade leader himself and he had taken up the case personally. In this household, the father was one of four brothers whose wives had so far all given birth to daughters. Hence, he wanted to have a second child in order to try for a son. He had eventually been persuaded to change his mind and sign the certificate. In the third 'difficult' case, the mother of a daughter was represented as extremely stubborn, so that even her husband was said to be in some awe of her. He had been visited by the production brigade leader, but he felt unable to stand up to his wife who worked in a factory outside the production brigade, and therefore beyond its jurisdiction. Eventually it was the factory cadres who had put pressure on the wife, and so the case had not been as difficult to resolve as the production brigade leader had initially feared. He had only to visit the husband a few times before they both signed the certificate. On the whole, he thought his job was becoming easier, now that the entire commune and outside enterprises had all combined to exert pressure on recalcitrant and reluctant couples.

Again, as in the first commune, the most recent task of the Women's Federation had been to investigate cases of discrimination against female infants and conduct as educational campaign to enhance the status of daughters. The worst case of prejudice against the mother of a baby girl uncovered by the Federation during its recent investigation, had concerned a typist in the commune office. While she was pregnant, a fortune teller had predicted that the baby would be a boy, and hence expectations surrounding the birth were high. Once a girl was born however, relations between the mother and her disappointed mother-in-law, who felt extremely let down, rapidly deteriorated. The Women's Federation had subsequently drawn attention to the problems and publicised cases which proved that daughters could continue to care for their parents after their marriage, either because their husbands had moved into their households or because they still lived nearby. As a result of these campaigns, the leader of the commune Women's Federation expected to reduce the incidence of discrimination and to further the cause of female equality.

GENERAL OBSERVATIONS

Beijing is a large capital city and the single-child family policy has probably been implemented there to a degree not shared by many of the smaller cities or most of rural China. The percentage of certificated one-child families in Beijing is very high standing at more than 90 per cent in many neighbourhoods and enterprises. In looking at implementation at the local level more closely, several observations can be made about the single-child family programme in Beijing. The high acceptance rate can be attributed to a number of factors. The first is the educational level and socio-political make-up of the city's population and the existing patterns of 'small' family size which were already common by the late 1970s. The higher concentration of cadres, intellectuals and skilled factory workers in the state economic sector must have eased the implementation of the policy in the capital. A second factor is the increase in incomes and the sharp rise in consumption and living standards over the past four years. One of the important rationales behind the policy is the relation between a reduction in population and a rise in standard of living and the quality of life of the single child and its family. Over the past four years the residents of Beijing, like those in other large cities and their rural suburbs, have experienced such an improvement and have been able to appreciate the idea of such a relationship for themselves. This was clearly evident in many answers to questions about the policy. Indeed, it is arguable whether this radical family-planning policy could have been pushed to the degree that it has if it had not been for the coincidental and quite dramatic increases in incomes and opportunities for consumption. Nevertheless the government has not depended on these advantages alone, and family-planning personnel in Beijing municipality have worked very hard to attain high acceptance rates particularly in what they saw as the very difficult first years. The educational programmes accompanying the policy are still immensely detailed and painstaking, and family-planning workers are in constant contact with residents both in groups and individually.

A very important milestone in this respect and one constantly mentioned in the commune, the factory and urban neighbourhood seems to have been the 'Open Letter on the Question of Controlling China's Population Growth', sent from the Central Committee of the Communist Party to all members of the Party and Youth League in September 1980.[11] It explained the reasons for the single-child family policy, outlined the means by which it was to be achieved and concluded by urging all family-planning workers to implement the policy to the best of their ability. It seems as if this letter officially confirmed that the new policy, far from being a tentative or temporary phenomenon was here to stay. Although family-planning personnel thought that the implementation of the policy was much easier after The Open Letter and had continued to be so following a change in expectations, none of them underrated the difficulties involved in achieving these high rates of acceptance or the vigilance required to maintain them. Given that much of the Beijing population would have been accustomed to a four-year space between children, it may be that these rates of acceptance have yet to be tested.

The main problems did not vary from locality to locality. They were the continuing preference for sons, the influence of the older generation and fears for the physical well-being of the only child. The propagandists' greatest concern was the marked desire for sons. With this new policy the sex of the first-born became crucial and was much discussed by potential parents, kinship groups and the community at large. The recent enquiries of the Women's Federation into the incidence of female infanticide and violence against mothers and daughters suggested that they did not occur in Beijing and its immediate suburban areas, but what did emerge was evidence that lesser forms of prejudice and discrimination delaying certification existed in the capital city and the incidence of these must provide some measure of the iceberg elsewhere in the country if Beijing is but the tip.

Another of the fears of both parents and grandparents is that the quality of life for both the oldest and youngest generations will be reduced as a result of the small or single-child family. The old, and potentially old, fear for the future of their family line and their welfare and support in old age. If family provision for old age seems to be at risk, the government has attempted to allay fears and create a new institutional provision and care for the elderly. In each of the urban and rural communities visited, the leading cadres emphasised the current moves to improve the welfare of the old by establishing homes for the old and in the suburban communes such provisions extended to the introduction of new pension schemes for the retired. The message was that children need not be the sole form of support in old age. What worries many parents though is that economic support is not the only thing the elderly hope for from their children. Moreover it is many years before today's parents will become grandparents and present guarantees of support may well not materialise.

So far as the youngest generation is concerned parents fear that the single child may be lonely, spoilt and selfish or may suffer ill-health, an accident or even death. Indeed, concern for the well-being of children has generated a whole new interest in child-development in Beijing. In part this interest has been encouraged by the government in its bid to sell the one-child policy, and in part parents have themselves chosen to invest all the resources at their command into the one child allowed. This joint investment by both state and parents has led to a demand for theoretical knowledge and practical aid in child-rearing which may benefit young children. Doctors in the Beijing Farm commune hospital cited examples where parents had very closely questioned the credentials of the doctors arranging for their obstetrical care. However, not all the attention and expectations centred on the single child are likely to be to its benefit. Because of their widespread fear that the child will be spoilt and selfish, the demand for child-care outside the family unit has increased in the past four years both because parents want company for their child and because of greater trust in professional care. In the Evergreen Commune the belief in the superiority of professional care had risen to such heights that many peasants there preferred to place their children in the village kindergarten as weekly boarders rather than leave them all day with doting and untrained granny.

Perhaps it is easier to identify the main problems, fears and reasons of the small minority in Beijing who do not accept the policy than it is to identify the various factors making for its high acceptance rates. What evidence there is suggests that differences between the incentive and disincentive packages of various enterprises and neighbourhoods may not be a deciding factor influencing the certification rates of one-child families. In some localities the incentives and disincentives lose their efficacy once certification is widespread and preferential treatment is no longer feasible. It is quite evident that in Beijing more households could afford to pay the penalties than choose to, thus suggesting that other economic factors and ideological prescriptions are still very important. Yet it is also not without significance that Beijing Farm has recently raised its penalty for an out-of-plan birth to 3500 *yuan* as a disincentive to the newly-prosperous. Gradually, as more and more data becomes available it may be possible to discuss in greater detail this and other attempts to implement the single-child family policy and its likely implications for the family, the community and society. Beijing and its richer suburban communes represent the most privileged regions of China in terms of political and socio-economic resources and it is perhaps not surprising to find that, if success is measured in terms of certificate rates, the policy has so far been implemented there with a measure of immediate success tempered by the continuing presence of many problems delaying fundamental acceptance. The degree of success in Beijing cannot be assumed to be representative of the implementation of the single family policy elsewhere. However, if even in Beijing the problems in implementing the single-child family policy are perceived to be tenacious and difficult to resolve then the scale and their tenacity elsewhere is certainly far greater.

NOTES AND REFERENCES

1. 'Beijing Discussion on Population Control', *Beijing Daily*, 5 August 1979, in *SWB*, 16 August 1979 (FE/6195/B11/12).
2. Ibid.
3. 'Report on an Investigation into Beijing's Birthrate', Beijing Municipal Family Planning Committee, October 1982, mimeographed Report.
4. Family Planning Work in Beijing. Beijing City Service Broadcast, *SWB* 13 February 1979 (FE/6041/B11/17).
5. 'Capital Population Growth Study', *New China News Agency*, 9 September 1980.
6. 'Family Planning in Beijing', New China News Agency, 20 July 1979; 'More Couples Decide to have Only One Child', ibid, 11 October 1979.
7. 'Population Control in Beijing', New China News Agency, 7 November 1979.
8. 'Penalties for Birth Control Offenders in Beijing and Tianjin, *SWB*, 16 August 1979 (FE/6195/B11/11).
9. 'One-child Family Becoming Norm in Beijing West District', *Renkou Yanjiu* (Population Research) no. 1, January 1981, 29–34.
10. 'Worker Sentenced for Deserting Wife and Daughter', *SWB*, 12 April 1983 (FE/7305/B11/6).
11. For English translation of 'Open Letter on Birth Control', 25 September 1980, see *SWB*, 30 September 1980 (FE/6336/B11/4–7).

Index

233